BEGINNING LIVES

To my parents,
Jay and William Hursthouse

BEGINNING LIVES

ROSALIND HURSTHOUSE

Basil Blackwell
in association with
the Open University

Basil Blackwell Ltd
108 Cowley Road, Oxford OX4 1JF, UK

Basil Blackwell Inc.
432 Park Avenue South, Suite 1503
New York, NY 10016, USA

British Library Cataloguing in Publication Data
Hursthouse, Rosalind
Beginning lives
1. Abortion
I. Title II. Open University
179'.76   HQ767

ISBN 0–631–15327–6
ISBN 0–631–15328–4 Pbk

Library of Congress Cataloging in Publication Data
Beginning lives.

Bibliography: p.
Includes index.
1. Abortion—Moral and ethical aspects I. Title.
HQ767.15.1187   1987   363.4'6   86–10344

ISBN 0–631–15327–6
ISBN 0–631–15328–4 (pbk.)

This book forms part of an Open University course, A310 *Life and Death*. For further information about this course, please write to the Student Enquiries Office, The Open University, PO Box 71, Walton Hall, Milton Keynes, MK7 6AG, UK.

Typeset in 11 on 12½pt Bembo
by Photo-graphics, Honiton, Devon
Printed in Great Britain

Epitaph on a Child Killed by Procured Abortion

O thou, whose eyes were closed in death's pale night,
Ere fate revealed thee to my aching sight;
Ambiguous something, by no standard fixed,
Frail span, of naught and of existence mixed;
Embryo, imperfect as my tort'ring thought,
Sad outcast of existence and of naught;
Thou, who to guilty love first ow'st thy frame,
Whom guilty honour kills to hide its shame;
Dire offspring! formed by love's too pleasing pow'r!
Honour's dire victim in luckless hour!
Soften the pangs that still revenge thy doom:
Nor, from the dark abyss of nature's womb,
Where back I cast thee, let revolving time
Call up past scenes to aggravate my crime.
Two adverse tyrants ruled thy wayward fate,
Thyself a helpless victim to their hate;
Love, spite of honour's dictates, gave thee breath;
Honour, in spite of love, pronounced thy death.

Anonymous, 1740

Contents

Preface

I have found this book very difficult to write for several reasons. One is that it is impossible, inevitably, to please everyone on a topic such as abortion, and wrong, I think, even to try. But in writing this book I have had to fight a constant temptation to soft-pedal, to go for the 'on the one side this, but on the other side that' approach which does try to please everyone, but in which one winds up not having committed oneself to anything at all. Looking at it now (introductions are usually the last things to be written) it seems to me that perhaps I fought the temptation too hard and have wound up sounding much more certain about a number of points than I am. One thing I am certain of is that one's moral knowledge on such topics is constantly subject to modification in the light of increasing age and experience.

The second reason I have found the book difficult to write is that it is hard to write about the most central cases of abortion without giving justifiable offence or understandable pain to certain people. The cases in question are those in which an abortion is suggested or requested because there is a certainty, likelihood or risk that if the pregnancy runs its full course a baby will be born with some degree of disability. The particular difficulty in writing about such cases is to find an inoffensive vocabulary in which to do so.

We have, available in our language, a number of words which describe states one does not want, and would not wish visited upon anyone. Some commonly used terms are 'abnormal', 'handicapped', 'disadvantaged' and 'disabled'. Correspondingly, there are words which describe ways we like to be – normal, having lots of advantages, being able to get about and lead a life of one's own. But, some of us who use this common language are blind, or confined to wheelchairs, or have haemophilia or rheumatoid arthritis, *and* are leading full, busy, happy, contented lives. Now if one is such a person, one may well want to repudiate any and every one of the first set of descriptions. So, where is the description of these ways which succeeds in conveying that, though of course one thinks it is far from ideal, one is not complaining, but is happy with one's life?

As far as I can see there simply is not one, hence the difficulty of writing inoffensively in this area. To talk of having a handicap or disability, or being handicapped or disabled would be all right if only everyone would keep the literal meaning of these terms clearly in mind. But unfortunately this is not clearly appreciated, so 'handicapped' and 'disabled' can have the same offensive overtones as 'abnormal'.

I hope that any offence or hurt my language causes, particularly when I am summarizing positions, where I have found myself forced to talk baldly in terms of 'the disabled', may be partly eased by the line I take on 'euthanasia', a term which has become much abused in current usage. It should be restricted to the cases in which someone is killed or allowed to die *for their own sake* because *they* truly would be better off dead, their lives are not worth going on with. But, as I emphasize again and again in this book, many cases which are described as euthanasia or mercy-killing are no such thing. The death of a baby with Down's syndrome, for example, may well be a mercy to its parents and to other children in the family and to society at large, but it is not necessarily a mercy to the baby, nor sought for *its* sake when doctors and parents choose that it should die. Some babies born with Down's syndrome are capable of playing games and enjoying affectionate relationships. Unless we are prepared to say of such children, and of people who, for instance, are confined to wheelchairs or who have haemophilia, that they would be 'better off dead', that for *their* sakes one

wishes they would die, that death would be a mercy to
them, we cannot appeal to 'euthanasia' or 'mercy-killing' as
the justification for infanticide or for abortion in the cases
where it is predictable that a baby may be born with one of
these conditions.

That is not to say that *abortion* cannot be justified in such
circumstances. According to one's view of the moral status
of the fœtus, one may think that infanticide and abortion
stand or fall together, but one may think rather that abortion
is justifiable in many cases in which infanticide would not
be. It *is* to say that any such justification must be very
carefully phrased. I do think that abortion is justifiable in
some cases of suspected disability, but would want to
disassociate myself entirely from those who justify it on the
'better off dead' line. I hope that in what follows, I am never
betrayed into sounding as though I would judge that anyone
would be 'better off dead' simply in virtue of a disability.

Finally, and most generally, the book has been difficult
to write because it involves thinking constantly about
suffering, both past and ever present. I have been haunted
throughout by the knowledge of what people have gone
through and are enduring – painful and unwanted pregnancies, decisions about abortion, infertility, sterility, miscarriages, the sight of one's child in agony, the constant burden
of looking after children with severe disabilities, the constant
burden of pain.

This emotional involvement on my part is not, I think,
apparent. The book is written (mostly) in a style of
detachment; it also contains as much abstract, 'theoretical'
moral philosophy – about Aristotle, about utilitarianism,
about the concept of a person – as 'practical' or 'applied'
discussion of concrete moral issues. Does this mean I am
being 'clinical' and 'academic'? Well, yes, and I make no
apologies for it, since in an academic book of moral
philosophy, which this is, a certain level of cool detachment
and abstraction is precisely what is called for. 'So much the
worse', someone might say, 'for academic books on moral
philosophy.' But that, I would say, is a mistake. Time spent
thinking coolly about painful moral issues is not time
misspent. For one thing, we need to do it if we are to

understand other people's points of view and live without hatred and strife in a society which contains such variety of opinions and attitudes. Secondly, anyone who has children, or who teaches, or who has family or friends or colleagues who pay any heed to what they think, has the power to exert some small influence on the way our society will develop, and that influence, if it is to be for good, rather than ill, needs to come from cool thought as well as good feelings. And thirdly, some of us will find ourselves forced to make painful decisions concerning these tragic matters very quickly, in precisely those circumstances in which one's emotions are most deeply involved; to have thought earlier about them in the abstract, when it was possible to do so, may save one from the bitter regret and remorse that follows on making the wrong decision in the stress of the moment.

Quite generally, we owe it to ourselves to try to make our moral convictions our *own*, the product of our own reason and reflection, and not the product of misfortunes that chance has sent our way, nor solely determined by our upbringing, or the influence of the media, or what is vaguely referred to as 'the social environment'. So it is important, I think, that there should be academic books of moral philosophy. But I have realized how particularly fortunate one is to be in a position even to contemplate reading, let alone writing, such a book. Since the beginning of philosophy, the pursuit of truth or knowledge has been upheld as one of the supremely worthwhile activities that we can go in for. Someone who agrees with this, as I do, must count themselves fortunate indeed that their lives are sufficiently free from care or suffering to permit them to pursue it.

Acknowledgements

I am grateful to the many people who have influenced this book, some for the frank discussion of their own views and experience, some for painstaking commentary on various drafts, and some for extensive philosophical debate. In at least one, and quite often in all of these ways, I have been generously helped by Alison Davis, Roy Blackman, Oswald Hanfling, Andrew Goodfellow, Michael Kelar, Gavin Lawrence, Caroline Lewis, Betty Shumener, Tom Sorell, Christine Swanton, Peter Wright and Godfrey Vesey.

Special thanks must go to Don Locke, who, as my external reader, read the second draft of the whole thing most conscientiously and guided me into substantial revision and improvement of it. I have benefited from the advice and factual information provided by David Barlow of the Nuffield Department of Obstetrics and Gynaecology, and from the efficient organization of Shirley Coulson, without whose endeavours the book would still be lost in the Open University word processors.

Finally, I should like to express my great debt to Elizabeth Anscombe and Philippa Foot, though neither of them was able to read this material while I was writing it, and though each of them, in their different ways and for different reasons, would disagree with much that I say. Reading and listening to them over the last twenty years has provided me with a source of inspiration, and a standard to aim at in thinking seriously in philosophy, without which this book would have been immeasurably the poorer.

The author and publishers are grateful to Cambridge University Press for permission to use Rosalind Hursthouse, 'Aristotle, Nicomachean Ethics', in Vesey, Godfrey (ed.) (1986) *Philosophers Ancient and Modern*, Cambridge University Press. This article is drawn on throughout Chapter Six.

CHAPTER ONE

Introduction: the issues, their context and strategy

1 PRELIMINARIES

This book is a text book in applied and theoretical moral philosophy, concentrating on the issue of abortion. It is a text book in the sense that it both assumes no familiarity with philosophy and aims to introduce the readers to this academic subject and teach them something about it. In doing so, it treats in an academic way the far from merely academic topic of abortion; it treats it as a topic that can be discussed dispassionately and, moreover, as a topic falling under not history, or psychology, or sociology, or politics, or medicine or legal philosophy, but under moral philosophy. It thereby presupposes in the reader some willingness to regard the topic in this way.

Such willingness is not incompatible with regarding the subject in all the other ways too. It is not only all right, but quite right, to recognize that abortion is, as I said, far from being a merely academic topic; it is one which should engage the emotions. It is, furthermore, a topic with so many facets or aspects that an interest in it which is (not merely but also) academic could appropriately take many different forms – historical, psychological, sociological, political and so on. One's interest in it might also be simply practical. But my interest in it is theoretical, and is that of a moral philosopher; though I know it has all these other aspects, they are not, in this book, my concern.

Hence, in particular (and for reasons I give at some length later in this chapter), there is not much in the book about legislation, actual or proposed. Nor are there many sociological facts about numbers of abortions past or present, nor statistics about the ages at which women have them, nor historical facts about say, the lives of women in the nineteenth century, nor many medical facts. Such facts as are appealed to are mostly of the sort that one might reasonably expect to be common knowledge.

The exceptions to these are to be found in four appendices and a glossary. This book touches on the issues of *in vitro* fertilization and surrogacy insofar as they relate to abortion, and the facts that are relevant to these have been discovered too recently to be common knowledge; so there is one appendix on methods of overcoming infertility, and one on the 'Warnock Report'. I also discovered in the course of researching for this book, and having successive drafts of it criticized and queried, that my own knowledge, and the knowledge of many people I knew, concerning the facts of prenatal development and of methods of abortion, had a surprising number of gaps in it. So I thought it appropriate to supply basic information on these two topics as well in two more appendices. The glossary contains technical terms relating to the facts outlined in the appendices.

The duties of someone writing a text book in applied moral philosophy are, I take it, at least two: (a) to acquaint the reader with at least some of the standard literature on the moral topic at issue and to subject it to critical appraisal, and (b) to present what one believes to be true about the topic. As it happens, the prevailing intellectual orthodoxy on abortion at the moment is extremely 'permissive', so a *critical* examination of some of the current standard philosophical literature is bound to consist of attacks on permissive rather than conservative views. And since my own convictions are out of sympathy with the prevailing orthodoxy, my attempts to fulfil (b) honestly are bound to consist of presenting a rival non-permissive view, not of trying to work out better versions of the permissive views which evade the criticisms I have made.

It may seem that I thereby flout a third requirement it is

sometimes thought that a philosophy text book, particularly one on moral philosophy, should meet, namely that the author should 'give an unbiased view' or 'present both sides of the question'. If this is supposed to rule out the author's coming down on one side rather than the other, then indeed I flout it, but make no apologies for doing so. Refusing to come down on one side rather than the other is incompatible with fulfilling (b), and I do not see why it should be regarded as any more obligatory in moral philosophy than it might be thought to be in mathematics. If it means only that the author should make it clear that her own position is not the only one available, and describe the rival views in sufficient detail to provide ammunition for readers who disagree with her, then I would agree that an introductory book in applied moral philosophy ought to do this, and also claim that I have done it. Three central chapters are devoted to giving the current permissive lines a good run for their money; each is outlined thoroughly before it is attacked.

My conclusions may offend not only the radicals but also arch conservatives who will find them still too permissive. If their views on abortion are founded on their religion then offence, I think, is not the appropriate reaction. The arguments throughout this book are entirely secular; if their more conservative conclusions need premises provided by religion, it is not surprising that those conclusions are not yielded by this book. If, on the other hand, more conservative conclusions can be got from purely secular arguments, then I have not avoided mention of these arguments deliberately; I simply do not know what they are.

Although this book is about abortion, it is also, to a lesser extent, concerned with embryonic and fœtal research, surrogacy and infanticide. That might seem a fairly natural grouping of topics. But the book hardly touches on women's rights, the abortion law, the 'Warnock Report' (though this is described in Appendix Four) or any of the subsequent debates there have been about legislation governing *in vitro* fertilization and surrogacy, despite the fact that these topics might reasonably be thought to form part of the same natural group. But as well as being about abortion, the book is about the concept of a person, speciesism, utilitarianism, and Aristotle.

To a reader familiar with current academic philosophy, I could probably explain my selection (and rejection) of topics by mentioning just two points: (a) that this is a book in moral philosophy, not in legal or political philosophy, and (b) that, as an academic book, it is deliberately set in the mainstream of current, Anglo-American, philosophical literature. The purpose of this chapter is to make this cryptic explanation intelligible to a reader who is not familiar with philosophy. In it I outline a distinction between the concerns of moral philosophy and those of legal or political philosophy, discuss what one can expect moral philosophy to achieve, describe some of the general features of the current academic literature on abortion, and try to make clear how these various factors have shaped the contents of this book.

2 MORAL PHILOSOPHY: WHAT DOES IT YIELD?

What can one reasonably expect moral philosophy to yield on the issue of abortion? This is itself a difficult philosophical question, so let us approach it by considering instead what current philosophy *has* yielded on abortion.

The current literature has a curious history, and, to people unacquainted with philosophy, has some unexpected aspects, about which something should be said.

Until the beginning of the 1960s, few Anglo-American philosophy journals had any articles on abortion; but by the end of the 'sixties it had become a very popular topic, and has remained so. Why should philosophers, so silent on the topic before, suddenly have become so loquacious? To some extent, the explanation of this seems obvious. The 'sixties saw the upsurge of the women's liberation movement and the consequent debate over whether women should be given a legal right to abortion on demand. But relying on such a simple explanation might lead one to expectations about the current philosophical literature on abortion which would not be fulfilled.

It would, for instance, be natural to expect that much of

it would refer to women's rights, speaking either for or against them in relation to abortion. But much of the literature does not even *mention* women's rights, let alone discuss them. Unsurprisingly, in a male-dominated profession most of the books and articles are by men – but it would be a mistake to infer from this that because they ignore women's rights, they promote a conservative line on abortion. On the contrary – much of the literature supports a liberal or permissive line. But it does so in terms that make no reference to women's rights. This should not strike one as surprising; for if it could be established that abortion was morally innocuous, arguments within political philosophy for the right to abortion on demand would be on a particularly sure footing and could be made without reference to women's rights.

The tracing of cause and effect in the history of ideas is a dangerously speculative business, and fortunately, it is not an enterprise on which I have to embark here. For whatever reason (or reasons), the 'sixties saw the emergence of 'applied' or 'practical' moral philosophy – a shift from an almost exclusive concern with the logical features of moral judgements, to a concern with 'real' moral issues. Seeing the popularity of abortion as part of this quite general phenomenon in moral philosophy makes it easier to understand how it might be discussed without reference to women's rights or to other 'women's issues', and appear in association with topics such as euthanasia, infanticide and our treatment of animals. It has been approached, not particularly as a women's issue, but as an applied or 'real' one, and become naturally associated with other 'real' issues concerning the taking of life.

But at this point, someone unfamiliar with philosophical literature might reasonably wonder how philosophers ever get round to writing anything on abortion at all. If they have to consider all these other issues as well, how do they ever get started? Nor does the problem end there, for once again, medical technology has just presented us with a new set of issues. *In vitro* fertilization techniques now open the possibility of 'test-tube' babies, of growing embryos in laboratories for the purposes of research, of surrogacy – and it seems obvious that, in considering whether or not it is morally permissible to abort embryos or fœtuses, moral philosophers must now regard that question as an aspect of the more general one, raised in the 'Warnock Report', of how it is right to treat the human embryo or fœtus, and settle all these new issues too. And, one might reasonably wonder, how could any one moral philosopher even attempt such a thing?

In effect, this takes us back to one of the questions raised at the beginning of this section: 'What has current philosophy yielded on abortion?' There is, unsurprisingly, very much variety within it, but two particularly prevalent theoretical positions can be detected. One involves a totally comprehensive, albeit remarkably simple, moral theory, namely *utilitarianism*. According to this theory, roughly, no taking of life, human or otherwise, be it abortion, suicide, euthanasia, infanticide or murder is intrinsically wrong, since actions are wrong only insofar as they cause suffering or reduce happiness. The second position should not, perhaps, be described as a theory so much as relying on a particular theoretical concept, the concept of a *person*. A person may be roughly defined as a rational and self-conscious being, a definition according to which all of us are persons, but fœtuses, babies, and the extremely senile or brain-damaged are not. The theoretical significance of this concept is that it singles out (so it is maintained) those beings which matter morally, or which, in particular, it is wrong to kill. Since fœtuses, babies, the extremely senile, etc. are not persons, they do not matter morally, or at least it is not wrong to kill them, so there is nothing wrong with abortion, infanticide and the killing of the senile or brain-damaged.

These two positions could fairly be described as current 'orthodox mainstream' philosophy; hence we can answer the question 'What has this philosophy yielded on abortion?' by saying, rather generally, 'It has yielded a set of arguments in support of a permissive line on abortion, which provides equally good support for a correspondingly permissive line on infanticide and the killing of the senile or brain-damaged'.

I subject these two positions to very detailed criticism not merely because I think they are wrong in detail, but because

I think they are fundamentally wrong – that their exponents try to do something that moral philosophy cannot do. And that, of course, brings me back to the first question raised at the beginning of this section: What *can* one reasonably expect moral philosophy to yield on the issue of abortion?

It seems that a moral philosopher writing on abortion has to consider all the related issues; but is it then reasonable to expect her to be able to settle anything? Well, 'considering all the related issues' need not mean settling them. It might mean something like 'Taking it as a working assumption that the issues are more or less settled in the way recognized by conventional morality and ensuring that whatever one says about abortion is consistent with this working assumption'. So, for instance, in considering as a question whether abortion was wrong, one might take as a working assumption that infanticide was 'more or less settled' as being wrong (the 'more or less' registering the possibility of dispute about some particular examples). All argument has to start somewhere; one is not obliged to count everything as up for discussion simultaneously. Indeed, one cannot.

But the philosophers who support the two prevailing positions I described above are not only prepared to throw away the working assumption that many of these other issues are 'more or less' settled in the ways recognized by conventional morality, they are willing to regard them all as up for discussion and settlement (along with the issue of abortion) in ways that may be contrary to conventional morality and in strikingly simple black and white terms. In attempting to do this, they are, in my opinion, attempting the impossible. Moral philosophy cannot yield so much, and it is a fundamental mistake on the part of the exponents of these two positions to think that it can.

It should not be inferred from what I have just said that I am assuming at the outset that it is impossible for good moral philosophy to come up with conclusions that run counter to conventional morality (though I do take as working assumptions the conventional moral views concerning the wrongness of callous infanticide, involuntary euthanasia and many other issues besides). I am not opposed to the idea that moral philosophy should turn a critical eye on our familiar moral beliefs and consider our moral convictions and problems anew. But it is reasonable to oppose the idea that doing so is going to be a simple matter and yield simple cut and dried answers.

There is indeed a strong and natural temptation to think that moral philosophy ought to be able to come up with *the* answer to any moral problem and deliver it cut and dried. After all, one might think, if moral philosophy cannot solve our moral dilemmas, what does it do, and what possible point or value can it have? This is perhaps a temptation to which philosophers are particularly prone, since they have a characteristic tendency to fall for theories, and a corresponding optimism about what the application of rational thought to the recalcitrant world will achieve. This optimism is characteristic of the philosophers who support the two positions I mentioned. Equipped with just one moral standard or one theoretical moral concept (or, at most, with these plus a couple of extra principles), dispensing with any reliance on familiar moral beliefs, they expect to be able to deliver the solutions to the moral problems that vex us, and to resolve the disagreements between disputants on moral matters.

But could they possibly achieve so much? Can one theory, or one theoretical concept, in moral philosophy do that? It would be reasonable to be convinced, even in advance of looking at any such specimen of moral philosophy, that the answer to these questions is 'No'. For one might think that, in relation to many issues, there could not possibly *be* a straightforward, cut and dried answer. Questions about particular cases of abortion, or the treatment of babies born with Down's syndrome, or what can be done to give children to people who want them, or euthanasia, are not agonizing for nothing. They are often agonizing because there is not, within secular morality, a clear judgement as to what ought to be done. Rather, a number of different considerations, all of which are morally relevant, pull in different directions. When one considers the complex range of factors that may be relevant to just the one issue of abortion, and how differently these seem to weigh in particular cases, when one considers the sheer variety of cases, then it seems reasonable to be convinced in advance that there could not be any way of imposing any theoretical philosophy on this rich complexity which would yield black and white answers. And if moral philosophy, in trying to impose some system on this complexity which would clearly settle questions about abortion, has to be looking for something which would also settle all questions about euthanasia, infanticide, our treatment of animals, *in vitro* fertilization, embryo research, surrogacy and so on, then may we not be convinced in advance that it is not going to be possible?

That, at any rate, is my conviction, though not, it should be said, in advance of looking at any specimens of attempts. I am opposed to the philosophers I mentioned who are currently arguing that some simple answer can be given concerning the rights and wrongs of abortion, and, moreover, that the theories or concepts which yield this simple answer will also settle questions about euthanasia and infanticide (at least) in ways contrary to conventional morality. I discuss and criticize them at length in order to substantiate that conviction, and in the hope that readers who do not share it, and are still expecting moral philosophy to solve our problems, may come to accept that this is a mistake. With the clear intent to disparage, conventional morality is sometimes described as 'comfortable'. But in its recognition of many painful dilemmas to which no simple solution can be given conventional morality is, on the contrary, very uncomfortable, and it is the theorics offering the simple solutions which should be disparaged for offering the comfort of too easy a way out of them.

But this book is not simply negative. It is shaped by the belief that, although there are few cut and dried answers to be given, and although indeed the complexity that has to be dealt with is not confined to the abortion issue, it can be illuminatingly systematized, if the system of thought itself is sufficiently rich rather than over-simplified. Described at the most general level, the strategy of this book is to begin by looking at the most cut and dried answers and to introduce increasing complexity up to roughly the level I think is required. Even at that level, I do not 'give the answers'. It is, indeed, built into the theory I eventually present that moral knowledge – knowledge of what one ought to do and ought not to do in particular circumstances – is not something that can be taught adequately through the medium of books and lectures, but is something each one of us has to learn for ourselves. What books in moral philosophy can try to do is correct false ways of thinking about moral issues and encourage people to think rightly on them in the light of their own experience and development. And in my view one of the false ways of thinking about abortion is to think about it in over-simple terms.

Hence, the contents of the rest of this book are as follows. In the second chapter I begin one stage back from the current, mainstream philosophical literature, discussing the simplest view on the issue of abortion, namely that the moral rights and wrongs of abortion can be unproblematically settled by determining the moral status of the foetus. Non-philosophers who believe this underestimate the difficulty of proving that the foetus has one particular status rather than another and, more seriously, fail to 'consider all the relevant issues' in the way consistency requires. Almost any view on the moral status of the foetus, and its upshot for abortion, has consequences concerning issues such as euthanasia, infanticide, our treatment of animals and so on, and these consequences, far from being unproblematic, require further discussion and defence.

Those philosophers who aim to settle the abortion issue by showing that the foetus is not a *person* are, at least in theory, prepared to accept the consequences of their view and produce more elaborate arguments in support of it. So in the third chapter I try to show the inadequacy of the arguments and in this connection discuss the concept of a person and speciesism. The criticism of this, currently prevailing, radical position on abortion leads on naturally to a discussion of the other mainstream position I mentioned, namely utilitarianism, which occupies Chapter Four.

Both these positions, in defending a permissive line on abortion, involve rejecting conventional morality on other sorts of killing (for instance, infanticide). This could be seen as the inevitable result of one aspect of their extreme simplicity. For since both positions, in being simple, operate with so few notions, they take no account of what is special about, or peculiar to, abortion as a form of killing, namely that it is the termination of a pregnancy, something that essentially involves a woman's body. But the feminist insistence on the importance of this point is surely correct. So I turn, in Chapter Five, to discussing the one mainstream article which tries to support a permissive line on abortion, without rejecting conventional morality concerning other forms of killing, by emphasizing what is peculiar to abortion. This is an article by Judith Jarvis Thomson[1] which introduces the right to determine what happens to one's own body in relation to the issue of the morality of abortion.

Her article, as I argue, does not succeed in establishing a permissive position, but, more interesting than its failure is its implicit introduction into the discussion of abortion of what, I maintain, is the minimally necessary level of complexity. This is not merely because it introduces women's rights. It also allows that some abortions may be wrong *in different ways*, for instance, unjust or callous, and thereby begins to discuss the issue in the vocabulary of the virtues and vices.

Familiar as this rich vocabulary is, few people nowadays recognize the fact that it can be embedded in a particularly rich and complex moral theory. And here is the explanation of why the name of Aristotle appears in the list of topics at the beginning of this chapter: in a purely theoretical Chapter Six I outline a modified, modernized Aristotelian theory. I offer this as the rich, complex theory in terms of which we should be thinking about moral issues; a theory which, if it does not yield simple, right answers, at least does not yield simple, wrong ones, and illustrate the powers of its complexity in Chapter Seven.

Modernized Aristotelianism, like every other modern moral theory, regards the biological differences between men and women (officially) as morally irrelevant. The last piece of complexity, which I introduce in the final chapter, is the idea that we might try taking as intrinsically relevant to moral philosophy the brute fact that women bear children and men do not.

3 MORALITY, LEGISLATION AND ABORTION

Viewed one way, the issue of abortion is about killing or the taking of human life; viewed in another way, it is an issue about women's rights. Over the last twenty years or so, these two ways of viewing the issue have standardly been expressed as two opposing views about abortion: the so-called 'conservative' and 'liberal' (or 'extreme liberal' or 'radical') views. As the labels indicate, the views tend to be about what the laws governing abortion should be, the conservatives maintaining that the laws should be very restrictive, the liberals maintaining that abortion should be available in a wide range of circumstances.

So familiar has this opposition become that it is important for me to make clear at the outset that this book does not take up either of these two sides. This is not because it remains entirely uncommitted, nor because I argue for some moderate line on legislation, but rather because I concentrate on arguments concerning *morality* and do not consider the further complex range of considerations relevant to legislation. Concerning the first we can ask, 'Is such and such right or wrong or morally innocuous?' and the arguments belong to moral philosophy; concerning the second, 'Should we have laws covering such and such, and what form should they take?', the arguments belong to legal or political philosophy. Though hardly independent of each other, these questions are distinct; and there is no simple connection to be made between the rightness, wrongness or moral indifference of an act or practice, and the propriety or desirability of having a law which requires, permits or forbids it.

In some cases this is perfectly obvious and no one makes mistakes about it. There is nothing intrinsically right (or wrong) in driving on the left (or right) but we want laws to guarantee that everyone follows the same convention. Conversely, there is, it might be said, something intrinsically wrong in being spiteful, in telling cruel lies to hurt people, in betraying one's friends, but (apart from extreme cases) we do not have laws governing such acts, and nor would most of us want them. Such laws would do more harm than good, might well encourage spite and betrayal rather than discouraging them, would be open to abuse, might be impossible to enforce and so on; and all these considerations speak against having legislation against spite and betrayal though they do not in any way suggest that spite and betrayal are anything but morally wrong.

But what is obvious in one area may be forgotten in another, and it is noteworthy that in many life and death areas people do confuse the questions 'Is it (always) wrong?' and 'Should we have a law against it or should the law permit it?' So, for instance, it is easy to confuse the issue of whether euthanasia is always wrong with the question of whether legislation permitting it would be the first step towards a Hitlerian elimination of the unfit. Once the issues are distinguished, it can be seen that one might reasonably hold that euthanasia was sometimes morally permissible, but also be very chary of supporting legislation that permitted it. In arguments concerning capital punishment, it is easy to confuse the question of whether some human beings are so wicked that their lives are worthless, with the question of whether a fallible judicial system can be guaranteed to apply the death penalty only to those who putatively deserve it. Distinguishing the issues, one might agree with retributionists that some people deserve to die but continue to oppose capital punishment.

The mention of capital punishment may serve to remind us that, although we can often distinguish questions about legislation from questions about morality, it is not always possible to do so. For one of the most familiar objections to capital punishment is that it is legalized murder, and hence as morally wrong as the very crime for which it is supposedly an appropriate punishment. Indeed, arguments about what laws there should be must presuppose a background of decisions about the rightness and wrongness of certain sorts of acts, for (to a certain extent and in some very complicated way) the law is supposed to enshrine and reflect morality. By and large, we want serious moral injustices to be treated as serious legal injustices; by and large we do not want morally innocuous acts to be treated as crimes. Moreover, we do not, by and large, want the upholders of law and order to act in ways that are morally wrong in order to uphold or enforce the laws. Hence the objection I just mentioned to capital punishment; hence the arguments waged back and forth over the methods the police may use to secure confessions from known criminals.

There is a good illustration of how complicated the arguments concerning legislation can be even when there is perfect agreement about the morality of the issue. For suppose it is universally agreed that commercial surrogacy is morally quite all right, it certainly does not follow that commercial surrogacy should be legalized. The law must say something about what is to happen when the contracting couple and/or the surrogate mother change their minds during the pregnancy; and what should it say? What if the surrogate mother decides that she does not want to go through with the pregnancy after all – should the law restrict her access to abortion? What if it turns out that the baby is going to be born damaged in some way – should the law give the contracting couple any right to insist on abortion even if the surrogate mother does not want it? And what if the surrogate mother decides she wants to keep the baby after all – should the law permit this or not? Some quite general arguments concerning the connections between morality and the law support the idea that, where possible, we want serious moral injustices to be treated as serious legal injustices. Hence, in this particular area, we do not want there to be legally valid contracts which license people acting (morally) unjustly. There is no possible legally valid contract in Europe or America by means of which I can contract myself into slavery however eager I might be to do so. And one of the criticisms that is made of commercial surrogacy is that it involves legally valid contracts which are not morally binding, creating the possibility of people acting (morally) unjustly with the backing of the law.

Although arguments about what laws there should be presuppose, at least in a general way, a background of argument and decisions about moral right and wrong, the converse is not true. Arguments and decisions about moral questions are, with one sole exception, independent of questions about legislation. The sole exception is the issue of civil disobedience, of the moral rights and wrongs of breaking the law. In this context one may consider whether an act could be wrong because, and only because, it was against the law; if one decided that it could be, one would thereby have forged a direct connection between the morality and the legality of an act. But in general there is no such direct connection.

The confusion of questions about morality and legislation is particularly common in arguments about abortion, which is no doubt why this important distinction is glossed over by the familiar way of defining the opposing parties. One reason why the questions become readily confused in debate is because of the tactics of opposition. Many people, particularly women, do think there is something wrong about having an abortion, that it is not a morally innocuous matter, but also think that the current abortion laws are if anything still too restrictive, and find it difficult to articulate their position on the *morality* of abortion without, apparently betraying the feminist campaign concerning *legislation*. To give an inch on 'a woman's right to choose', to suggest even for a moment that having an abortion is not only 'exercising that right' (which sounds fine) but also 'ending a human life' (which sounds like homicide) or even 'ending a potential human life' (which sounds at least serious) is to play into the hands of the conservatives.

What happens to the conservative and the liberal sides of the debate once the distinction between questions of morality and questions of legislation is drawn? In theory, drawing the distinction opens up the possibility of four different positions.

Morality of abortion	Laws on abortion	Position
Wrong	Restrictive	Conservative
Innocuous	Restrictive	'Totalitarian'
Innocuous	Liberal	Liberal/Radical
Wrong	Liberal	Liberal/Moderate

The 'totalitarian' position is of merely theoretical interest. (It might be occupied by someone in an under-populated country, indifferent both to women's rights and to appeals to the sanctity of life, who thought it was necessary to increase the population quickly.) The first position is a familiar one. It is well known that the conservative position on legislation about abortion is based on a corresponding conservative position about its morality. According to the conservative view, abortion is morally wrong because it is the taking of human life, and hence, like any other case of homicide, justifiable in only a restricted range of circumstances, which should be laid down by law.

It is the possibility of two distinct liberal positions, which for want of better labels I will henceforth distinguish as the 'radical' and the 'moderate', which is not so familiar, and much that is said on the liberal side about women's rights leaves it quite unclear which of two views about the morality of abortion its supporters hold. Do they hold that abortion is morally quite innocuous – and hence that to have laws restricting women's access is as absurd and punitive as having laws which decreed, say, that women (though not men) were forbidden to cut their hair or smoke? Or do they agree with the conservatives that it is a morally very serious matter but hold that nevertheless the suffering and lack of freedom that women must at present undergo when abortion is not legally available not only justify but require our having laws which permit this wrong to be done whenever the woman wishes it? Is abortion a necessary evil as things are at present, or not an evil at all? Or are many champions of liberal legislation and 'a woman's right to choose' not clear about which position they hold?

Some liberals are avowedly radicals. They do indeed explicitly maintain that abortion is *not* a morally serious matter, not a matter of the taking of even potential human life, but simply something which removes a bit of living tissue from the woman's body, like an appendectomy, or the removal of a cancerous growth. If they maintain this, they can consistently claim that, in having an abortion, all that a woman is doing (which means 'all that is relevant to morality', for it is beyond dispute that having an abortion can be described in all sorts of ways) is exercising her right to choose what happens to her body, or her right to choose not to bear a child.

But this is a substantial position on the moral status of the fœtus, calling for substantial argument addressed to that issue. It is certainly not established merely by asserting a woman's (moral) right to choose; rather, the existence of such a right depends on whether the fœtus is morally on a par with a bit of one's body, like an appendix. Nor can the question of whether killing a fœtus is as morally innocuous as, say, having an appendectomy be settled by arguments concerning the propriety or desirability of past or existing legislation governing abortion. The past legislation may have caused women untold suffering, as well as driving them to back-street abortions. The present legislation may still be open to abuse in the hands of male chauvinist doctors; it may be inconsistent and expressive of the sexist belief that women, unlike men, should not have sex simply for pleasure; it may be part of a (consciously or unconsciously pursued) programme on the part of a predominantly male legislature to keep women subservient. Any or indeed all of this could be true, but its truth would have no bearing on whether abortion was morally innocuous or not. These are considerations relevant to what the laws governing abortion should be, not to whether abortion is morally innocuous or wrong.

In this connection, we might compare arguments concerning abortion legislation with arguments about women's rights in other areas. At the moment, many women's lives are cramped and confined not only by the fact that they get pregnant and have to bear the children if abortion is not available, but also by the fact that they, rather than men, are expected to nurse their aged parents. Many feminists have, I think rightly, protested at the injustice of allowing the burden of 'caring' to fall so heavily on women's shoulders rather than men's in these areas, pointed to inconsistencies in the legislation, argued that it is part of a conspiracy to keep women subordinate, but none, so far as I know, has argued that women should always be given the legal right to kill their children or aged parents as a way of shedding the burden, nor thought that such killings would be morally innocuous.

Although some liberals do explicitly maintain the radical position on the morality of·abortion (that it is morally innocuous), their arguments for that position concern the moral status of the fœtus, not, initially, women's rights. Once it is established (supposedly) that abortion is morally innocuous, comparable to cutting one's hair, or having an appendectomy, because of the status of the fœtus, then, and only then, can one move to arguing that, since this is so, a just legal system must allow women to choose whether or not to have an abortion. Such a position does not make the desirability of liberal abortion laws conditional on the present lack of effective birth control, or the plight of women burdened with children. It simply points to the obvious fact that it would be absurd, punitive and unjust to have laws restricting women's (but not men's) access to plastic surgery or appendectomies.

It is important to note that this 'radical' position leaves no room for the possibility that there might ever be anything wrong in my having an abortion. To agonize over whether or not to have one, to feel guilty about having one, or about having got pregnant in circumstances that necessitate having one, to make a solemn vow that one will never make that mistake again – any such reaction is, according to this position, simply a mistake. One should no more feel guilty about having an abortion than one should about having an appendectomy or being sterilized or using contraception or being chaste. For, according to this position, abortion itself is morally innocuous and all one is doing in having one is exercising one's right to choose to do something morally innocuous, such as cutting one's hair.

This 'radical' view is, I suspect, more often asserted than believed, and I think the reason for this is the one I mentioned above: that people committed to supporting liberal *legislation* concerning abortion fail to distinguish questions about that from questions about its *morality*, and think that somehow, the only available feminist position is the radical moral view.

That it is difficult for sincere campaigners for liberal legislation to express anything other than the radical moral view that abortion is morally innocuous is made clear in a most instructive book which I read while writing this one. Early in it, one woman is quoted as saying:

> I decided to have an abortion but I didn't like myself for doing it, I didn't feel good about it and the fact that I was exercising my right to choose did not heal the pain I felt at having ended a life.
>
> But when I tried to talk with friends who are involved with the abortion battle, as I have always been, about this they were really unsympathetic. One woman got very cross and said to me, 'It's not on to talk like this, you'll be joining the anti-abortionists next.'[2]

Another is quoted as saying:

> I used to belong to a women's group and they were all pro-abortion, but I didn't share the way they felt about it. I had suffered over the abortion, I felt damaged by it and not exactly jubilant at having had the opportunity to exercise this right to choose. So I didn't need the heavy political support. I really wanted people who felt the ambivalences as I did and who felt regret as I did.
>
> In a way it was this issue which brought me into conflict with the women's movement. I had always been involved with issues and groups before and I was as political as anyone but I supposed I realized that the business of abortion is much more complicated for women than just a legal right.[3]

The author comments on this as follows:

> Other women have expressed similar feelings and it is quite clear there is here a dilemma for feminism. On the one hand, it is essential that the struggle for abortion for those women who want it must continue. As the moral climate becomes more reactionary and anti-abortionists work hard to have the Abortion Act repealed, there is a very real danger of a return to a situation where women are forced to bear children they feel they cannot cope with, or resort to back-street abortions. On the other hand, it is important that the political battle for this right should not gag women, making them feel they must not speak out about their ambivalent feelings since

these can be taken as reasons for preventing abortion being available. Women who have campaigned for the right to choose need now to acknowledge that having ambivalent, distressing feelings is a legitimate part of the experience and in no way undermines the importance of allowing women who feel they need an abortion to have it with a minimum of trauma.[4]

It is not clear here just what the 'dilemma for feminism' is supposed to be. If abortion is a morally innocuous matter then it is indeed 'essential that the struggle for abortion for those women who want it', no matter how they are circumstanced or what their reasons are, 'must continue'. But believing that it is a morally innocuous matter should not, of course, lead anyone to 'gag' any women who are still too confused or socially conditioned to have realized this fact, nor any women who, although they appreciate it intellectually, have not yet managed to bring their emotions into line. Women who feel guilt or regret when they have had abortions should, like women who feel guilt when their husbands abandon them for younger or prettier women, be helped and supported, and shown they have nothing to feel guilty about, not gagged. There is no dilemma here.

If, on the other hand, abortion is not a morally innocuous matter, then feminism, at least as presently understood, may be faced not so much with a 'dilemma', i.e. a choice between two equally unfavourable alternatives, as a problem. If abortion is a morally serious matter, then the women who feel guilt and regret when they have had abortions are not merely having feelings which are 'a legitimate part of the experience' (whatever that may mean) but the morally appropriate feelings, and this certainly undermines in *some* way 'the importance of allowing women who feel they need an abortion to have it with a minimum of trauma'. If there is something wrong about abortion then it is far from obvious that morally responsible feminists should be 'struggling' to make it available to 'those women who [just happen to] want it', i.e. for abortion on demand as a legal right. It is far from clear that they should want it to be available to 'women who *feel* they need it', and not even obvious that it should be available to women who do in fact need it. It becomes important for morally responsible feminists to consider, concerning morality, what sort of wrong they think abortion may be, and, concerning legislation, whether it is the sort of moral wrong which the state may, or should, try to control.

For if, as conservatives believe, abortion is a form of homicide, no morally responsible person who shared that belief could think that women should be able to do it without any legal repercussions, however difficult their lives might be made as a consequence. (Compare again what would be said about women killing their children or aged parents when they are stuck with the burden of caring for them.) If abortion, though not as serious as homicide, is still wrong in some way, there is still a problem, for a morally responsible person who shares that belief, about whether women should be given a legal right to do this wrong thing under any circumstances.

Feminism 'as presently understood' is closely associated with the campaign for 'abortion on demand', i.e. a campaign for legislation which would give women the legal right to an abortion under *any* circumstances (not merely the 'justifying' circumstances at present cited in various abortion laws in Europe and America). And if abortion is a morally serious matter, the problem that feminism faces is to find arguments to justify that campaign.

It will not be enough simply to insist on a woman's (moral rather than legal) 'right to choose' if it is agreed that abortion is morally wrong in some way. For if abortion is morally wrong then it may be that a woman does not have a (moral) right to choose to have one. Can one 'have a moral right' to do what is morally wrong? People's intuitions about what is involved in 'having a right' vary a lot, and correspondingly there may be varying ways of answering that question. One might think that the answer was 'No' – and, in that case, if one thought that abortion was wrong in some way, one would have to give up saying that women had the 'right to choose'. One might think that the answer was 'Yes', or 'Yes, in a way' or 'Yes, in some cases'. But such an answer would call for elaboration – that one may have a right to do what is wrong has at least an apparent oddity about it which would need to be explained away – and the need for elaboration rules out a *simple* appeal to a woman's 'right to choose'.

Moreover, even if it were established that a woman does have such a (moral) right, it might still be morally wrong of her to exercise that right if abortion is wrong in some way. And if to exercise it may be morally wrong it is far from obvious that the moral right should be enshrined in and protected by law. So once again, if it is agreed that abortion is wrong in some way, a simple appeal to a woman's right to choose is not enough to justify liberal or permissive legislation on abortion. This is not to say that liberal legislation cannot be justified by people who think that abortion is wrong. But it is to say that their justification cannot be quickly and easily given in terms of the right to choose.

To say only that much should hardly count as 'joining the anti-abortionists'. And indeed, there are feminists who hold that abortion is a morally serious matter – and that, moreover, it is important that it be recognized as such – but who also argue that, given the existing set-up, liberal legislation is necessary. So, for instance, Joanna Chambers of the Birth Control Trust is quoted in *Mixed Feelings* as saying:

> None of us likes abortion; I certainly wish it did not have to exist. But there is little effort going into devising such effective forms of birth control that it will be eliminated. Until this happens and until life is made a great deal easier for women with children, abortion seems to me an absolutely essential right.[5]

It is not, indeed, clear from this whether Chambers is supporting abortion *on demand* in the phrase 'absolutely essential right'. Nor is it quite certain that she thinks abortion is actually wrong. But it seems tolerably clear that she thinks that if and when we have effective birth control and women with children are not thereby badly off, then something more akin to the conservative position on abortion laws would be the right one. It also seems that Chambers should agree with the conservatives that, in particular circumstances, particular women would be doing wrong in having an abortion even if they were thereby exercising this 'essential right'. Abortion, she must surely agree, is not an *alternative* to contraception; it is not morally all right for me to be feckless about contraception because I can always fall back on having an abortion. Nor is it obviously all right for me to have an abortion if I am a woman whose life with children would be easy. This position actually leaves open the possibility that, in certain circumstances, and despite the existence of the right to abortion, it would be utterly wrong of me to have one.

Chambers herself might well want to reject this possibility; nevertheless, it is clearly a tenable position, and for want of a better label I shall call the view that 'Abortion is morally wrong but liberal legislation concerning it is necessary as things are at present', the liberal/moderate position.

It is true that to occupy such a position requires giving up a certain sort of collective feminine self-righteousness about women who choose to have abortions – they can no longer be automatically congratulated on 'only exercising their right' – nor is it appropriate for people who occupy such a position to admire women who treat abortion as a minor event in their lives. Mira Dana, to quote once again from *Mixed Feelings*, says:

> Because abortion has become more freely available, it is sometimes fashionable and liberal to think of it as a minor event in a woman's life. One woman I remember said: 'I have written in my diary: Friday – 1. Put car in garage. 2. Abortion. 3. Shopping. 4. Take car out of garage ...'

and goes on to say that she thinks this attitude is 'almost as dangerous as that which seeks to claim that abortion is murder and, therefore, should not be available'. There is, she says, 'no way of avoiding the issue of an abortion being the termination of a potential human life ...'[6]

To cease to admire and congratulate women who regard their abortions as on a par with their shopping is, indeed, to lose out on a bit of feminine solidarity. But part of the point of *Mixed Feelings* is to bring out the fact that refusing to acknowledge as morally appropriate emotions the guilt, remorse, regret and pain that many women feel about their abortions is also (and probably to a much greater extent) betraying feminine solidarity. The woman I first quoted above (p. 19) – the one whose friend accused her of being about to join the anti-abortionists – went on to say, 'And I found myself feeling afterwards that this hard line is really cruel; it's absolutely not about sisters working towards a good world for each other',[7] and the second woman, as is revealed in the quotation, found herself forced to leave her sisters in her women's group. Mira Dana, if I understand her correctly, thinks that the 'fashionable and liberal' way of regarding abortion as a morally innocuous event is dangerous because of its tendency to harm women, a tendency which makes it almost as anti-feminist as that of the anti-abortion campaigners. Surrounded by upholders of the fashionable view, women who have had abortions will either express their grief and regret and suffer ostracism and rejection from the very people who should be giving them support, or suppress their feelings, to their psychological detriment. (The woman she mentions, who had casually listed '2. Abortion' before '3. Shopping', goes on to say, 'Not until four years later did I realize the full importance of what it meant for me to have had it.' I take it that Dana's point in quoting her is to illustrate that women can be conned into thinking of abortion as a minor event, and deceive themselves so successfully that their emotional reaction to 'the termination of a potential human life' may not emerge for years. It is not clear from what is quoted whether she thinks that the emotional reaction must take place even if it never does emerge (for some women do continue to say sincerely that it was no more to them than a minor inconvenience) or whether she holds more moderately that it is quite probable that it has taken place even in women who deny it.)

So the fact that the liberal/moderate position requires ceasing to encourage women to regard abortion as morally innocuous seems no betrayal of feminism; if anything, the reverse is true.

Occupying the liberal/moderate position also requires, as I mentioned above, finding arguments to justify women's being given a *legal* right to do what is acknowledged (by people who hold this position) to be *morally* wrong in some way. Such arguments would be squarely in the arena of *political* or *legal* philosophy, not in the arena of moral philosophy, and as such, as I said at the outset, beyond the scope of this book. That is why the book cannot be described as taking up either of the two standardly described sides. Like the liberal/moderate position, *and* the conservative position, it is opposed to the liberal/radical line that abortion is morally innocuous, maintaining instead that it is wrong. Like the liberal/moderate position, and unlike the most extreme conservative position, it does not go so far as to say that it is as wrong as murder. So on the *morality* of abortion, it is in agreement with the liberal/moderate position. But, thereby, it is also in agreement, concerning questions of morality, with many supporters of a fairly conservative position, and, unlike the liberal/moderate position, it remains uncommitted over legislation. In fact, I have only a few convictions, and many doubts and confusions, about what our present legislation should be; but even if I were perfectly convinced that there should be abortion on demand or, alternatively, that our present laws should be made rather more restrictive, such conviction would not be based on the arguments considered in this book. It would be based on arguments about the extent to which the state is justified in restricting individual freedoms, where the line between public and private morality is to be drawn, in what ways the laws of a democratic state should try to accommodate completely opposed moral views within society, which rights a just state must protect, whether women should be especially favoured now to compensate for past injustice – and no doubt several other theoretical issues in political philosophy. And this book gives no such arguments. It is concerned only with arguments in moral philosophy.

NOTES

1 Thomson, Judith Jarvis (1971) 'A Defense of Abortion', *Philosophy & Public Affairs*, vol. 1, no.1. Reprinted in Singer, P. (ed.) (1986) *Applied Ethics*, Oxford University Press.

2 Neustatter, Angela with Newson, Gina (1986) *Mixed Feelings*, Pluto Press, p. 38.
3 *Ibid.*, pp. 109–10.
4 *Ibid.*, p. 110.
5 *Ibid.*, p. 84.
6 *Ibid.*, p. 108.
7 *Ibid.*, p. 38.

CHAPTER TWO

The moral status of the fœtus

1 INTRODUCTION

The simplest view on the issue of abortion, the one often expressed explicitly or implicitly by non-philosophers in letters to newspapers, discussions on the wireless and so on, is that the moral rights and wrongs of abortion can be unproblematically settled by determining the moral status of the fœtus. Hence it is common to find people on the conservative side insisting that the fœtus is an unborn baby and hence that abortion is infanticide or murder and absolutely wrong, while people on the opposite side insist that the fœtus is just a clump of living cells and hence that abortion is merely an operation which removes some part of one's body and hence is morally innocuous.

Now it is certainly true that the question of the moral status of the fœtus is important, for according to what its status is, different arguments will bear upon the rights and wrongs of abortion.[1] If, as conservatives believe, the fœtus has the same moral status as a baby, then the mother's moral right to abortion is, to say the least, problematic; if there were any such right, a quite particular case would have to be made out for it. If, on the other hand, the fœtus has the same moral status as, say, a kidney, then the argument for the mother's moral right to abortion could proceed, quite generally, as an argument concerning the right, of both women and men, to decide what happens to their own bodies. But to agree that the question is important, even fundamental, is not to say that it is the only relevant question and that the issue of abortion can be settled by answering it.

There are at least two respects in which things are not as simple as many people who express either of the extreme views mentioned above seem to think. One is that neither side has a compelling argument for their position on the status of the fœtus. The second is that abortion cannot be treated as an isolated issue. No view about the moral status of the fœtus yields anything determinate about the rightness or wrongness of abortion unless combined with other, more general moral views (about killing, for example) and these bear on other issues besides abortion. As a consequence, anyone trying to move from a premise about the status of the fœtus to a simple conclusion of the form 'so abortion is always wrong' or 'so abortion is always morally innocuous' is likely to find themselves surprised by what they have committed themselves to on other moral issues.

Neither problem is easily avoided by taking some other line on the status of the fœtus, despite the fact that a variety of positions other than the two extreme ones are available. The aim of this chapter is to familiarize the reader with the range of possible positions and the simpler arguments concerning them, and to illustrate in what ways each of them is problematic.

This involves me in doing two things. I make a point, where possible, of laying out the arguments for the various positions very explicitly, stressing rather laboriously the distinction between questions concerning the truth of their premises and the question of their validity. The distinction between the truth of premises and the validity of argument is one of the most (if not the most) fundamental distinctions in philosophy so I take it this is worth doing for its own sake. But emphasizing it has a particular purpose here too. Abortion is one of the moral issues concerning which passions run particularly high. If we are to have any reasonable discussion, rather than impassioned slanging matches, with people whose views are different from our own, we must make an effort to understand why they believe what they do, rather than immediately dismissing their views as wicked or stupid. And to understand their arguments, to appreciate that they are, perhaps, as good as our own, to see that other people perhaps start with quite different premises from those which strike us as the obvious ones, all this may lead us to see that our own positions are not as unassailable, not as obviously virtuous or reasonable, as we might have thought.

Laying the arguments out explicitly is, inevitably, not always possible, for sometimes they do not even purport to be conclusive. Rather, they put forward considerations which make the position in question plausible. Here the important point to recognize is that the argument is not conclusive, but might be reasonable all the same.

Secondly, in the discussion of each of the various positions on the moral status of the fœtus, I raise its consequences not only for abortion but also for other areas. The point of doing this is to illustrate vividly why abortion cannot be treated as an isolated issue. The consequences cover quite a range of areas, varying according to which particular view of the fœtus is in question. So, for instance, euthanasia and killing in self defence come up in relation to the conservative view that abortion is like murder, but are not relevant to the extreme liberal view that abortion is like an appendectomy or hair cut. Surrogacy, on the other hand, is particularly relevant to the extreme liberal view so it gets discussed there but not in relation to other views, since they remain relatively uncommitted over it.

Embryonic and fœtal research

However, one issue that has consequences for all views is the new problem area of embryonic or fœtal research (see Appendix Four).

When, in 1984, the issue of research on human embryos hit the headlines, many people in Britain were surprised to discover that there was no existing legislation that, strictly speaking, governed fœtal research. A number of living fœtuses are obtained by spontaneous abortion, and also by 'hysterotomy' (an abortion procedure sometimes used after the fifth month of pregnancy which is like a Caesarean). In Britain, if such fœtuses are old enough to count as legally viable (twenty-eight weeks), they count as premature children and fall under the Protection of Children Act. But if they are younger than that, nothing in our existing law applies to them at all, only the 'less formal mechanism' of the guidelines suggested by the 'Peel Report' (1972).[2] So the following sort of experiment (which took place in the United States) is not ruled out.

> The living fetuses, ranging in weight from 300 to 980 grams, were then placed in tanks filled with warmed, saline solution (to mimic amniotic fluid). Small cannulas, or tubes, were inserted in the umbilical arteries and veins – for pumping and removing oxygenated blood ... The following is taken from the investigators' report, and details the death of the largest (980 grams) fetus used in the study:
> 'For the whole five hours of life, the fetus did not respire. Irregular gasping movements, twice a minute, occurred in the middle of the experiment but there was no proper respiration. Once the perfusion (i.e. the pumping-in of oxygenated blood) was stopped, however, the gasping respiratory efforts increased to eight or ten per minute ... After stopping the circuit, the heart slowed, became irregular and eventually stopped ... The fetus was quiet, making occasional stretching limb movements very like the ones reported in other human work ... the fetus died twenty-one minutes after leaving the circuit.'[3]

(It should be noted that premature babies weighing less than 500 grams have, with suitable care, survived to grow into healthy children.)

Any position on the moral status of the fœtus is bound to carry some commitment on embryonic or fœtal research, since both it and abortion count as raising issues under the general heading of 'how it is right to treat the human embryo or fœtus'.

The possibility of such research provides a searching test of the radical moral line on abortion. If abortion is to be defended as morally innocuous, calling for no special justification, on the grounds that the human embryo or fœtus is an entity of no moral significance, then all such research becomes morally innocuous too. But suppose, on the other hand, that one wants to say that such research is absolutely wrong. Or suppose one wants to say, more moderately, that much of it would be wrong, though some could be justified in special circumstances. Or suppose one wants to say no more than that it calls for *some* justification – that it could not be undertaken for a whim. Then one must say the same about abortion.

It is, in fact, only as a test of various positions on abortion that I discuss embryonic and fœtal research. Naturally, this is not because I think there is nothing more to be said about them; rather, there is too much. A thorough discussion of the morality of the research would involve, amongst other things, questions about what counts as 'serious' or 'important' research, what sorts of means are justified by the ends of relieving suffering and acquiring knowledge, and the extremely difficult topic of what sort of justification can be given for using other animals rather than human beings as research subjects. And discussing all these issues would have taken me too far from my central concern with abortion (though an aspect of the 'animals issue' does crop up and gets some discussion – see pp. 61–2).

2   THE CONSERVATIVE VIEW

According to the conservative view, the fœtus is in most if not all morally relevant respects like an average adult human being from the moment of conception. This is sometimes expressed as the view that 'human life begins at conception or fertilization', or that what we have from the moment of conception is, as I have heard it said, 'not (just) a potential human being but a human being with potential'.

There are two arguments for this position.

The theological argument

The argument begins from premises about the existence and nature of God, and the existence of the soul; and fixes conception as the time at which the entity acquires a soul.

The further premise required is that (roughly) it is the possession of a soul that matters morally and is what distinguishes human beings from other entities. From suitable premises of this sort it does indeed follow that, from the moment of conception, the fœtus is, in at least many morally relevant respects, on a par with a fully-developed, adult human being. In other words, the argument is *valid*, that is, its conclusion does indeed follow from its premises. But this leaves open the further question of whether the premises are true.

The discussion of this further question would take us well beyond the area of moral philosophy into those of theology and metaphysics, and beyond the scope of this book. In fact, the view commonly identified as 'the' Catholic view – that the fœtus is ensouled at the moment of conception – is not the only Catholic view and, in particular, was not held by Thomas Aquinas. For complicated reasons, in part derived from Aristotle, Aquinas held that the human soul was infused into the fœtus only when the latter developed to the point of having a human shape and basic human organs. Moreover, since ensoulment requires a divine act it could not even be said that, in its earliest stages, the fœtus is a potential human being, for it is not in its own nature to develop the soul. Of course, it does not follow from this that Aquinas held abortion in the early stages to be morally permissible. I mention the point only to illustrate how very far afield the discussion would have to go if I were to enter into the details of different theological premises of the argument for the conservative view.

The secular argument

This argument does not depend on any theological or metaphysical premises. It begins from the premise that a newly born infant is morally on a par with an adult. It then adds, as a second premise, that working backwards in time from the birth of the infant, there is no point at which we can draw a line and say 'This is the morally significant point'. There is no morally significant difference between a newly born infant and a baby about to be born, no morally significant difference between a baby about to be born and a baby of eight months two weeks, between a baby at eight months two weeks and at eight months . . . and so on all the way back to the moment of conception, for the development of a fœtus is so gradual. (Of course, there are physical differences, but this is not the sort of difference that counts as morally significant.) So, assuming that a newly born infant is morally on a par with an adult, so must the fœtus be, from the moment of conception.

Objections to the secular argument

The premises Unlike the theological argument, this is an argument about which we can raise the further question about the truth of its premises without going far afield. Some people do not accept the premise that a newly born infant is morally on a par with an adult. (We shall be considering this view shortly so all I shall say now is that this roughly is the view that the morally significant feature of most adult human beings is that they are *persons* and newly born infants are not persons and hence not morally on a par.)

Many others have wanted to deny the second premise, that the development of the fœtus is so gradual that there is no point at which we can say, 'Here is the place to draw the boundary line'. So let us consider this premise.

Birth Is it true, as was claimed, that there is no morally significant difference between a newly born baby and a baby about to be born? Could one not say instead that, on the contrary, the difference between being born and not yet being born *is* morally significant?

What reasons could one give for that? A very straightforward argument is that after birth we have an independently existing creature whereas before birth we do not. After birth we have an entity separate from the mother which we can see and touch independently of seeing or touching her. Moreover, in seeing and touching it we are not simply relating to an object. After birth, we have a new member of the human community which we smile or frown at, see

as adorable or repulsive or amusing, which we pinch or
fondle, are cruel or kind to, are responsible or irresponsible
about and so on. After birth we have something to which
we can ascribe its own personality, its own interests or
rights.

But against this it could be objected that a mistake has
been made about what is making the difference. We may
think it is the difference between being born and not, but
on further consideration it seems to come down to the
difference between being visible and tangible, especially
perhaps the former, and not. According to a variety of
reports, many people's whole attitude to fœtuses changes
after they have seen good photographs or films of the
developing fœtus in the womb. Hitherto, they report, they
had thought of babies as babies and fœtuses as things; now
they have actually seen the fœtuses they think of them, at
least in the later stages of development, as babies.

The main objection to finding a morally significant
difference between a newly born infant and a fœtus about
to be born comes from the fact of premature birth. (One
might regard this main objection as grounding the above
point about the irrelevancy of what one can see. Anyone
who has seen a baby born prematurely at seven months
knows exactly what a fœtus in the later stages of its
development looks like.) For it seems strange we should say
of a baby born prematurely at seven months and in an
incubator that it has acquired its moral status as a result of
the accident of the mother's having given birth prematurely,
and that in a normal pregnancy at seven months it would
not have had that moral status. How can the moral status of
something depend on the accident of where it is – in an
incubator or in a womb? This raises another issue which has
affected where people have wanted to draw the boundary
of moral significance.

Viability   A fœtus is said to be viable at the point where it
could survive independently of the mother. It seems obvious
to some people that although there is no morally significant
difference between a newly born baby and one about to be
born, and none between a two months premature baby in

an incubator and a seven-month fœtus in the womb, there is a significant difference between the seven-month old fœtus, wherever it is, and, say, a three-month-old fœtus that could not possibly survive independently. And, it might be said, this is the real difference that the birth criterion required. After viability we have, not an actually independently existing creature, but a potentially independently existing creature, and this potentiality makes all the difference. Before viability all we have is something that is part of the woman's body, with no life independent of her life. After viability we have something that happens to be living and developing in the woman's body, but could be living and developing elsewhere. And, as we said before, it seems absurd to say that a creature has a different moral status according to where it happens to be living and developing.

Unfortunately, as we now know only too well, medical technology is shifting the viability boundary line, and might, for all we know, shift it back all the way to the moment of conception. Reflecting again on the viability criterion it can be seen that there are problems inherent in the phrase 'could survive independently of the mother': 'could survive', but under what conditions? Given the best available medical resources? Of course, 'available' brings its own difficulties – are the best medical resources available to someone too poor to afford them, or too far down the waiting queue to get them? But putting those difficulties to one side we are still left with the problem of medical technology progressing all the time. And if it seems absurd to say that a creature has different moral status according to where it happens to be living and developing, it seems equally absurd to say this can change according to when it can live and develop independently. But if we limit 'could survive independently of the mother' to 'could, given the best contemporary medical resources . . .' this absurdity will be the result. We could imagine the case where a six-month fœtus conceived in a particular year would not be viable and thus not have the same moral status as a newly born baby and adult, yet a six-month fœtus conceived at some later date, when medical technology had progressed, would be viable and thus would have the same moral status as a newly born baby. But if we do not limit 'could survive independently of the mother' in this way, but take it to mean something like 'the fœtus is morally significant from the moment it might one day be able to survive independently of the mother' then, as noted above, for all we know that 'moment' might be the moment of conception, which would be the conservative view.

More can be said about the drawing of a boundary line, but the difficulties inherent in the above two most plausible attempts make it clear that drawing one is not a simple matter. And we should remind ourselves at this point what such a boundary line is meant to do, in the context of debates about abortion. It is meant to mark not just a difference, but a difference of such significance that it can bear the weight of our saying: 'Before this point it is all right to kill, and after this point it is wrong to kill'. (Or, in more neutral terms, 'Before this point abortion may be permissible, but after this point it is *killing*'.) But given the uncontrovertible fact that, from the moment of conception, the fœtus's development is a gradual process, the possibility of there being such a line seems remote.

The argument's validity

However, a further objection can be brought against the second argument. Unlike the first argument, it is, as it stands, invalid. Expressed more abstractly, the argument goes like this:

First premise   At some stage, we have something, call it x, with a certain property, call it F. (E.g. we have a newly born baby with the property of having the same moral status as an adult being.)

Second premise   Tracing x back through its development there is no point at which we can find a change in it which justifies our saying that at this point it changed in such a way that it acquired F when it had not had it before. (The premise of the process being gradual.)

Conclusion   So it must have the property F right from the beginning.

But now suppose that:

First premise   We have something with a certain property, namely a patch with the property of being blue (which used to be green).

And let us suppose that:

Second premise   Tracing it back through its gradual changes as it faded in the sun to a slightly less pure green to an increasingly blue one, through a particularly green turquoise and so on to blue, there is no point at which we can find a change in it which justifies our saying that at this point it changed in such a way that it became blue when it had not been before.

Conclusion   So it must have been blue right from the beginning.

This shows that something is wrong with the argument. For if it was of a valid form then any pair of true premises of the right form would necessitate a true conclusion. But here we have imagined true premises of the right form and got a conclusion which is obviously false.

This formal objection provides the support for the common objection that even if there is nowhere precisely to draw the line in the fœtus's development, nevertheless there obviously is a morally significant difference between a newly born baby and a two-week-old embryo, just as there is obviously a visually significant difference between blue and green. It is a mistake to infer from the fact that something which (a) changes gradually, and (b) definitely has a certain property at some stage, therefore had that property all along. Rather, we should infer that the property itself (being blue, having a certain moral status) is a matter of degree. Turquoise things are not true blue but almost blue; six-month fœtuses (say) do not have quite the same moral status as a newly born baby but have almost that status. Green things simply are not blue; month-old embryos simply do not have the moral status of a baby. An ancient version of this point is known as the paradox or puzzle of the heap. One grain of sand is not a heap of sand. And just one grain of sand cannot make the difference between something's being a heap and its not being a heap. But if one adds grain after grain, eventually there will be a heap of sand. (The view that the status of the fœtus is a matter of degree can be seen as implicit in many abortion laws which put different, and increasingly strong, conditions on abortions in the first, second and third trimesters.)

Against this objection it can be maintained that moral status is quite unlike the property of being blue and does not admit of degree. (When abortion is discussed in terms of the right to life and whether or not the fœtus has such a right, this point is sometimes made by saying that one either has the right to life, absolutely, or one does not – nothing can have the right to life 'to a certain extent', or 'to a certain degree'.) But it is very difficult to maintain this position without being committed to quite extreme views about animals. Must I say *either* that animals have the same moral status as babies and adult human beings *or* that they have no moral status at all and that the wanton killing of any animal is morally insignificant? May I not say that, faced with a choice between saving the life of a chimpanzee and the life of a duck I should choose to save the chimpanzee (and should save both if I can)?

Consequences of the conservative view

So much for the (preliminary) arguments for and against the conservative view. What are its consequences?

Abortion   The consequences for abortion are, simply, that killing a fœtus, from the moment of conception, is as wrong as killing a human being. Clearly, it is in order to secure this consequence that the view holds the fœtus to be in 'most if not all morally relevant respects' like an average adult. Now I do not think that anyone literally holds that view. Most adults, for instance, have duties and responsibilities, vices and virtues. These are 'morally relevant' if anything is, and no one thinks that even infants are like adults in those respects. The point of maintaining the (literally absurd) view that the fœtus is in 'most if not all morally relevant respects' like an average adult is to guarantee that, as far as taking its life is concerned, the only possible justifications would be those, if any, which would justify taking the life of an average adult.

This is intended, at least traditionally, to rule out two distinguishably different sorts of grounds for abortion. One sort of ground involves not regarding the fœtus as like a human being at all, but as more akin to an animal, or part of the woman's body. The other involves regarding the fœtus as like a human being but not on a par with an average adult human being. (This latter view is, as we shall see later, often expressed as the view that the fœtus is not a person. The fœtus, unlike the average adult or person, can (allegedly) be readily replaced, is not enjoying any particularly valuable quality of life, has no expectations about its future, cannot be said to want to go on living – and these respects are morally relevant to the question of whether or not it may be permissibly killed.) To insist that, as far as taking its life is concerned, the fœtus is to be regarded (a) as a human being and (b) as an average *adult* human at that, is to maintain that these cannot be given as grounds justifying abortion.

When, if ever, is abortion justified on this conservative view? It is usually supposed that, on this view, abortion is justified only in the case where, without it, both mother and child will die, this being taken to be the Catholic position. But it is possible to hold the conservative view without being a Roman Catholic, and then upholders of this view may hold differing positions about when abortion may be justifiable.

Let us, to clear away one confusing issue, put to one side the fact that women do not usually abort themselves, but get someone else to do it for them. (This fact is too significant to be *left* to one side, but we know that miscarriages can be self-induced and can envisage easily a medical technology that has produced a pill which will do this at any stage.) If we put that fact to one side we can consider some abortions as a form of self defence and ask, 'What is one permitted to do in order to preserve one's own life, one's physical and mental well-being?'

It has seemed to many that one is justified in killing another human being in order to preserve one's own life. If this is so then, on the face of it, a woman would be justified in aborting if she did so to preserve her life, supposing that continuing the pregnancy or giving birth would kill her.

However, we need to think how far this so-called 'self defence' justification is intended to carry. The example that we mostly have in the forefront of our minds when we think 'Yes, it's justifiable to kill in self defence' is the case in which someone is trying, or threatening, to kill me and thereby (it might be thought) manifesting his indifference to the value of my life. But if the other human being is endangering my life involuntarily or unknowingly, do we still think it obvious that killing in self defence is justified? Suppose that a child is about to set off a booby-trap which will kill me, or is making noises which will lead the enemy to my hiding place. It is quite innocent of any intention to endanger my life but it is endangering it, and perhaps my only real chance of survival is to kill the child. Those who believe that killing in ordinary self defence is justified do not necessarily think that killing is justified here.

In other cases too, it might seem that self-sacrifice, albeit heroic, is the only decent way to make the choice between 'Me or you'. When small groups of people are faced with the fact that only some of them can survive on the food available till rescue arrives, they sometimes draw lots to determine who will be killed. Many people feel qualms about whether what the survivors did was justified – and yet they did draw lots, they did not just kill without consent. And finally, we might wonder whether it does not make an important difference if I am responsible for our being in the position such that only one out of two (or more) can survive, and the other person (or people) is not responsible. If I am the experienced mountaineer and responsible for packing the food, and you follow me trustingly into fatal circumstances in which it is either you or me – if one of us has to die – should not it be me? Some people would say yes, since I am responsible for our predicament.

Of course, I do not mean to imply by analogy that women whose lives are under threat through pregnancy are always responsible for getting themselves in that position, only that this is sometimes so, whereas the fœtus, regarded as morally on a par with an adult, will always be unlike an adult in being necessarily innocent. It will also be unlike most adults in being totally helpless and defenceless, as a baby is, and this itself may be seen as a reason for giving it special protection. It is not clear that if my choice lies between my life or an infant's it is straightforwardly permissible for me to kill the infant.

The so-called 'self defence' justification becomes even more problematic when we bring in again the fact that usually doctors perform abortions for women. For the doctor is not killing in self defence but in defence of the woman. On the conservative view, this amounts to killing one human being to save another and we do not in general hold that this is something that doctors are permitted to do, even if one of the human beings is the doctor's patient and the other one is not. (We do not, for instance, think that doctors should kill some human beings in order to use their organs to save others.)

What about abortion on grounds other than saving the mother's life – cases such as pregnancy due to rape or incest? Except for fœtal euthanasia, considered below, none of these cases would be permissible on the conservative view.

One could hold that a woman who was pregnant as a result of rape and aborted herself had acted forgivably or excusably on analogy with people who kill when half-crazed by grief or under certain sorts of duress. But the excuse would not extend to any outsider who performed the abortion for her. Similarly an eleven-year-old child might be excused a murder on the grounds of youth, and by analogy excused aborting herself, but the excuse would not extend to someone who murdered or aborted on her behalf. For in both these cases, the fact of rape, or extreme youth, or even the combination of the two, does not license or justify the killing of an innocent human being; it remains wrong and the fact of rape or extreme youth is held to excuse or mitigate the doing of something wrong.

On the conservative view these cases, and all others like them, are best thought of in comparison with infanticide. That a baby is the result of rape, or the result of incest, or the offspring of an eleven-year-old child, does not make it all right to kill it. Nor would it usually be thought permissible to kill a baby because it has a fifty-fifty chance of developing some debilitating disease later in life. (At present, in Britain the law allows pregnant women who are carriers of haemophilia to abort male fœtuses; the male offspring of such carriers have a fifty-fifty change of being born haemophiliac.) Nor would it usually be thought permissible to kill two out of a set of born triplets on the grounds that the family was going to be made too large. So abortion would be equally impermissible on any such grounds (i.e. a statistical likelihood of disability, over-burdening a family, etc.).

Fœtal euthanasia   However, abortions (and some infanticides) might be permissible on the conservative view *if* euthanasia was held to be permissible. A detailed discussion of euthanasia cannot be given here, but I shall make just two points.

The first is that it is particularly hard to argue for the permissibility of euthanasia (in the case of adults) without consent. Some people think that all euthanasia is wrong, but amongst those who do not, many believe that the only really unproblematic case is the one in which a fully informed rational adult wishes to die and consents to being killed – indeed, requests it. Cases where people say, while rational, that they want to be killed or allowed to die if and when they degenerate into a certain state, but say otherwise when they are in that state are more problematic. Cases where people have never made their views known about whether they want to live in certain conditions or not are more problematic still. Since the fœtus could not possibly have any view about whether it wants to live in certain conditions, the issue of whether killing a fœtus for its own sake is permissible falls, on the conservative view, into this latter, more problematic class – there is no present or even past consent to being killed, and, regarding the fœtus as on a par with an adult human being, this lack of consent is morally significant. Of course, this is not to deny that one may hold that euthanasia of adults is permissible in some cases without present or past consent – where, for instance, it seems certain that no one could want such agony to be drawn out. And then, on the conservative view, one could consistently regard abortion as permissible in certain cases.

The second point concerns the proper definition of 'euthanasia'. I mentioned in the Preface (p. xi above) that this is a much abused term; strictly speaking, something is an act of euthanasia only if the death brought about is *for the good* of the one who dies – i.e. when life is, or is shortly to become, an evil for them. Now, there are many adults around with terrible physical disabilities, people who habitually endure a great deal of pain, people who cannot do or enjoy a number of things that people with an average physical constitution can do, but who nevertheless lead lives that they, and anyone else with an unbiased eye, regard as normal and worthwhile. No one thinks it would be all right to kill them, or that their lives are an evil to them and that they would be better off dead. So, on the conservative view, it would not be permissible to abort a fœtus that was predictably going to become such an adult.

Moreover, there are people with severe mental disabilities for whom life is clearly a good; people with brain-damage who need constant care but who can still enjoy being alive – not many people think that it is all right to kill such people and no one could properly describe killing them as an act of *euthanasia*, i.e. done for *their* sake. So, on the conservative view it would not be permissible to abort a fœtus that was predictably going to be disabled in such a way.

Fœtal research It is generally agreed to be wrong to make use of people as the subjects of medical research without their informed consent. Regarding fœtuses as morally on a par with adults, the same holds true for them, and since they cannot give informed consent, fœtal research is ruled out on this view. The prohibition may not extend to cover research on *dead* fœtal tissue, for some people hold that it does not matter what happens to their bodies after they are dead. So just as one might allow that adult dead bodies, unclaimed by family, could be used in medical schools and research laboratories, so one might allow that dead fœtuses, unclaimed by family, could be used in the same way.

In vitro fertilization   Clearly, on the conservative view, it would be completely unacceptable to create embryos in test-tubes with a view to research. However, to create them with a view to implantation and successful pregnancy is not clearly ruled out. If and when implantation techniques become much more successful than at the time of writing, there would be no intrinsic objection to IVF on this view. The present difficulty is that a number of embryos are created in the full knowledge that few if any will survive. At the time of writing, IVF procedures often result in a number of spare embryos (see Appendix Three), and on the conservative view it seems that the only permissible thing to do with these would be to freeze them intending to implant at a later date. (Compare infanticide again: if someone gives birth to triplets we would think it completely wrong that she should kill two, or allow two of them to die, on the grounds that she wants only one child now.) So given current procedures, IVF would be permissible on this view if the woman was intending to have any spares implanted at later dates, or if everyone concerned knew of other women eager to have them implanted.

It is also true of current procedures that a large number of the embryos that are transferred to the uterus (see Appendix Three) do not implant successfully and of those that do over a third do not survive. Is this a further reason, on this view, for regarding IVF as wrong? This brings us to a further rather odd consequence.

Fœtal deaths   On the conservative view there is a fundamental moral difference between different sorts of so-called contraception. The sort that simply prevents conception (e.g. the contraceptive pill, the sheath) is not ruled out by this view (though it might be objected to on other grounds – it might be said, for instance, that contraception is unnatural, or contrary to the purpose of the sexual act). But the sort that prevents the fertilized ovum from implanting in the wall of the uterus (e.g. the coil, the 'morning after' pill) is comparable to a murderous weapon, and is therefore ruled out. For to use this sort of 'contraceptive' method is to ensure that any fertilized ovum in one's body is bound to die, and if, from the moment of conception what exists is morally on a par with an adult or child, this is comparable to putting death traps around one's house into which any adult or child might fall.

One might think it odd to draw such a sharp distinction between different sorts of contraception. 'Surely', it might be said, 'contraception is either permissible or it isn't. It's ridiculous to quibble about the details of the mechanics of it, saying that they make an important difference.' But this objection is surely an objection to the conservative view itself, not to this particular consequence of it. If one rejects the conservative view about the fertilized ovum, of course one will find nothing in the distinction but irrelevant detailed differences. But on the conservative view the details are made relevant by their relevance to whether or not what is going on is murder, and that is hardly a quibble.

Still, there seems to be something more in the objection. Perhaps it is this: suppose that using the second sort of 'contraceptive' device is running a fair risk of committing murder, as, according to the conservative view it is. Then it must be the case that a lot of women have committed quite a few murders without knowing it. And what is odd is the thought that something as serious as murder can quite commonly be done without anyone even noticing.

Of course I might rig up something fatal (intending it to be so) in a remote spot and as a result kill someone and it be the case that I never found out I had done this (because I never went back to look) and no one else ever missed the hermit I had killed. It is *possible* to kill someone without ever knowing that one has, and without anyone else ever knowing. But on the view of the second sort of 'contraception' just considered, this is going on all the time.

A related oddity is this. Apparently something like forty per cent of very early embryos are lost before the woman ever knows she is pregnant (see Appendix One). If the early embryo has the same moral status as an adult this fact should surely be a matter of acute concern and great efforts of medical research should be directed towards saving these lives.

One reason why some women find it very difficult to

have children is that they have a tendency to have very early miscarriages, so early that they are readily mistaken for ordinary menstruation. Once such a woman has discovered this about herself, what, on the conservative view, should her attitude be? Should she immediately take steps to ensure that she never conceives again, on the grounds that to do so is to run the likely risk of being responsible for a human life being lost? Would it be outrageously immoral of her to continue to try to have a child, given that probably many lives will be lost in the process? On the conservative view, it seems that this must be so, and once again, it is a distinctly odd consequence.

Finally, we should, as in several cases above, compare fœtal death with the death of a child. Suppose a madman has got hold of a baby in one hand and a ten-day-old embryo in a test-tube in the other and is about to kill them both. Suppose you can save only one of them. On the conservative view there is no intrinsic difference between the two which would ground your saving the baby rather than the embryo. Of course you might go for the baby instead of the embryo for extrinsic or consequentialist reasons – the baby has parents who will be heartbroken, the embryo was generated for purposes of research and will not be missed. But such reasons could weigh the other way: perhaps the baby has been abandoned whereas the embryo represents some woman's only chance of bearing her now dead husband's child, and in such a case, on extrinsic or consequentialist grounds, one would save the embryo and not the baby!

It is not implausible for the conservative view to hold that you should do your utmost to save both – though the same might be said if the madman were proposing to destroy both a baby and a work of art. But it might well be thought implausible to suppose that only extrinsic differences (which in any case could weigh either way) could ground saving the baby instead of the embryo as, it seems, the conservative view has to hold.

Summary

Someone who holds the conservative view about the moral status of the fœtus will tend, pending further arguments, to be committed to the following views:

Abortion (at any stage)

(i) to save the mother's life	possibly, but not necessarily permissible
(ii) on social or psychological grounds	impermissible
(iii) as fœtal euthanasia	possibly permissible
(iv) to avoid the possibility or certainty of a child with disabilities	impermissible

Fœtal research

(i) on live fœtuses	impermissible
(ii) on dead fœtal tissue	possibly permissible

Breeding fœtuses for the purposes of research	impermissible

In vitro fertilization and embryonic research

(i) creating embryos and deliberately allowing them to die	impermissible
(ii) keeping embryos as living tissue and using them for purposes of research	impermissible

Infanticide	impermissible

3 THE EXTREME LIBERAL VIEW

According to the extreme liberal view, the fœtus is in most if not all morally relevant respects like a piece of tissue or a bit of the human body. It should be said at the outset that I think not many people actually hold this view explicitly about the status of the fœtus right up to the moment when it is about to be born (or perhaps until the umbilical cord is cut?). However, it is the only view about the status of the fœtus which makes possible the justification of abortion which quite a lot of people do hold. Many people say that it is permissible for a woman to d~mand an abortion at any stage for any reason because (and simply because) she has a right to choose what happens to her own body. Now the fact (if it is a fact) that we have a right to choose what happens to our bodies would not *on its own* justify abortion 'on demand' unless the fœtus were indeed part of the mother's body. So people who claim that abortion is permissible on this *single* premise of the woman's right over her body may be said to hold implicitly the extreme liberal view about the status of the fœtus.

I emphasize the 'single' for the following reason. Suppose I hold that abortion is permissible at any stage and give as a reason the right to do what I choose with my own body. Can I also hold that the fœtus has a right to life? Only if, for example, I *add* a premise about my right to do as I choose with my own body *overriding* the right to life. Or could I hold that, though fœtuses do not have rights, it is nevertheless wrong to destroy them wantonly, as it is wrong to destroy plants and animals wantonly? Again, only if I *add* a premise about my right to choose what I do with my own body being superior to the wrong of wanton destruction. But if I am going to maintain as my single premise that the woman has a right to do as she chooses with her own body and that simply because of this abortion is permissible at any stage if the woman wants it, the only view I can consistently hold of the fœtus is that it is on a par with a part of the woman's body.

The argument for this view is basically the same, surprisingly enough, as the non-theological argument for the conservative view, but starts at the other end of the process. It begins from the premise that the unfertilized ovum is part of the woman's body – a cell of it. Hence, it is morally on a par with any other part of her body. It then adds, as its second premise, that working forwards from the ovum, through conception, implantation, gradual growth, etc., there is no point at which we can draw a line and say, 'This is the morally significant point'. There is no morally significant difference between an unfertilized ovum and a fertilized one, no morally significant difference between a fertilized ovum (a single cell) and a clump of sixteen cells, no morally significant difference between that and a month-old embryo, ... and so on, until the baby is actually born and the umbilical cord severed. (There are minor variations on this argument – some for instance taking as their starting point the embryo attached to the side of the womb – and corresponding variations in the objections.)

Familiarity with the conservative version of this argument makes it easy to see some initial objections that can be brought against this one.

As before, the truth of the second premise (that there is nowhere to draw the boundary line) can be questioned, but here, perhaps, with a little more initial plausibility. Is there really nowhere between the unfertilized ovum and the fœtus about to be born that a boundary line can be drawn? A line *can* be drawn, it will be said, at the moment of conception or fertilization, for that involves something that is not part of the woman's body, namely the sperm. From then on what we have is not simply part of the woman's body, but a new composite with its own genetic constitution. As people sometimes say, 'conception is the magic moment'.

As before, the validity of the argument can be questioned, independently of the truth of its premises. Agreed, it can be said, that there is no one point where we can draw the line; nevertheless, a one or two-week-old fœtus clearly is like a part of the woman's body, morally on a par with any other part, and an eight-month-old fœtus, although it may be physically part of her body, is morally on a par with a new-born baby. We cannot draw a line at 'the' point at which blue things become green either; nevertheless some things really are green not blue, and some are blue not green.

A new objection can be brought against the extreme liberals' reliance on the premise that the fœtus is morally on a par with part of the woman's body. It is claimed that if this is so, and if I have a right to do as I choose to my own body, it follows that abortion on demand is permissible. But suppose that I do 'have a right' to do as I choose to my own body. It does not follow that it is always morally permissible for me to exercise that right. Perhaps it would be wrong of me wantonly to destroy some part of my body, or my health; perhaps there are some things I cannot do to my body without degrading myself. Or, to take another example, suppose that I maim myself to avoid fighting in a just war, not because I am a pacifist, but out of cowardice; some would say I was wrong to treat my body that way. This objection takes us on to the disconcerting consequences of maintaining the extreme liberal position.

Consequences of the extreme liberal view

A number of the consequences of the extreme liberal view are perhaps rather unexpected, and some, I am sure, would not be explicitly held by its upholders.

Abortion, of course, becomes as permissible, indeed as morally neutral, as anything else one might choose to do to or with bits of a human being's body. A woman might choose to have an abortion from motives of pure vanity, as one might choose to have a tooth out for such a reason, and this would be no more wrong (at *any* stage) than would be acts promoted by trivial vanity. Someone might even maintain that since pregnancy does wonders for the complexion, apparently often regulates malfunctioning menstrual cycles and is claimed by some to increase one's libido, one might choose to be pregnant for a while in order to clear up one's spots or give oneself a lift.

Abortion, on this view, becomes an essentially trivial matter, deriving such importance or seriousness as it has only from the present incidental fact that medical technology has not yet made it as safe and painless as having one's teeth done. For pregnancy becomes equivalent to the development of a benign growth and the termination of pregnancy simply the removal of this growth.

However, one aspect of this view I have not seen discussed in the literature is what holders of it believe should be done about the attitudes that many currently hold about this growth. Should fathers be positively discouraged from thinking of women as carrying their unborn *child* and thereby ceasing to regard them as the proper object of a range of particularly intense emotions, amongst them respect gratitude, tenderness and even awe? Should women who have conceived as a result of rape be discouraged from making a fuss about the rapist's *child* growing in them? Should women who miscarry be discouraged from making a fuss about losing their *child*? The only options, on this view, are either to agree that these emotional reactions are quite out of place in relation to a piece of tissue, or to maintain that they are appropriate, given how very special this particular sort of bit of tissue is. But the latter option concedes too much. If this bit of tissue (in virtue of being, unlike any other bit, a part of the woman's body which is growing into a child) is so special it is thereby *not* morally on a par with all the other bits.

I suspect that upholders of this view will have to insist that this part of a woman's body is special in at least one respect, namely that a woman has an extremely important and unique right in relation to it – the right to grow it into a child if she wants to. (Or, eschewing talk about rights, that it would be particularly wrong to do anything to harm or inhibit the growth of this part of her body without her consent.) For without this, the view leaves women startlingly badly off. If I forcibly cut off your hand or blind you, I have indeed done you a terrible injury, for, quite aside from the pain, you are permanently damaged. But if out of spite or jealousy I shave off your hair or beard while your are unconscious, though it is certainly very mean of me, it can hardly be said that I have done you a terrible injury or wrong. You are not damaged, and you can grow some more, even if it will take you another nine months. So either it must be agreed that a woman is not done a terrible wrong if one induces a miscarriage in her (supposing, of course, that it is a safe one) out of spite or jealousy, against her will, or something special about this part of her body must be invoked to explain the wrong done.

But if it is allowed that this part of a woman's body is special in this way – namely that it can be grown into a child – the moral permissibility of a woman's exercising her right to choose what happens to her body becomes particularly problematic. For now it is not any old part, but a special one, and, moreover, one which is special in that the father might legitimately take a special interest in it. And once it is allowed that one does a woman a terrible wrong by depriving her of the chance of growing this part into a child if she wants to, the way is open to saying that she does herself a terrible wrong in throwing away this chance. Even if one continued to maintain that there is nothing morally wrong with harming yourself if you want to, there would still be a problem about maintaining that other people can help you to do it. That is, even if it is morally permissible for me to blind myself, or cut off a foot because I want to, and it is my body, it does not follow that it is morally permissible for a doctor to blind me or cut off my foot at my request, just because I want her to.

Viable fœtuses   It is hard to work out what, on this view, the status of the viable fœtus is after it has been separated from the mother. Let us ignore for the moment the point about viability as a moving boundary and consider the aborting of a viable fœtus in the present state of medical technology. It can be done in such a way that the fœtus survives, or not. Suppose it is granted that, while the woman is still carrying it, the viable fœtus is morally on a par with an organ of her body, and hence that she has the right to say whether the operation to remove it should remove it dead or alive. And now suppose that a viable fœtus is aborted and lives. Is the fœtus still morally on a par with an organ of her body, so that she still has a right to say that it should be killed simply because she wants it dead? If so, then since in fact what we are talking about here is premature babies, it seems that on this view a woman has a right to say of her premature baby that it should be killed simply because she wants it dead, given that it is morally on a par with an organ of her body. But then it seems quite arbitrary to say that *non*-premature birth and the severing of the umbilical cord is the boundary line between being morally on a par with an organ of the body and being of the same status as an adult.

Alternatively, it might be said that, like ordinary premature babies and non-premature babies, an aborted, living, viable fœtus is not morally on a par with an organ of the human body since it is something which is itself growing and developing into a human body independently of attachment to the mother's. But this creates a difficulty we have noted before, namely, that it seems odd to say that something has different moral status according to where it is living and developing. A viable fœtus in an incubator counts as a baby; a viable fœtus that, as it happens, is not in an incubator but in a woman's body just counts as morally on a par with one of her organs.

It is true that where an organ of one's body happens to be can make a moral difference. While my kidneys are in my body I have the right to say what becomes of them. It is up to me whether or not they are operated on, and, if one is removed, it is for me to say whether I want to have it destroyed or to take it home in a jar, or to let the hospital do with it as they will. Suppose I say the last and the hospital puts it in someone else. The fact that my kidney is in this person's body not mine, certainly makes a moral difference – it is no longer for me to say whether it is to be operated on or left to science. Indeed, it is no longer *mine* in the rights-supporting, *meum* and *tuum*, property sense at all. So could it be maintained that, after all, it is not so odd that where the fœtus happens to be (in the woman or the incubator) makes a moral difference?

The kidney example shows that *where something happens to be* can make a moral difference. However, what was needed was an example to show that where something happens to be can make a difference to its *moral status*. The kidney retains its moral status as an organ of a human body wherever it happens to be, but the viable fœtus supposedly changes from being morally on a par with the kidney to being morally on a par with a baby.

Fœtal research This difficulty about the status of the viable fœtus after it has been separated from the mother also carries over into questions about fœtal research. If an aborted viable fœtus is said to be still in the morally relevant respects like a part of the woman's body then it is up to her to say what may be done with it – if she does not mind its being kept alive and being experimented on, there is no further intrinsic objection to this that can be brought. However, something further in the way of a restriction would have to be admitted here since the viable fœtus, in virtue of being viable, will develop into, not just a baby, but a child, if kept alive too long. Perhaps we could say that it would always be wrong to allow an organ of a human body to grow into a baby (or a human being at any stage) in laboratory conditions for the purposes of research, and hence that a viable fœtus, being in the morally relevant respects like a human organ, should never be allowed to grow into a baby in laboratory conditions for the purposes of research.

In vitro fertilization   What about the non-viable fœtus? If we put to one side the problem of viability as a shifting boundary, we do not encounter the same problems about the non-viable fœtus or embryo; it can non-arbitrarily be regarded as morally on a par with a bit of tissue whether in or out of the mother's body. However, the possibility of *in vitro* fertilization makes it unclear *whose* bit of tissue it should be regarded as on this view, and suggests that whether we take the starting point to be the ovum or implantation matters a great deal.

If the ovum is (morally on a par with) a part of the woman's body whether in her, or in a test-tube, fertilized or unfertilized, then no new problems arise concerning research on *in vitro* embryos. They are, on this view, to be regarded in the same way as the non-viable fœtus. But what now should be said about surrogacy?

Surrogacy   In discussing surrogacy we distinguish between the *genetic mother* (whose ovum is fertilized) and the *carrying mother* (in whom the fertilized ovum is implanted and who, when things go according to plan, carries the resulting baby to term – see Appendix Three). It may be that the carrying mother is also the genetic mother, her ovum having being fertilized *in vitro* by sperm from the husband of the couple to whom she intends to hand over the baby. (At the time of writing, cases where fertilization was brought about by normal sexual intercourse between the husband and the woman who had contracted to hand over the resulting baby are being discussed as cases of surrogacy, but subsequent legislation may well find it necessary to classify them as cases of adoption and reserve 'surrogacy' as a term implying *in vitro* fertilization.)

It is sometimes assumed in the literature that the moral permissibility of surrogacy is completely established by the premises about a woman's right to do as she chooses with her own body and the premise that the fœtus is a part of it. However, this is not so, for two reasons.

Assuming that the fœtus does have that status and the woman that right, it still does not follow that women are not degraded by acting as commercial surrogates.[4] So an extra premise is needed. One possibility, which many have argued for, is that women are not thereby degraded if their choice to act as surrogate mothers is informed and not made under financial pressure. Another much more abstract possibility is to add a premise to the effect that it is morally permissible to degrade oneself.

Even with such extra premises the moral permissibility of surrogacy does not follow. For describing commercial surrogacy as 'womb-letting' conceals the fact that the former involves not only being paid for being pregnant but also (when things work out as all parties intended) handing over the born baby. Whether this is described as 'abandoning', 'giving away', 'selling' the baby, or 'placing the baby in a good home', it is unavoidably an act that involves a baby, and hence not an act whose moral nature could be determined solely by a woman's right over her own body and the status of the fœtus.

It is sometimes claimed that 'logically' there is no relevant difference between surrogacy and AID (artificial insemination by donor – see Appendix Three) and that the fuss about the former is simply due to sexism. However, this is not a position that anyone remotely interested in women's rights ought to agree with. Presumably, the idea is that each sex makes an equal contribution to the final product – a baby is genetically just as much its father's as its mother's – and we do not make a fuss about artifice concerning the male contribution (AID) so only sexism could prompt us to make a fuss concerning the parallel female contribution.

But as an argument concerning surrogacy rather than egg donation the flaw in this is obvious. Genetically each sex makes an equal contribution to the final product, but only females can also contribute nine months of carrying the baby to term. Of course, someone could stubbornly maintain that this was not important and did not make a difference, but it is ridiculous to claim that only sexism prompts one to say that it is important and does make a difference.

The issue that was raised above was, in effect, what sort of difference does it make? While we are discussing ordinary conception and pregnancy, the extreme liberal view does not need to commit itself to whether the release of the ovum or the implantation is the starting point from which moment on we have something morally on a par with a part of the woman's body; for in the ordinary cases it will not make any difference. But clearly it will make a difference in the case of surrogacy. If implantation is the relevant starting point then the fœtus counts morally as part of the carrying mother's body, regardless of whose ovum (or sperm) has made the genetic contribution. If the release of the ovum is the starting point and the carrying mother is not the same as the genetic mother, then presumably the fœtus counts morally as part of the genetic mother's body even though it is in the carrying mother's body. Does this mean the genetic mother can insist that the carrying mother has an abortion, even if the latter does not want one?

Consequences for surrogacy of different starting points   We should note that, perhaps surprisingly, nothing specific follows, concerning the overriding rights of the carrying mother, either during or after pregnancy, from taking implantation as the starting point. That is, her right to abortion may, for all that has been said so far, be overridden by the contract-generated rights of the commissioning couple. Moreover, if before birth we do not have an unborn *child* belonging to its (carrying) mother (only something morally on a par with part of someone's body) for all that has been said so far the carrying mother might have no rights at all in connection with the born child.

Whether or not her right to abortion can be overridden

by the contract-generated rights of the commissioning couple depends on whether the right to determine what happens in and to one's own body is inalienable. ('Inalienable' rights are rights that you cannot lose or waive. Of course, this does not mean that it is somehow impossible for the law to deprive you of them, for people to violate them, or for you to offer to give them up. It means that you cannot *justly* be treated as if you did not have them.) If it is inalienable, then no contract with the commissioning couple would be morally binding however legally water-tight it was.

Whether the carrying mother has any rights at all in connection with the born child is not straightforwardly settled. Indeed, this is another consequence of a fundamental weakness in the extreme liberal position – that in its anxiety to secure the right *not* to have children it has overlooked the need to secure some sorts of rights in connection with having them. I noted above (p. 51) that upholders of this position surely needed to invoke something special about the fœtus-part of a woman's body in order to guarantee that a woman who wanted to carry a child to term had some right to do so. But I did not then press the point that this still would not guarantee any parental rights.

What does or does not follow from taking the ovum as the starting point is unclear for a different reason. We said above that when the genetic mother is not the same as the carrying mother the fœtus counts morally as part of the genetic mother's body even though it is in the carrying mother's body. But the difficulty here is to attach a clear sense to 'the fœtus counts morally as'.

Our usual method for doing this is to take an actual example of the sort of thing the fœtus is being compared with (an adult, a piece of tissue) and see what would be said about it in some parallel situation. So, for example, if it is not morally permissible to kill a person who was conceived as a result of a rape, and if the fœtus 'morally counts as a person' then it is not morally permissible to abort a fœtus conceived as a result of a rape. But now the difficulty is that nothing seems to count as a parallel situation.

When I donate part of my body it ceases to be 'mine', morally speaking, and becomes the property of whoever I gave it to. But surrogacy is not a matter of ovum donation. In the sort of case we are concerned with, the genetic mother does not donate an ovum to someone else who wants a child; *she* wants a child and asks the surrogate mother to house her ovum in such a way as to produce one. A parallel situation would have to be one in which I asked you to look after some detached part of my body for me, returning it to me some period later considerably developed and in peak condition. To be genuinely parallel it should also be the case that, while you are looking after it, it is actually physically part of your body. And since nothing *like* this in fact ever does happen we have no intuitions about what to say about it. Would I still have a right to it after you had looked after it for a time? Or would you acquire a right to it because of its having been part of your body? Who knows?

Summary

Someone who holds the extreme liberal view about the moral status of the fœtus will tend, pending further arguments, to be committed to the following views.

Abortion (at any stage, for any reason)	permissible
Fœtal research	permissible (with the woman's consent)
Breeding fœtuses for the purposes of research	permissible
In vitro fertilization and embryonic research	
(i) creating embryos and deliberately allowing them to die	permissible
(ii) keeping embryos as living tissue and using them for purposes of research	permissible

Infanticide   probably impermissible
                                     (infanticide of premature
                                     babies possibly permissible)

4   THE ANIMAL VIEW

According to another quite liberal view, the fœtus is in most morally relevant respects like an animal, such as a dog or a chicken. More, or less, liberal versions of this view can be held, depending on what extra premises are added about the moral status of animals.

Suppose I hold that morality is essentially about human beings, that they are the appropriate objects of moral attitudes, that they have virtues and vices, rights and duties and that though there can be other objects of moral concern (animals, even plants, the environment, etc.) these are not of central importance. Then, clearly, if I add that the fœtus is in most morally relevant respects like an animal, such as a dog, I am saying that it is not of such central importance as an adult human being, or indeed of a baby. On such a view, since infanticide is the killing of a human being it would be wrong, but abortion would be on a par with killing an animal and thereby either not wrong at all or not as wrong (depending on what I thought about the seriousness of killing animals).

Many people who hold this animal view of the moral status of the fœtus do so because they see it as encapsulating two fairly common moral beliefs: (a) the belief that (contrary to the extreme liberal view) abortion is morally significant, but (contrary to the conservative view) not as serious a matter as infanticide, and (b) that if, for example, from a burning house I can save only the baby or the embryo in the test-tube but not both, then it is completely obvious that I must save the baby. Or, similarly, that if my choice as a doctor lies between saving the woman and saving the fœtus it is completely obvious that I must save the woman. It would also be a standard part of this view (the reason for mentioning this will be obvious later) that if, from a burning house I can save only a baby or an animal – any animal, no matter how intelligent – then of course I must save the baby.

The argument

The argument for the animal view is not as precise as the earlier arguments we have looked at. It involves emphasizing the ways in which fœtuses (at no particular specified stage, but let us say roughly in the middle of their development) are unlike mere pieces of tissue or human organs but also unlike independently existing babies. It then adds the premise that working forwards or backwards we can find only two boundary lines: conception (before which what there is is (just like) a piece of human tissue) and birth (after which what there is is an independently existing baby). This argument is subject to objections we have discussed earlier.

It appeals to two boundary lines as having distinctive moral significance, but as we saw above (p. 33), it is not perfectly clear that either birth or conception do make an absolute moral difference. It infers, from the lack of clear boundary lines to be drawn within the gradual development of the fœtus, that it has the same moral status from beginning to end. But it has already been shown that this is invalid (p. 36).

Consequences for the animal view

Abortion and infanticide   Abortion at any stage for many of the usual liberal reasons would be permissible according to the animal view. It would be held to be permissible on the grounds that it is permissible to kill an animal (*any* animal) for the sake of a human being or for the same sorts of reasons. Hence this view cannot justify infanticide in the same way.

What about abortion solely for vain or self-indulgent reasons such as not wanting a pregnancy to interfere with a holiday or one's figure? Here the consequences vary according to what other views are held about human exploitation of the animal kingdom. If I believe that it is wrong to kill baby seals for their fur, or tortoises for their shells and so on, then on the animal view I would conclude that it is wrong to have abortions for trivial reasons just as it is wrong to kill animals for trivial reasons. However, I might think that if something is '*just* an animal' then its life is of no value whatsoever and that no wrong is done by killing it for whatever reason. And then on the animal view I would conclude that abortion is permissible for no matter how trivial a reason.

Fœtal research Here again consequences about the extent to which fœtal research is permissible and what form it may take vary according to what view is taken about experimentation on such animals as mice and chickens. On a very strong anti-vivisectionist line a great deal of it would be ruled out, in particular, any experimentation on late living fœtuses. However, to object to the dissection of living animals (which is what 'vivisection' literally means) is, so far, to remain uncommitted about research on dead animals, and further, on breeding them for the purpose of such research. So if I believe that it is all right to experiment on dead mice and chickens and that it is all right to breed such animals in order that they may be killed and used in dissection classes in schools and research laboratories, then, on the animal view of the status of the fœtus, I will hold that it is all right to experiment on dead fœtuses and further that it is all right to grow them in test-tubes or for women to carry them for the same purpose.

In vitro fertilization On the animal view, once again, one can draw a variety of consequences concerning this issue. It would be odd to object to *in vitro* fertilization for the sake of childless couples (one would need an irrationally strong premise about its being wrong to interfere with nature – something that would rule out even dentistry and amputation in the case of gangrene) and the discarding of surplus embryos would not, on this view, matter particularly.

However, *in vitro* fertilization and different sorts of subsequent research could be regarded in different ways. A premise about the wrongness of, or dangers inherent in, tampering *in certain ways* with nature (or playing God) would lead to condemnation of varieties of genetic research involving, say, the growing on of either human *or* other animal embryos and perhaps the 'artificial' growth of tissue. Such a premise can be just the irrationally strong one about its being 'wrong to interfere with nature' mentioned above; but it need not be, for it can be far more specific.

It is clear from letters to newspapers and elsewhere that many people have a particular horror about the deliberate production of creatures that could not survive and flourish under natural conditions – for example, hybrid half-this-half-that animals. But this horror can co-exist with a delight about other prospects for genetic research – for example, our recreating various species of animal and plant life that, in our earlier folly, we have made extinct. So it would be possible to condemn some sorts of research while welcoming others. Alternatively one might adopt a utilitarian approach and, bearing in mind the great advantages to be derived from embryonic research, maintain that, as long as the embryo is incapable of feeling pain, it does not matter what you do to it in the way of research.

The upshot of classifying fœtuses and embryos with animals is that research on fœtuses is not special in any way. In particular, there is, on the animal view, no reason to say that research on fœtuses should be carried out as a last resort, and only when results cannot be obtained by alternative means, for example, by research on the lower animals. Similarly, there is, on either version, no reason to say that research on fœtuses should be directed towards the medical benefit of humans; we are also interested in the biology of other creatures and may experiment on fœtuses in order to find out, for example, how to improve the success rate in lambing.

Fœtal euthanasia   It is sometimes said that in one respect we treat animals better than human beings, since we will humanely kill an animal to put an end to its suffering, but refuse to do the same for human beings. Whatever one's views on whether euthanasia for adult human beings is permissible, it is possible to hold that euthanasia-type abortions are permissible if one holds the animal view about the status of the fœtus. I say 'euthanasia-type' because part of the point of holding this view of the fœtus is to allow a number of abortions which are not strictly for the sake of the child (see the discussion of fœtal euthanasia in Section 2 above, pp. 42–3) but which are, loosely speaking, 'to avoid suffering'. We put down animals that are suffering, but also animals that might suffer (because they might have a disease or a defect) or will suffer a little (for similar reasons) and we may claim that all this is humanely done. So if we regard the fœtus as morally comparable to an animal we shall think that not only genuine euthanasia but much more weakly-grounded cases of 'putting down' a fœtus are permissible.

Summary

Someone who holds the view that the fœtus is morally on a par with an animal will tend to be committed to the following views.

Abortion (at any stage)

(i) to save the mother's life	permissible
(ii) on social or psychological grounds	permissible
(iii) as fœtal euthanasia	permissible
(iv) to avoid the possibility or certainty of a child with disabilities	permissible
(v) for vain or self-indulgent reasons	impermissible
Fœtal research	permissible
Breeding fœtuses for the purposes of research	permissible

In vitro fertilization and embryonic research

(i) creating embryos and deliberately allowing them to die	permissible

(ii) keeping embryos as
living tissue and using
them for purposes of
research   permissible

Infanticide   impermissible

I should mention here that there is another extremely radical view which might, casually, be described as 'the view that the fœtus is in most morally relevant respects like an animal such as a chicken'. This is the person view mentioned in the first chapter (p. 6.), according to which fœtuses and most animals are alike in not being persons.

The argument for this view is quite unlike any of the others considered in this chapter. It usually consists of a premise which defines 'person' in some way (as, say, 'a rational, self-conscious being') and a second premise to the effect that fœtuses (at any stage), in common with babies, the very senile and brain-damaged, and the less intelligent animals, are not persons according to the definition. Finally, it adds a third premise which amounts to the claim that killing non-persons is not wrong, since morality is essentially about (not human beings but) persons.

The second premise is usually beyond dispute, because the first premise (the definition) is usually framed in such a way as to guarantee that fœtuses (and babies) are not persons. But arguments can rage back and forth about the claim that morality is not about human beings but persons and become very complicated. This is why discussion of this view on the status of the fœtus is not treated in this chapter, but given individual attention in the next. At this point it is just worth bearing in mind that anything the animal view allows as permissible for (say) mice and fœtuses (killing them, using them for experiments, breeding them for laboratory purposes), the person view will allow as permissible for mice, fœtuses and babies. So infanticide comes out as perfectly permissible, and so, rather startlingly, does the deliberate breeding of babies for use in laboratories.

5 THE MIXED STRATEGY

According to the mixed strategy view, the fœtus has a varying moral status. Initially it is, in most morally relevant respects, like a bit of tissue or an organ of the body. As it develops it gradually becomes, in most morally relevant respects, like a lower animal, then like a higher one, and in the later stages of its development it is, in most if not all morally relevant respects, like a baby, and hence on a par with fully-developed, normal, adult human beings.

The argument

This view, it might be said, is the only reasonable reaction to the difficulties that we have encountered with the previous ones. If we want to hold on to the premise that infanticide is wrong, and research on babies and breeding them for that purpose totally impermissible, then any of the liberal views about the status of the fœtus need birth as an all-important boundary line. But the fact of premature birth tends to shift the birth boundary line back to viability, and the open-ended possibility of increased medical sophistication threatens to shift the viability boundary line all the way back to conception. Hence, in trying to maintain that babies are, as the conservative view maintains, like adult human beings in the respects morally relevant to killing or experimentation, the liberal views are actually driven towards the conservative one. But anyone who wants to hold on to the belief that to have an early abortion for such reasons as to avoid risk to one's life or because one is pregnant as the result of rape, for example, is not *at all* on a par with killing a baby for the same reasons, needs to be able to draw a distinction between the fœtus in its early and in its late stages, and hence cannot accept the full conservative view. And so we are led to the seemingly sensible compromise of the mixed strategy.

The mixed strategy strikes many people as such obvious commonsense that they think it stands in no need of argument. Nevertheless, there is an intrinsic interest in seeing what the argument looks like.

It borrows a premise from each of the conservative and extreme liberal views. It agrees with holders of the conservative view that there is no morally significant difference between a newly born baby and a baby about to be born. And it agrees with the holders of the extreme liberal view that there is no morally significant difference between the fertilized ovum or the embryo in its early stages of development and a piece of tissue or organ of the human body. It also agrees with both views that the development from fertilized ovum to born baby is gradual but, unlike the other views, it does not try to infer from this that the fœtus has the same moral status throughout its development. On the contrary, from the fact that the development is gradual, it infers that so too is the development of moral status or standing. This, we should note, is to take account of the objection to the validity of the argument which both the conservative and extreme liberal views relied on, *viz.* that no boundary line could be drawn during pregnancy.

Consequences for the mixed strategy

Given the nature of the mixed strategy view, the consequences inevitably turn out to be a mixture of those that follow from the conservative and liberal views. However, these are not always strictly adhered to by proponents of this view. As I noted above, p. 38, this compromise position is the one that is roughly embodied in a variety of abortion laws which are permissive about abortions in the first trimester, and become increasingly restrictive about abortions in the second and third trimesters. But the embodiment is indeed rough; I do not know of any set of laws governing abortion and related practices (fœtal research, etc.) which achieves strict consistency.

Abortion Abortion in the early stages of pregnancy, say the first trimester, has on the mixed strategy, no more moral significance than any other minor operation. So in itself abortion is morally insignificant, although it could count as morally indifferent, wrong, or indeed even heroic solely on account of the reason for which it was done.

Abortion in the later stages of pregnancy, say the third trimester, should, on this view, be of the same moral significance as infanticide. However, most upholders of this view want to qualify this consequence in *some* way since, as it stands, it either rules out abortion (in the late stages) to save the mother's life, or at best leaves it open (see Section 2, p. 41), and few non-conservatives want this as a consequence. (This is the first point on which, I think, the real consequences of this view are not strictly adhered to by its proponents.) But a reason for a qualification seems fairly easy to find; a fœtus, even at the late stage, is parasitic upon the mother in a way in which an infant is not, and 'that parasitic relation will justify late abortion more liberally than infanticide, for they do not occur under the same circumstance'.[5]

Abortion during the middle stages, say the second trimester, contains some clear-cut cases, but also some genuinely borderline and indeterminate cases. An abortion that would be justifiable in later stages is a clear-cut case of an abortion justifiable in the middle stages. But an abortion justifiable in the early stages and unjustifiable in the later (e.g. that having the child will seriously affect one's standard of living) may simply become less and less justifiable during the middle stages and it may be genuinely indeterminate whether abortion during this time is permissible or wrong.

Now it might seem that this view can satisfy the most extreme liberal desire to support a woman's right to decide whether to have a child but without thereby allowing her a right of infanticide. And people who offer the mixed strategy usually see themselves as tending well towards the liberal rather than the conservative side. The woman can exercise the right to decide, on any grounds she chooses, during the early stages, and, assuming that she must know during the early stages (a) whether she is pregnant and (b) whether she wants the (or a) child, this will in fact guarantee just what the extreme liberal was after.

But this is not so for the perhaps small but by no means insignificant number of women of whom that assumption is not true. Amongst the ones of whom it is not true that they *must* know during the early stages whether they are pregnant are the particularly young and/or the ignorant and innocent; and amongst these some will be pregnant as a result of rape, and some will have their health impaired by carrying the child to term, and all will run some risk of dying in childbirth, and these are all reasons that an extreme liberal wants to justify abortion even in the late stages. But by the mixed strategy, with its admixture of conservatism in the latter stages, it seems that abortion would not be clearly justifiable in these cases, if, through lack of knowledge, the pregnancy had not been recognized until late on. (As with the conservative view, we could regard mental condition or physical youth as a mitigating circumstance in someone who performed an abortion on herself, but no doctor would be justified in doing it for her.)

There are also some cases of women becoming pregnant in late middle age and attributing the signs of it during the first four or so months to the onset of the menopause – not implausibly when their last child is, say, twenty years old. Here too, any extreme liberal will want to say that such a woman has a right to an abortion regardless of how late it will be, but according to the mixed strategy she does not.

The other half of the assumption requires that the woman does not change her mind but decides in the early stages whether she wants the (or a) child. Upholders of the mixed strategy want to avoid the extreme liberal view that a woman might permissibly have a late abortion simply because she has changed her mind as a matter of whim, and the assumption succeeds in ruling that out. But what if the woman changes her mind in the later stages for a serious reason? Perhaps most changes of mind will depend on discoveries about the normality of the fœtus (to be considered under 'Fœtal euthanasia' below), but some will not, relating rather to changes in circumstances. For example, another member of the family suddenly develops an illness and will need a lot of care; one suddenly is faced with the prospect of being homeless. Upholders of the mixed strategy are committed to saying that in these circumstances, abortion, though morally insignificant in the early stages, is completely unacceptable in the late stages, just as infanticide as a way of alleviating these circumstances would be. And this will not satisfy the extreme liberals.

Fœtal euthanasia   Views about the acceptability of euthanasia and hence some cases of infanticide make a difference, on the mixed strategy, only at the conservative, late-stage end. If infanticide is permissible, for the sake of the child, in some cases of severe abnormality, then late abortion, for the sake of the fœtus, is permissible in such cases. If no such infanticide is permissible, then no such late abortion is either. But whatever view was held about euthanasia, on the mixed strategy any woman could permissibly choose an early abortion because, say, there was a risk that the child might be born with a severe abnormality, or indeed for any reason at all.

Supposing euthanasia to be permissible, what is to be said about late abortion where there is a risk of severe abnormality? As I noted above (Section 2, p. 43) abortions in such cases are often described as being 'for the sake of the fœtus' when this is merely specious. As is well known, if a woman has German measles (rubella) in the early stages of pregnancy there is a high risk that the fœtus is affected at the time, and consequently a high risk that if she carries it to term it will turn out to be a severely deformed baby. But to say this is not to deny that it is perfectly possible for the fœtus not to be affected at the time; it may get through quite unscathed. Now such a fœtus is not running any risk at all of becoming a severely deformed baby and it is not spared a miserable life by our killing it, it is simply deprived of what is likely to be a worthwhile one.

So it cannot be said on this (or any other) view, that abortion counts as fœtal euthanasia when the abortion is done to avoid the risk of severe abnormality. Hence on this view late abortions of this sort cannot be justified as being cases of fœtal euthanasia. However, it is open to this view not only to justify abortions of this sort in the early stages (along with every other sort), but also in the middle stages, at least towards the earlier end. Of course, they would not be justified as cases of fœtal euthanasia, but rather by analogy with justifiable killings of higher animals.

Fœtal research and in vitro fertilization   On the mixed strategy view, the embryos that result from *in vitro* fertilization are, if anything is, absolutely guaranteed to be of no more moral significance than any other bit of human tissue. In emphasizing the significance of the developmental nature of the fœtus, the mixed strategy accepts that many cases, maybe even any cases between three and seven months, are borderline and indeterminate. But the starting point of the strategy was that, despite all this indeterminacy in the middle, things were perfectly determinate at either end – an eight or nine-month-old unborn baby is a baby, not just a bit of human tissue; a two or three-week-old embryo is just a bit of tissue, not a baby. So the consequences for embryonic research, on the mixed strategy, are just the same as they are on the most extreme liberal view. The only restrictions on what can be done to the tissue, and for what reasons, come from considerations about the consent of the person whose tissue it is. Nor will there be any intrinsic objection to embryos being generated purely for the purposes of research, either *in vitro* or through ordinary conception and abortion.

It is worth noting that the mixed strategy view is (at the time of writing and as far as I know) expressed by people only in connection with, or embodied in laws that cover only, abortion. It *can* of course be extended to cover fœtal and embryonic research, but many of its upholders may not subscribe to the consequences if this were done. This inconsistency is enshrined in some legal systems. So, for instance, the USA has an abortion law which reflects the mixed strategy but its National Commission for the Protection of Human Subjects makes recommendations imposing strong restrictions on research involving fœtuses at *any* stage, and suggests that even research on dead fœtal tissue should be 'consistent with . . . commonly held convictions about respect for the dead'. It is maintained there that 'considerations of respect for the dignity of the fœtus [once again it is not suggested that this is limited to the fœtus at middle or later stages] continue to be of paramount importance'. Clearly, aborting the early fœtus in the usual ways (which involve violent dismemberment or salt-induced osmotic shock) cannot be taken as reflecting 'considerations of respect for the dignity of the fœtus'.

Similarly, Britain, at the time of writing, operates a roughly mixed strategy abortion law, but has recently received the Report of the Committee of Inquiry into Human Fertilization and Embryology (the 'Warnock Report' – see Appendix Four) which, while far more liberal in its recommendations than many people were happy with, is still considerably more restrictive than any mixed strategy view would be.

There is, in theory, nothing to prevent an upholder of the mixed strategy from giving up the claim it shares with the extreme liberal position – that a two or three-week-old embryo is just like any other bit of tissue – and granting the fœtus some sort of moral status right from the moment of conception. In practice this has not (yet) been done, in part, no doubt, for the reason I mentioned above, that upholders of the mixed strategy have seen themselves as tending well towards the liberal rather than the conservative side, wanting to preserve a woman's 'right to choose' an abortion during the early stages of pregnancy and for any reason. But it is also, perhaps, in part because the issue of embryonic research is so new and most of the existing literature has been exclusively concerned with the issue of abortion. The final view of the status of the fœtus that I shall consider has always had its advocates in discussions of abortion, but is also the one that is most usually supported by people with qualms about embryonic research.

Summary

Abortion at an early stage,
for any reason   permissible

In the middle stages:
  (i) to save the mother's
      life   permissible
 (ii) on social or
      psychological grounds   permissible
(iii) as fœtal euthanasia   permissible

(iv) to avoid the possibility
or certainty of a child
with disabilities   permissible
(v) on trivial grounds   impermissible

During the late stages of pregnancy:

(i) to save the mother's
life   permissible
(ii) on social or psychological
grounds   impermissible
(iii) as fœtal euthanasia   permissible
(iv) to avoid the possibility
or certainty of a child
with disabilities   impermissible
(v) on trivial grounds   impermissible

Foetal research   permissible

*Breeding fœtuses for the
purposes of research*   permissible

In vitro fertilization and embryonic research

(i) creating embryos and
deliberately allowing
them to die   permissible
(ii) keeping embryos as
living tissue and using
them for purposes of
research   permissible

Infanticide   impermissible

6   THE POTENTIALITY VIEW

According to the potentiality view, which can be either conservative or liberal, the fœtus, from the moment of conception, is morally unique, unlike anything else in being not an actual but a potential human being or person.

The reason why I describe the potential human being view as one that can be conservative or liberal is this. In giving the fœtus unique moral status, this view rules out our appealing to parallel or comparable cases in order to determine what is or is not morally permissible. So there are hardly any consequences concerning the rights and wrongs of abortion, fœtal research, *in vitro* fertilization, etc. which follow *directly* from taking this view of the fœtus. Insofar as it is, uniquely, not an actual but a potential human being, it is (a) trivially, unlike an actual one, (b) unlike any other piece of human tissue – a kidney is not a potential human being, and (c) unlike any (other) animal – (other) animals do not turn into human beings. But someone who holds this view can, quite consistently, rank any potential human being over any animal and very close to an actual human being; hence moving very close to the conservative position. Or they can, quite consistently, rank any potential human being very low, below many if not all animals and quite close to a bit of human tissue; hence moving close to an extreme liberal position. Or they can take up a variety of positions in between.

However, it is true that the point of assigning this moral status to the fœtus, for most of the people who do so assign it, is to try to sum up a number of moral convictions they have which incline towards the conservative rather than the liberal views. The point of specifying the fœtus as a potential human being is not so much to emphasize that it is *merely* potential as to pick it out as potentially a *human being* (or whatever our essential moral category is) and hope thereby to avoid some of the extremes of the liberal and conservative views. Insofar as the mixed strategy in practice tends towards the extreme liberal view and inherits some of its consequences, the potential human being view can also be seen as a modification of it – one which pushes the mixed strategy towards a more conservative line by granting the fœtus a definite moral status right from the moment of conception. But it remains much less specific than an 'upgraded' mixed strategy. It can agree that the moral status of the fœtus becomes more and more significant the closer its potentiality approaches actuality, but at any stage it is still morally unique, not comparable to, say, an animal at any stage.

The argument

This is the by now familiar one, with suitable modifications. It begins from the premise that the fertilized ovum, unlike the unfertilized ova and sperm, is a potential human being. It then adds the gradual development premise that, working forwards from conception through the various stages, there is no point at which we can say 'Now it is an actual human being' until the baby is born. It is of course open to the by now familiar objections to taking birth as a cut-off point and also to the objection about the argument's validity (that even if there is no point at which we can say 'Here the fœtus changed from being a potential to an actual human being', nevertheless it may be true that a two-day-old embryo is (merely) a potential human being and an eight-month-old fœtus is an actual one – cf. 'The argument's validity' in Section 2, p. 36.

What about the premise that conception provides a starting point? Unlike the claims that the fertilized ovum is immediately morally comparable to a human being (the conservative view) or simply part of the woman's body (the extreme liberal view), the claim that it is immediately a potential human being seems beyond dispute. However, it can be disputed on the grounds that the ovum and sperm also have the potential for becoming a human being. This move can in turn be questioned, as involving a misapplication of the concept of *potentiality*. I will defend this below.

Consequences concerning abortion

One point of specifying the fœtus as potential is to avoid the particular consequence of the conservative view that many non-religious (and indeed many religious) people cannot accept, namely the idea that even if abortion is needed to save the mother's life it is not thereby permissible. Historically, potentiality was held to be inferior to actuality (this ranking is still implicit in the use of the word); so it can be said that when the lives of an actual and a potential human being are in conflict, the life of an actual human being wins out. So one consequence that does follow from this view is that abortion is permissible to save the mother's life.

But many other consequences are still left wide open. If the fœtus's life is very important, albeit not as important as an actual human being's life, is it less, or more, or as important as an actual human being's health? Or suffering? Or several actual human beings' happiness? According to what one believes about when abortion is permissible, one can decide to say 'less' or 'more' or 'as', but this is a stipulation, not the drawing of a conclusion from a premise.

Assigning the fœtus this status does provide a premise for ruling out abortion on trivial or self-indulgent grounds. For it can plausibly be said that deliberately to destroy a potential human being, thereby preventing it from realizing its potential, is a morally serious matter and that if and when it can be justified, the justification must be serious.

Abortion to secure the perfect baby   The view of the fœtus as a potential human being is at its haziest over the question of whether abortion is permissible to avoid the certainty or likelihood of a less than perfect baby. If one holds, as it is possible to hold even on the conservative view, that genuine euthanasia is permissible in the case of actual human beings, adults or babies, then one can certainly hold that euthanasia for potential human beings is permissible, since what is (merely) potential is not quite as important as what is actual. But what if one holds that euthanasia of actual human beings is never permissible? Then one might hold the same was true of potential ones; and on the other hand one might not – either would be consistent.

To hold the first would be to come very close to the conservative position and would presumably entail sharing the conservative position on *in vitro* fertilization and embryonic research. If it is wrong to kill potential human beings even for their own sake then it would also be wrong to create them with a view to killing them in research, or to do anything with spare ones that had been created to enable a woman to have a child except freeze them (see Appendix Three).

In fact, many people who regard the fœtus as a potential

human being do not approach the conservative view so closely; regardless of their views on euthanasia for actual human beings they tend to think it is permissible, perhaps even morally required, in the case of potential ones. But it is this position that leaves everything so indeterminate regarding the question of abortion in cases where what is at issue is *not* euthanasia, but the certainty or likelihood, or some risk of a less than perfect baby – a baby who will be, say, haemophiliac, or blind, or have Down's syndrome.

On the one side there is a strong pull towards saying that, although human beings with such conditions are as precious and their lives are as valuable as any other, nevertheless no one would choose to have such a condition, and, given the choice, no one would choose to have anything but a perfect baby. If a couple knew that if the woman conceives now, they will have a baby who is, say, deaf, whereas if they stop trying to produce a baby (stop trying to conceive) for a month and undergo some course of medical treatment, any baby that results will probably be perfect, we would all expect them to wait for a month and have the treatment. So it would seem to follow that if one knows of a potential human being that it is not going to become a perfect actual baby, and knows that one might easily generate another potential human being which would become a perfect actual baby, the right thing to do is to stop trying to produce this baby (i.e. have an abortion) and have another go later on. (I am leaving to one side for the moment all the cases in which there is only a likelihood, or a risk, that the baby will not be perfect.)

On the other side there is also a strong pull towards saying that to regard potential human beings as things one can pick and choose between, rejecting some as sickly specimens which are not worth allowing to live, and keeping only the perfect, is not to regard them seriously as potential human beings at all. If one can pick and choose this way, then why not agree that it would be morally permissible to abort fœtuses because of their gender in the cases where the couple particularly want a girl rather than a boy or vice versa?

To this it might be replied that it was never suggested that something as morally serious as the killing of a potential human being could be justified by selfish concerns. Nor was it suggested that the 'rejected' fœtuses are necessarily 'not worth allowing to live'. All that was said was that, other things being equal, it might be better not to let them develop if they are not going to become perfect babies.

But if it is allowed that killing a potential human being is a serious matter and hence calls for suitably serious justification (which would exclude, for instance, merely the desire for a child of a certain gender) what is the serious justification supposed to be in these cases? That the birth of a less than perfect baby will be avoided? Obviously, it seems. But then the birth of a less than perfect baby must be a terrible thing, something to be avoided even if the cost is the serious matter of killing a potential human being. 'Well', it might be said, 'isn't that right? Isn't it a terrible thing?' But the difficulty in agreeing with this is to find the right thing to say about the past births of lots of people around one, or indeed, depending on one's condition, about one's own birth. Suppose I was born, as Alison Davis was, with spina bifida, and am leading, as she is, a 'very full, happy and satisfying life by any standards'.[6] Am I going to say that my birth was a terrible thing? That hers was? No, I am not. So how can I agree that the birth of a less than perfect baby is a terrible thing?

The only thing to be said here, I think, by an upholder of the potential human being view is (a) that disabilities should be prevented if they can be, and (b) that although there are many things that cannot (morally) be done to prevent them (such as experiments on adult human beings without their consent, or infanticide), the killing of potential human beings is one of the things that can (morally) be done. But, to return to the point I left aside above, it is very unclear to what extent one can (morally) kill a potential human being when there is no certainty but only a risk of something wrong, or even a likelihood, and *justify* this as trying to prevent disability.

An upholder of the potential human being view might also justify the killing of potential human beings for the sake of the happiness of actual human beings. (I read an article by a woman who had had German measles while she was pregnant; she knew this meant there was a fair possibility she would give birth to a baby with disabilities. She thought that, had she been on her own, there was no doubt but that she should go on with the pregnancy, hoping for the best. But she thought that perhaps it was wrong to run the risk of bringing a disabled child into her family, and wondered whether, for their sakes, she should have an abortion. In fact, she didn't and the baby was perfect.) But clearly, this is a justification that would have to be handled with great care if it is not, once again, to involve upholders of it in outrageous claims about the people around them. Parents of, for instance, spina bifida babies, may be happy with their offspring, and quite generally, the parents of children who, for one reason or another, need a great deal of special attention and care are often to be heard saying that they would be *perfectly* happy if only it were not for the attitude and behaviour of other people: it is clear that some actual human beings would be happier if everyone born less than perfect were locked away out of sight – but that is not the sort of happiness that one could justifiably do anything to secure or encourage.

Fœtal research   In this context, the point of specifying the fœtus as a potential human being is to suggest a certain range of restrictions on fœtal research. Upholders of the view may vary in the extent to which they condemn or condone particular forms of it, but they share the view, as over abortion, that it is a morally serious matter which calls for justification and restriction. So, for instance, it is usually agreed, first that the research must be for the purpose of important biomedical knowledge. 'Important' allows scope for the variation I mentioned above. Where, for instance, does research into the particular reasons why smoking causes lung cancer fall, when it is our own fault that we smoke? But few would deny that in general research into the causes of cancer is important and research into shampoos that will not cause scalp irritation is not. Secondly, it is usually agreed that fœtuses should only be used as a last resort – that is, that wherever possible alternative means of acquiring the knowledge, such as experiments on consenting adults or animals, should be used instead.

In vitro fertilization   As I noted at the outset the potentiality view can be very conservative. It is possible to hold, with the conservative view (see p. 44), (a) that it is completely unacceptable to create potential human beings with a view to using them for research and never allowing them to realize their potential, and (b) that the only permissible thing to do with 'spare' embryos is to freeze them with a view to implantation at a later date, so that they can realize their potential.

According to a small but significant modification of (b) the spare embryos may be allowed to die, or be killed, this presumably being regarded as a serious matter but justified by their being unwanted. (I say this is significant since it puts the emphasis more on the (merely) potential, bringing the fœtus's status closer to that of an animal. Someone who thinks it is wrong to kill animals for pleasure or trivial reasons might still agree it was quite justifiable to drown unwanted kittens, but few people would agree that one could justify killing babies *simply* on the grounds that they were unwanted.)

According to a more substantial modification of (b) it is also permissible to do research on spare embryos (subject to the above restrictions on fœtal research). Can this be held consistently with (a)? It seems that it can.

One could plausibly claim that intentionally creating potential human beings that will be used for research and never allowed to realize their potential is not justifiable when one's only reason for doing so is the research itself, but is justifiable when one is trying to enable a woman to have a child. Of course, something more would then need to be said about why it is justifiable in the one case and not the other, but this does not seem impossible – the reasons one has for doing things frequently make a great difference to the morality of the action. So, for instance, one might hold that it was wrong to kill animals in order to eat them but that if one had to kill an animal for some other reason, say to put it out of pain, it would be all right to eat the carcase rather than waste it.

Potentiality   Some people maintain that, when we are talking about the *in vitro* fertilization cases, there is no difference between spare and deliberately-generated-for-research embryos. Neither, it is maintained, have a potential for life, since neither are going to be transferred to a uterus. A similar argument is often put forward in relation to aborted non-viable fœtuses. That is, it is agreed that abortion is a morally serious matter, at any stage, since it involves the destruction of something with the potential of becoming a human being. But, it is said, after abortion the fœtus no longer has that potential (for we said it was non-viable); so there are no bars, on that score, to experimentation.

These arguments embody a confusion about the concept of potentiality, partly brought about by shifting from 'being a potential human being' (where 'potential' is an adjective) to 'having the/a potential for/to' (where 'potential' is a noun). To say that a fœtus is a potential human being is not like saying that it has a chance or opportunity to become a human being, an opportunity/potential that may be lost. It is to say something about its natural development, and its natural development can be perverted or prevented but it cannot be lost.

If 'being a potential human being' was like 'having an opportunity to become a human being' then some human fœtuses would be potential human beings and some would not, but the point of describing fœtuses as potential human beings is to group them all together into a natural class, with a certain natural development. A thing is potentially F if it will become F of its own accord, if nothing external intervenes. So (all) acorns and chestnuts are potential trees (not potential climbers, like beans); and (all) acorns are potential oak trees, not potential chestnut trees or bean plants, and these distinctions between acorns, chestnuts and beans are not undercut by the possibility, for example, that some particular acorn may have as little chance of growing into an oak tree (i.e. none, because it is in my souvenir collection) as a bean has. Similarly, human fœtuses and rabbit fœtuses are potential mammals (not potential amphibians like frog spawn); and human fœtuses are potential human beings not potential rabbits and these distinctions between human fœtuses, rabbit fœtuses and frog spawn are not undercut by the possibility that some particular fœtus (say, a non-viable aborted one, or a spare embryo in a test-tube in a research laboratory) has as little chance of growing into a human being as a rabbit.

The only way, I think, in which a human fœtus or human fertilized ovum could possibly fail to be a potential human being would be if it were, from the start, genetically so abnormal as to make it impossible that it would ever develop to term and survive. Apart from this possible exception, all human fœtuses are potential human beings, from the moment of conception.

At this point I should discuss the common claim that the ovum and sperm also have the potential for becoming human beings, i.e. are potential human beings. I said above that this can be said to embody a confusion about the concept of potentiality, and indeed it often does. It does when the argument for it simply involves emphasizing what might (possibly) become of the ovum/sperm/fertilized ovum. Thus someone may argue that a human ovum/sperm is, after all, something such that *if* it combines with a sperm/ovum and *if* the result is implanted and if . . . then a human being will result, and that this is all that is required for being a potential human being. When it is objected that the ovum or sperm alone is not a potential human being because it needed to combine with the other in order for the process to be got going, it will be replied that this is no different from the fertilized ovum which has to combine with, i.e. absorb, other things from its environment in order to develop into a human being.

But, according to this argument, a human ovum/sperm/ fœtus might be said to be potentially all sorts of things – a potential tree or rabbit, for example. For *if* the ovum/sperm/ fœtus dies and is buried in the ground and *if* it decays naturally and in doing so combines with other things and *if* it nourishes, i.e. combines with, a sapling (which may be eaten by a rabbit), then it might be said the ovum/sperm/

fœtus was potentially a tree (or a rabbit). Here we have lost the idea of natural development which the concept of potentiality involves.

Avoiding this mistake, someone might still claim that the human ovum and sperm are potential human beings on the grounds that, unlike say rabbit ova and sperm, and like the human fertilized ovum, they would naturally develop this way. But that really does amount to no more than saying that the human ovum and sperm *are* human, actually not potentially (unlike rabbit ova and sperm and like the human fertilized ovum): or else it says something usually thought to be false, that human beings (like bees and some aphids) can reproduce by parthenogenesis (i.e. that the ovum can develop into a fœtus without being fertilized). (If parthenogenesis is possible in human beings then indeed some ova would count as potential human beings. But sperm would not. So it would still be a mistake to try to classify the fertilized ovum or embryo with 'the ovum and sperm' as all potential human beings.)

Of course, it is open to someone to reject the concept of potentiality which I claim is being misunderstood above. It is open to someone to say that there is not a clear concept here to be understood; that the arguments I say embody confusions really enunciate all that can be salvaged from a concept that relies on such dubious notions as 'natural development', 'natural class', 'of its own accord' and so on.

This could be part of a quite general scepticism about relying on any sense of 'nature' or 'natural'. Or, remaining fairly tolerant about that, it could relate specifically to the difficulties of trying to apply this way of talking to the machinations of modern science. How can we hold on to the idea of a natural class or natural development when we can generate hybrid creatures? How can we maintain the distinction between a thing's intrinsic nature and external intervention in its life-cycle when we can 'intervene' and begin a life-cycle by so doing – as we do in the case of *in vitro* fertilization?

According to the general scepticism about 'nature', etc., the notion of 'being a potential human being' will, insofar as it makes any sense at all, single out a great ragbag of entities: some, but not all, fœtuses or embryos and also human ova and sperm, and perhaps anything that humans can digest and so on. According to the specific worry about whether 'being a potential *F*' makes sense in the context of modern science, 'being a potential human being' would single out only human fœtuses or embryos, but, once again, some, not all; it would not apply to embryos generated *in vitro*.

This is a plausible position, and can form a strong part of a criticism of the view about the fœtus under discussion. It amounts to an attack on the premise of this view, that *the* (i.e. any) fertilized ovum is a potential human being whereas the unfertilized ova and sperm are not. It represents a threat to this premise by maintaining that the notion of potentiality *either* lets in the unfertilized ova and sperm *or* does not cover those ova fertilized *in vitro*. So it is an argument for giving up this particular view about the moral status of the fœtus.

It is important to get clear about the fact that it is a *criticism* of the view that the fœtus is a potential human being and thereby morally and importantly unique. To try to hold simultaneously that (a) *the* fœtus is a 'potential' human being in this watered down sense of 'potential', and (b) that *it* is thereby morally and importantly unique is just to get into a muddle. For, obviously, if some human fœtuses are 'potential' human beings and some are not, then, on this view some are morally unique and some are not, and then we have not got a view about the status of *the* fœtus at all. Moreover, if the decision of a pregnant woman, or a scientist with an embryo in a test-tube, that she is not going to let the fœtus or embryo live, can remove its potential for life, then the consequent moral view is simply absurd. Before a woman decides to have an abortion it is wrong, because it is the destruction of something with a potential for life. But after she has decided, it is all right, because the fœtus lost its potential with her decision. Similarly, before the scientist decides not to freeze or implant the embryo, using it for research and eventually killing it would be wrong, because it would be the destruction of something with a potential for life but once she has decided to use it for research, it loses that potential, so it is all right! I stress the point that this is a muddle because it is one which people quite commonly get into.[7]

Summary

Someone who holds the view that the fœtus is morally unique in being a potential human being is hardly committed to anything but may consistently hold the following views.

Abortion (at any stage)

(i)	to save the mother's life	permissible
(ii)	on social or psychological grounds	permissible (but perhaps only during the early stages of pregnancy)
(iii)	as fœtal euthanasia	permissible
(iv)	to avoid the possibility or certainty of a child with disabilities	permissible (but perhaps only during the earlier stages of pregnancy)
(v)	on trivial grounds	impermissible

Fœtal research

(i)	on live fœtuses	impermissible
(ii)	on dead fœtal tissue	possibly permissible

Breeding fœtuses for the purposes of research impermissible

In vitro fertilization and embryonic research

(i)	creating embryos and deliberately allowing them to die	permissible
(ii)	keeping embryos as living tissue and using them for purposes of research	impermissible

Infanticide impermissible

7   CONCLUSIONS

What I hope to have made clear in this chapter is that there is no position about the moral status of the fœtus that is unproblematic. The problems take a variety of forms.

(1)   One problem shared by all the positions is the lack of a conclusive argument to establish what the moral status of the fœtus is. Some of the arguments have questionable premises; some are invalid; some of them do not even purport to be conclusive but merely mention considerations that make the position plausible. This problem need not be regarded as particularly damaging. All argument has to start somewhere and perhaps one's own position on the issue of abortion simply has to start from the unproved premise or assumption about the moral status of the fœtus.

   Now *if* one thought that settling the issue about the status of the fœtus was all that was needed to settle the issues about abortion, simply making such an assumption about the status would seem to be begging the question. But, as we have seen, the issues about abortion are not settled so simply. And this leads on to the other varieties of problems.

(2)   No position on the moral status of the fœtus settles the issues about abortion without the addition of extra premises. This problem was particularly noticeable in the case of the view that the fœtus is morally unique in status in being a potential human being. This view is, I think, the most plausible in relation to (non-conclusive but good) arguments that can be given for it, but what it gains in plausibility it loses in commitment, requiring hefty extra promises or straight stipulation about how potential human beings compare with adults, babies, dogs and bits of tissue in order to yield any conclusions about abortion at all. But the problem was not peculiar to this view. Every view required some extra premises such as 'killing human beings is wrong' or 'people have a right to decide what happens to bits of their own body' and so on.

   Why, one might ask, does the necessity for extra premises count as a problem? Well, the problem for each one of us trying to work out our own position on the issue of abortion is to get clear about *which* extra premises one wants. And this inevitably turns out to involve thinking about a whole lot of other moral problems – euthanasia, self defence, how animals should be treated, what we may do to prevent suffering, what people have a right to do and why, fœtal research – to name but a few of those that have come up. So there is no position about the moral status of the fœtus which is unproblematic in the sense that it unproblematically settles the issues about abortion. Each position requires further premises in order to settle anything about abortion, and these premises raise further issues about other moral problems.

(3) The third variety of problem I have in mind is less easy to specify than the other two, and may in any case be disputed. It is that each position is problematic insofar as it has difficulties with its consequences. The potentiality view's difficulty is that it hardly counts as having consequences at all. The other views all yield (given further simple premises) consequences that may be thought unacceptable – for example, on the conservative view there is nothing to ground saving a baby rather than a ten-day-old embryo from a fire; on one extreme liberal view no great wrong is done to a woman if a safe miscarriage is induced against her will; on another liberal view there is nothing wrong with infanticide and so on.

'Consequences that are unacceptable to whom?' one might ask. Not unacceptable to anyone who is prepared to accept them, obviously, and that is why I said that this third variety of problem may be disputed. But some of the consequences that I have drawn from the different views are such that I expect them to come as a surprise – consequences that someone who held a certain position about the moral status of the fœtus is unlikely to have accepted in advance and is, moreover, likely to find it difficult to accept. I will just record here, as a matter of possible interest, that I used to hold the mixed strategy position but found myself compelled to move to something more like the potentiality view when I discovered that the mixed strategy had as a consequence that there was nothing wrong with producing embryos solely for purposes of research. The point of drawing out these surprising consequences is not to engage in some exercise of intellectual one-upmanship, sniping at any and every position, but rather to encourage anyone, regardless of which position they hold, to think very carefully about how strongly they want to hold on to it. To a certain extent, this just brings us back to the second problem again— which extra premises does one want? Can one produce a set sufficiently complicated and subtle to rule out the unacceptable consequences after all? Or will one add as a premise that the 'unacceptable' consequences *are* acceptable, and look for an argument to justify this?

I said at the beginning of this chapter that one of its aims was to familiarize the reader with the range of possible positions about the moral status of the fœtus and some of the simpler arguments concerning them. Its other aim was to make clear that even at this fairly simple level, there is no position about the moral status of the fœtus, *vis-à-vis* the issues of abortion, which is unproblematic. I hope these aims have been achieved. I shall now turn to look at some areas in which the arguments get more complicated.

NOTES

1 I owe the idea of distinguishing a variety of positions on the moral status of the fœtus in the way I do in this chapter to an admirably clear article by Wasserstrom, Richard, 'The Status of the Fetus', reprinted in Rachels, James (ed.) (1979, 3rd edn) *Moral Problems*, Harper and Row.

2 The 'Peel Report' was the (1972) *Report of the Committee of Inquiry into 'The Use of Fetuses and Fetal Material for Research'*, HMSO.

3 Scarf, Maggie (1975) 'The Fetus as Guinea Pig', *The New York Times Magazine*, 19 October, 1975. Reprinted in Rachels, *op. cit.*

4 I shall be considering the view that commercial surrogacy is wrong because it is degrading in Chapter 8, pp. 323–7.

5 From L. W. Sumner's outline and defence of the mixed strategy which occurs in Sumner, L.W. (1981) *Abortion and Moral Theory*, Chapter 4, Princeton University Press, and a revised version of it is reprinted as 'A Third Way' in Feinberg, Joel (ed.) (1984, 2nd edn) *The Problem of Abortion*, Wadsworth Publishing Company.

6   Mrs Alison Davis, Organiser of the SPUC Handicap Division, regularly writes to newspapers and journals describing her condition. The quotation comes from a letter to the *New Scientist*, 31 October 1985. 'I was born with severe spina bifida, and am confined to a wheelchair as a result. Despite my disability and the gloomy predictions made by doctors at my birth, I am now leading a very full, happy and satisfying life by any standards.' In another letter, to the *Journal of Medical Ethics*, vol. 9, no. 3, September 1983, she responds to an article proposing law reform concerning disabled newborn infants as follows.

> I am 28 years old, and suffer from a severe physical disability which is irreversible, as defined by the bill ... [the bill] suggests several criteria for predicting the potential quality of life of people like me, and I note that I fail to fulfil most of them.
>
> I have suffered considerable and prolonged pain from time to time, and have undergone over 20 operations, thus far, some of them essential to save my life. Even now my health is at best uncertain. I am doubly incontinent and confined to a wheelchair and thus, according to the bill, I should have 'no worthwhile quality of life'. Despite my disability I went to an ordinary school and then to university, where I gained an honours degree in sociology. I now work full-time defending the right to life of handicapped people. I have been married eight years to an able-bodied man, and over the years we have travelled widely in Europe, the Soviet Union and the United States. This year we plan to visit the Far East.
>
> Who could say I have 'no worthwhile quality of life'?

7   See, for example, Wasserstrom, *op. cit.* and the 'Warnock Report', Section 11.22 together with 11.28.

CHAPTER THREE

Trying to prove the fœtus does not matter

1 INTRODUCTION

The main conclusion of the last chapter was that there was no position on the moral status of the fœtus which was unproblematic. The chapter formed the opening move in my general strategy of showing that abortion is far from being a simple issue to which simple cut and dried answers can be given.

But it might fairly be said that the conclusion has not been established and hence that the opening move has not yet been made. For there *is* a view about the moral status of the fœtus which claims to be unproblematic and to settle the abortion issue quite simply once and for all – and it is the very view for which I refused to give the arguments. So something more must be said.

The view in question was 'the person view', according to which the fœtus has the same moral status as one of the lower animals, such as hen, because like hens and unlike ordinary adult human beings, fœtuses are not *persons* (p. 64 above). On this view, abortion and fœtal research are permissible, and quite unlike killing people or experimenting on people without their knowledge or consent, because the fœtus is not a person. I pointed out that one consequence of this view was that not only abortion but also infanticide came out as perfectly permissible, and that 'rather startlingly' another consequence was that not only embryos but also fœtuses and babies could be bred solely for purposes of research.

Now one might think that showing that the person view has these unacceptable consequences was enough to show that it was problematic. But I mentioned in the conclusions of the last chapter the possibility of someone's regarding a particular position on the moral status of the fœtus as *unproblematic* despite its 'unacceptable' consequences, because she was prepared to accept them. And this, apparently, many supporters of the person view are prepared, at least in theory, to do.

This is not, I think, because prior to philosophical argument they were in general pro-infanticide (as many of them were certainly pro-abortion) and thereby inclined to accept these consequences. It is rather that they believe themselves to have found an argument so rationally compelling in relation to abortion that any convictions from conventional morality which are inconsistent with it (such as that infanticide is wrong) are thereby thrown into question. After all, if an argument in which one can find no flaw proceeds from premises which one finds beyond question, but unfortunately yields a conclusion one finds 'unacceptable', what can anyone rational do? If one is certain about the argument for the person view, and certain that it makes infanticide all right, the only thing to do is to try to accept that and produce arguments to support this acceptance.

Some upholders of the person view have tried to do this, but the arguments defending the 'unacceptable' consequences of their view are nothing like as interesting or challenging as the arguments which supposedly establish the person view in the first place. These arguments are quite unlike any that we looked at in the last chapter, for they embody a distinctively new line of thought, involving the idea that it is the concept of a *person*, rather than the concept of a *human being*, which is of central importance in morality. This idea is not in itself at all new, as we shall see later, but in the context of both the abortion debate and arguments reflecting the recent upsurge of concern over our treatment of animals, it has suddenly taken on a new life, as having a most significant role to play.

This chapter will chiefly be devoted to those arguments that have been put forward to establish the person view on abortion. In the concluding sections of the chapter I shall briefly criticize arguments from some upholders of the person view justifying infanticide and also consider what such philosophers should say about fœtal research. I reserve the further complications of the person view in relation to our general treatment of animals for the following chapter; in this one I shall leave unquestioned the common assumption that there is nothing wrong in our killing animals such as chickens, sheep and cattle for food, using them for experimental purposes, and so on.

One particularly interesting feature of the person view in relation to abortion is that, as I mentioned above, its proponents believe that it is unquestionably rationally compelling. Its conclusion, that abortion is morally neutral or acceptable, is said to follow from claims about persons and quite general claims about moral relevance; claims which, in the words of one of the proponents, are 'perfectly obvious ... [and] which ought, indeed to be obvious to both friends and foes of abortion'.[1] Foes of abortion (and indeed infanticide) persist in their error either because they have still not realized that these obvious, unquestionable, truths about persons and moral relevance entail that abortion and infanticide are morally neutral or because they are being irrational and emotional.[2]

I should say at the outset that I am strongly opposed to the person view, and do not agree that this is because I am being irrational or emotional. I shall try to show that the claims that are made about persons and moral relevance would only be obvious or unquestionable to those people who believe already that abortion and infanticide are morally innocuous. But I shall begin by making as plausible a case for the person view as I can.[3]

2 'PERSON' AS OPPOSED TO 'HUMAN BEING'

The word 'person' is an odd one. A lot of the time it functions simply as a synonym for 'human being' or 'man' (where the latter names the species, not simply the male members of it); the dictionary defines it as 'an individual human being, man, woman or child'. Though 'persons' is its grammatical plural, idiomatically 'people' is more usual (as in 'one person, two people') and 'How many people are here?' is asking 'How many human beings are here?' But since at least as far back as the seventeenth century it has been used to express a concept which is not simply that of a *human being* – a member of the species *homo sapiens* – but a less scientific ones.

In *An Essay Concerning Human Understanding* (1689), John Locke discusses the question of personal identity – what makes it true that I am the same person, Rosalind Hursthouse, now, as I was ten years ago? It cannot be that I am the same collection of cells, because I am not – they all change (we are told) every seven years or so. Nor, so Locke maintains, can it be because I have the same body – which I do, despite the change in the cells. That I have the same body, albeit older, as I had ten years ago is what makes it true that I am the same *human being* – the same member of the species – but this is not enough to guarantee that I am the *same person*. 'For', Locke argues in a famous passage, 'should the soul of a prince, carrying with it the consciousness of the prince's past life, enter and inform the body of a cobbler as soon as deserted by his own soul, everyone sees he would be the same *person* with the prince, accountable only for the prince's actions; but who would say it was the same *man*?'[4] This shows that 'human being' (or 'man') does not always mean the same as 'person', so, Locke says, '. . . we must consider what *person* stands for; – which, I think, is a thinking intelligent being, that has reason and reflection and can consider itself as itself, the same thinking thing, in different times and places; which it does only by that consciousness which is inseparable from thinking . . .'[5]

Fascinating as Locke's view of personal identity is, we must not allow it to distract us. I quote it to illustrate the fact that he is able, in a way presumably comprehensible to his seventeenth-century readers, to draw a distinction between the concept of a *human being* or *man* and the concept of a *person*. The concept of a human being is the scientific or biological concept of an organism with a particular body, with all that that entails. The concept of a person is the concept of something that perhaps has to be embodied, but it does not have to be in a particular body, nor even in a body of a particular sort. Locke imagines what we would say if we came across a cat or a parrot which could 'discourse, reason and philosophise' and says that even if this were to happen we still would not say that the cat or parrot was a man, or a human being. No amount of intelligence or self-consciousness would make it the case that they belonged to anything other than their own species, but, he implies, self-consciousness and rationality might make it the case that a cat or a parrot was a *person*. So although 'person' often functions as a synonym for 'human being', there are contexts in which it does not. Hence, although it is trivially true that all human beings are human beings, it is not trivially true that all human beings are persons — perhaps some are not.

It is not clear that Locke envisaged this possibility, but in defining 'person' in terms of rationality and self-conscious-ness, he certainly allowed for it, whether he realized this or not. An anencephalic (see Glossary) human infant would not be a person according to his definition for instance.

Conversely, although it is trivially true that no non-human beings (other animals, extra-terrestrials, robots, etc.) are or could be human beings, it is not trivially true that no other creatures (or robots) are or could be persons. And this possibility Locke clearly does envisage in imagining a philosophically inclined cat or parrot.

Now imagining that is perhaps too much like imagining a children's story in which all sorts of things, including teapots and spoons, or flowers and snails, can talk. But the idea that some sorts of animals might be able to use language is not at all fantastical. As is now well known, some chimpanzees and gorillas have been taught to use a sign language; the chimpanzee called 'Washoe' is said to under-stand about 350 different signs and herself to be able to use about 150 of them correctly. She can answer questions, and put the signs together to form new sentences (so her mastery of language is not merely parrot-like); she can make her thoughts and wishes known. She is not, of course, a human being, but she is a *person*. It is thought to be possible too that the noises that whales and dolphins make are a form of language; that although we cannot, and perhaps will not ever, understand what they are 'saying' to each other, they are nevertheless communicating. And if they are, it seems clear that they too must be persons, and the reason we would so much like to understand their language is so that we could find out what sort of people they were.

We should not take this as showing that *being a language-user* is the defining characteristic of being a person. This would amount to assuming that 'reason and reflection' and self-awareness are impossible for a creature without a language, and many philosophers, amongst them many supporters of the person view, do not find this a plausible assumption. We might say that being a language-user definitively settles that a creature *is* a person; if it is not a language-user, whether or not it is a person is harder to establish and it is hard to define what would be needed, but it might be a person none the less.

We can all employ the concept of a person, even if we cannot on the spot produce a tight definition of it, and notwithstanding the fact that in some cases we might be very uncertain about whether something was a person or not. In some other cases we can apply the concept with certainty, and it is clearly *not* the same concept as the biological one of a human being. But what is its point? What do we need it to do which the concept of being a member of *homo sapiens* will not do?

It seems that what it does is single out what is special or important about being a human being – a member of *homo sapiens*. As Kant said, 'The fact that man can have the idea of "I" raises him infinitely above all other beings living on earth. By this he is a *person*.' Now we may not agree with Kant that we are the only beings living on earth who can 'have the idea of "I"', i.e. be self-conscious or self-aware; for instance, maybe chimpanzees and dolphins can too. But he is surely right that the point of the concept of a person is to capture the fact that the really important differences between human beings and most other things living on this planet is not simply that we belong to one species and they all belong to different ones, but that we are a species of *persons*. We are rational and self-conscious.

In Kant's day, the natural extension of 'person' beyond human beings would have been to angels and to God but no further. We have come to think rather differently about animals such as dolphins and chimpanzees and have also become accustomed to the idea that there might well be beings living on other planets somewhere in the universe. They might be no more than plants, or only like prawns or hens, but the exciting possibility is that they might be 'like us' – not like us biologically, in being very like *human beings*, but like us in being *persons*. This is what we are thinking of when we wonder if there is intelligent life on other planets.

Now suppose we are wondering whether dolphins are persons. Or let us imagine finding things living on other planets and trying to find out whether they are just plants, or like prawns or hens, or whether, despite the fact that they look like plants or prawns or hens they are really persons. The interesting fact here is that when we do wonder whether dolphins are persons, or imagine wondering whether strange things living on other planets are persons, we find ourselves wondering about something of crucial *moral* importance. If dolphins are persons, we are doing them a terrible wrong in keeping them captive in 'Marinelands' and teaching them to do tricks; but if they are not persons there is nothing wrong with this (assuming it does not make them suffer). It would be terrible if we were treating persons with this sort of lack of respect, but if dolphins are not persons the question of 'respecting' their freedom or autonomy does not arise. Although people's reactions to imaginary examples vary a lot, even the most pragmatic can see the point of the many science-fiction stories and films in which we begin by putting the 'mere aliens' in cages, or experimenting on them, or using them to work for us, or eating them, or killing them for other reasons – in general, treating them as we treat animals and not with the respect we think is due to human beings – without thinking that we are doing anything wrong. But then we discover, to our shame, that these things are *persons*, and we feel shame because in treating them in this way, we have been treating them terribly wrongly.

So it seems that the concept of a person does two things. It distinguishes us (and no doubt other sorts of things) as rational and self-conscious from things that are not rational and self-conscious, such as plants and most other animals. And in doing so, it might be said, it pinpoints what it is about us that makes us members of what may be called 'the moral community'. The moral community is defined as the set of beings that moral rules such as 'Do not kill' or 'Killing is wrong' apply to. So, for instance, when we say that killing is wrong, we do not mean that it is wrong to kill plants, for plants are not members of the moral community. Do we mean that it is wrong to kill chickens and cattle and use them for food? No (bearing in mind that I said above I would leave this assumption unquestioned), animals, or those sorts of animals anyhow, are not members of the moral community. But nor, when we say that killing is wrong, do we mean that it is just *human beings* that it is wrong to kill. For we intend the prohibition against killing to apply to dolphins *if* they are persons, and to any non-human aliens who are. The moral community consists of all, and only, *persons*, and we are not members of it because we are human beings but because we are persons.

The obvious point seems to be that it is *being a person* rather than *being a human being* which is of moral significance. So two claims can be accepted, according to the person view, as quite uncontroversial.

(A)   That we have two distinct concepts, the biological concept of being a human being, or a member of the species *homo sapiens*, and the non-biological concept of being a person, or having rationality and self-consciousness.

(B)   It is whether or not something is a person which matters morally. Whether or not something is a human being is morally irrelevant.

I shall consider later whether these two claims are as

uncontroversial as they seem.[6] For the moment I shall continue to try to make the person view as plausible as I can.

The abortion debate

According to the person view, we may, once we have appreciated the truth of (A) and (B) above, come to understand why the abortion debate has been waged so fruitlessly for so long, and why liberals and conservatives have rarely, if ever, managed to convince each other hitherto. The explanation is that those taking part in the debate have been misled by the term 'human being', mistakenly supposing that it is always synonymous with the term 'person'. They think we have just one concept, that of *human being or person*, whereas in fact we both have and need two – the biological one and the other, morally significant, one. It is easy to understand why people may overlook the fact that we have these two distinct concepts since both the terms 'human being' and 'person' can be used in certain contexts to express either. As we noted at the outset, the dictionary indeed defines 'person' as 'an individual human being'. Conversely, we may use 'human being' or 'human' in a completely unscientific way. When we praise someone as 'a real human being' we are not commenting on their biological status but on their personal qualities; when we say of our pets that they are, or are nearly, human, or like another human being, we are commenting on their psychological qualities or their personalities, not suggesting that they are walking upright or developing opposing thumbs.

This vagueness in our language, it is claimed, lends a spurious plausibility to the conservative case. The standard conservative argument, at its simplest, is as follows:

(1) The foetus is a human being or person.
(2) It is wrong to kill human beings or people.
(3) So it is wrong to kill foetuses.

But, it is said, this position is plausible only because of the ambiguity of 'human being or person'. What we may have from the moment of conception is a new human being *in the biological sense.* That, it may be conceded, is settled by the facts of biology. But insofar as it is agreed amongst us that human beings or persons have the right to life, or that it is wrong to kill human beings or persons, it is human beings or persons in the *non-biological* sense that we have in mind.

If we explicitly reserve the term 'human being' for the biological concept, and likewise reserve the term 'person' for the non-biological one, the inadequacy of the anti-abortionist's argument can be clearly displayed as follows. She says:

(1a) The fœtus is a human being.
(2a) It is wrong to kill persons.
(3a) So it is wrong to kill fœtuses.

Clearly this is no argument against abortion at all; the two premises (1a) and (2a) fail to connect with each other. But until this simple fact is realized, the only thing for the liberal to do is to attack her opponent's premises in their old version, (1) and (2). Her attempts to do so are bound to fail to convert the conservative in any but the most minor way, for, without realizing it, she will be battling against the almost incontrovertible truths of (1a) and (2a).

Trying to falsify (1a), she may argue that the fœtus is not a human being for at least the first ten to fourteen (or whatever) days after conception. But at best this will not establish the liberal abortion policy she wants; it will hardly do more than justify the 'morning-after' pill. And at worst, since the biological facts simply do not yield a *better* clear boundary point than conception to determine when 'human life' begins, she will find her conservative opponents maintaining that all she has shown is that we cannot be sure when the fœtus becomes a human being, and hence must forbid all abortions in case we are killing a human being.

Trying to falsify (2a) the liberal may argue that it is not *always* wrong to kill persons, mentioning, for instance, self defence. But once again, such an argument will at best make out a case for a very few abortions being permissible. Moreover, such an argument will not truly reflect what extreme liberals believe. For, as one proponent of the person view has put it:

> their conviction (for the most part) is that abortion is obviously *not* a morally serious and extremely unfortunate, even though sometimes justified, act, comparable to killing in self-defense ... but rather is closer to a morally neutral act, like cutting one's hair.[7]

Trapped in the old terms of the debate, the liberal does not have the vocabulary with which to express her view. What she wants to say is that the fœtus is not a person, not rational and self-conscious, a fact so obvious that it does not need elaborate considerations of embryonic development to establish it. But she continually finds herself trying to deny that the fœtus is, biologically, a human being, and being forced to manipulate the biological facts. With hindsight, we can see why the abortion debate has continued so fruitlessly for so long hitherto. It is not because, despite shared knowledge of the facts of embryology, two sets of rational people have, incomprehensibly, arrived at diametrically opposed views about what these facts add up to. Nor is it because liberals are so morally corrupt that they think there is nothing morally wrong with murder. It is because, without realizing it, each side has been insisting on a view which does not contradict their opponent's while thinking that it does. According to the conservatives, the fœtus is, biologically, a human being; according to the liberals the fœtus is not a person, and between *these* two views there is no contradiction.

So, according to the person view, we now understand why the abortion debate went on for so long without resolution, and why neither side managed to convert the other. We also see that the conservative has no simple argument against abortion; once 'person' and 'human being' are clearly distinguished, her premises fail to connect.

And, finally, we see that the liberal has a conclusive argument justifying abortion, namely:

(1b) The fœtus is not a person.
(2b) Killing non-persons is morally neutral or unobjection-

able (*cf.* our killing of plants and chickens).
(3b) So killing fœtuses is morally neutral or unobjectionable.

Further complications

However, as I noted before, this same form of argument works equally well for infanticide. A new-born baby is not a person, so if abortion is morally neutral so, by the same token, is infanticide. What should we take this as showing?

(1)   We might take it as showing that perhaps we have set the conditions for personhood too high. If we agree (a) that you and I – ordinary adult human beings – certainly are persons, and (b) that fœtuses certainly are not, then could we not find some criteria for being a person, less demanding than rationality and self-consciousness, which would make (a) and (b) true but also guarantee that new-born infants were persons? I do not know of any writer who has tried such a move, and since it seems an unpromising one, this is perhaps unsurprising. Given what it is trying to do, namely keep abortion as morally neutral, no matter how late in the pregnancy, while preserving infanticide as murder, it will be compelled to treat birth as in some way relevant to personhood. But how could it be? The whole point of the concept of a person, as we have seen, is that it abstracts from any biological details and concentrates on a creature's conceptual (or 'mental' or 'intellectual') capacities. And these do not change suddenly when a fœtus is born.

So there is no point in trying to lower the criteria for personhood to let babies in *unless* one is prepared to let at least later-stage fœtuses in, i.e. to admit, in effect, that the person view does not justify abortion in the way claimed. For lowering the criteria (to, for example, sentience – the capacity for sensations or feelings, perhaps particularly feelings of pain or pleasure) in effect takes us back to something very like the mixed strategy discussed in the preceding chapter. But this is a far cry from the extreme liberal view that killing fœtuses at any stage is morally neutral since they are not persons. (It also, we should note, commits one to a particularly compassionate view of animals.

If having the capacities of a new-born baby is sufficient for personhood, then Kant was utterly wrong in thinking that it is our being persons which raises us above even most of the other animals. Mice, chickens, sheep, cattle – all of them are sentient, and in general may be said to have the same, if not greater, conceptual abilities than a new-born baby. So if we define 'person' to include babies, we shall include all of them too.)

(2) If we are certain that the person view correctly establishes that abortion is morally neutral, we can take the fact that by the same argument infanticide is also morally neutral as showing that, startling as this conclusion may be, it must, nevertheless, also be correct. What is then called for are some independent arguments to make such an apparently unacceptable view acceptable. Attempts at such arguments have been made by proponents of the person view, as I mentioned at the beginning of this chapter, and I shall be discussing them shortly.

(3) Alternatively, we can take the fact that this startling conclusion, that infanticide is morally neutral, has emerged as a compelling reason to suspect that there is something wrong with the person view. What is called for then is to show what is wrong with it. And that is what I shall now try to do.

3 SPECIESISM

The argument for abortion (and infanticide) on the person view was, as we have seen:

(1b) The fœtus (or the new-born baby) is not a person.
(2b) Killing non-persons is morally neutral.
(3b) So killing fœtuses (or new-born babies) is morally neutral.

What can one find wrong in this? The argument is formally valid, so our options are reduced to attacking the premises, (1b) or (2b). It might be thought that the thing to do was to go for (1b). But at this stage of the debate that would be, I think, a retrograde step, tending to fall back into the old terms in which one confuses 'person' with 'human being'. That leaves (2b). Suppose I were to attack it as follows.

'I agree', I say, 'that fœtuses and new-born babies are not persons, for I agree that they lack rationality and self-consciousness. But many other human beings also fail to be persons, for instance, some human beings suffering from brain damage and some of those who have had strokes, and the very senile, and the severely retarded or disordered. It may be that it is morally permissible (though hardly neutral) to kill some of these human beings – about that I am not sure. But I am quite sure that there are some of them it would be absolutely wrong to kill, even though they are *not* persons, because they *are* human beings. So (2b) is false.

'Moreover, when we replace the false (2b) with the correct premise about killing, namely:

(2c) Killing human beings is wrong

we reveal this liberal argument for abortion as suffering from exactly the defect it found in its opponent's. The two premises fail to connect.'

If I object to (2b) in this way, what can an upholder of the person view reply? Is there a plausible objection?

The objection any upholder of the person view makes to this is to say that I am being *speciesist* in maintaining that it is wrong to kill these non-persons because they are *human beings*, and replacing (2b) with (2c). Speciesism, it is said, is just like interplanetary or interstellar racism. Racists think that, for instance, the death or enslavement of someone of their own race matters, but that the death or enslavement of someone of a different race does not, despite the fact that a difference in skin colour does not make for a difference in how much one wants to live or be free, or how worthwhile one's life might be, or anything else relevant. Similarly, it is said, a speciesist would be one who thought that the death or enslavement of a member of their own species mattered, but that the death or enslavement of a member of a different species, say, an extra-terrestrial *person*, did not, despite the (imagined) fact that the difference in species does not make for a difference in how much the two beings want to live or be free, or how worthwhile their lives might be.

To lapse into speciesism, appealing to the wrongness of killing *human beings*, is to overlook, or to refuse to accept, the second of the supposedly uncontroversial claims that the person view made, namely that 'it is whether or not something is a *person* which matters morally. Whether or not something is a human being is morally irrelevant.' (See (B) above p. 96, where I promised to return to the question of whether the two claims were indeed uncontroversial.)

Now this claim may well seem uncontroversial initially, before one realizes that it has such startling consequences with regard to fœtuses, infants, the senile and the severely retarded or disordered. Now it is revealed that it does have these consequences we should look again at just why it seemed plausible in the first place.

The argument about the aliens

The claim gains much of its plausibility from the thought-experiment about our treatment of extra-terrestrial aliens. So let us go over this imaginary example again with rather more care than before. Let us imagine that some future space project gets us to a planet where we encounter another species of living things. Our question is: what settles how we ought to behave in relation to these things? Can we use them as a source of food or energy? And if so, why? Or would that be terribly wrong? And if so, why?

We may agree that the question is not settled by taking one look at these things and realizing that they are not *human beings*. To suppose that this on its own were sufficient to settle that it was morally all right to treat them as a source of food and energy, as though they were just like plants or hens or cattle, really would be viciously speciesist. Surely, what the person view says is right: if they are persons it would be terribly wrong to treat them as plants or cattle. But if they *are* like plants or cattle, in being not merely non-humans, but in being non-persons, then it must be morally all right to treat them like plants or cattle. What matters, and the only thing that matters, is whether or not these aliens are persons; that is what we have to decide when we encounter them.

But now that we are bearing in mind the examples of infanticide and the killing of the senile and severely retarded, we can locate a crucial ambiguity in the question of whether 'they', this species of alien beings, are persons or not. Once this ambiguity is revealed it becomes clear that in one sense, the claim that 'it is being a person which matters morally' is not uncontroversial at all.   The ambiguity lies in whether what we have to decide is if they *as a species* are persons, i.e. is this alien species sufficiently like our species in that respect for us to include them in our normal moral community? Or are they persons *as individuals*?

Which is the important one to decide? This is not uncontroversial. Indeed, we may expect that which one thinks is the important one to decide will be determined by one's prior convictions about abortion, infanticide and so on.

Suppose that I am against killing persons, and also against abortion, and infanticide, and the extermination of the senile and retarded. And suppose that, having encountered some of these aliens, I have discovered that, like us, they are a species of persons, but that, also like us, not every member of the species is a person throughout its life. Might I think that though infanticide and the extermination of the senile mattered in the case of human beings, they could not possibly matter in the case of these aliens? Surely not, for that would once again be vicious speciesism. It would be to think that the killing of a non-person who was a member of my own species mattered, but that the killing of a non-person who was a member of another species did not matter, even though both species were species of persons.

If I am not a speciesist and think abortion and infanticide and so on in the case of human beings are wrong, I shall certainly not assume that, if I encounter one of these aliens which happens not to be a person it is all right for me to kill it or enslave it or experiment on it. For to do so might be killing or enslaving or experimenting on an infant alien, or a senile one, or a severely retarded one, and I shall think that that would be wrong.

Indeed, for all I know (until I know a great deal more

about their biology), it might be doing something else wrong. We take it as obvious that we do not cease to be persons while we are asleep or unconscious after a faint (though it is quite difficult to produce a tight definition of a person which guarantees that this is so). No proponent of the person view thinks that it would be wrong of you to kill me while I am awake but all right to do so when I am not, despite the fact that while I am deeply asleep or unconscious I am exhibiting as little rationality or self-consciousness as a fœtus. But we are familiar with our own patterns of consciousness and unconsciousness; we sleep but do not hibernate; we faint and have strokes and often recover consciousness quite quickly; some people can go into trances, but we do not lapse into unconsciousness or semi-uncon-sciousness for months or years and come to again as part of our natural life-cycle. But for all I know these aliens do, or do something similar. So when I encounter an alien which does not happen to be exhibiting rationality and self-consciousness I shall treat it with the same sort of respect (in relation to not killing it, or experimenting on it, etc.) as I treat those aliens I encounter who are *persons*. So for me, the question of whether *any* member of this species of aliens can be treated as a plant or an animal is settled by discovering that *some* of them (or none of them) are persons, i.e. that they are persons (or not) as a species.

If, on the other hand, I am someone who already thinks abortion, infanticide, the elimination of the senile, experiments on them, and so on, are all morally neutral in the case of human beings because none of these human beings is a person, then presumably I will think the same about the aliens. In that case, the question of whether any member of this species can be treated as a plant or an animal is settled by discovering that this individual member of the species is (or is not) a person.

So let us return to the claim which was supposed to be so uncontroversial, namely that 'it is whether or not something is a person which matters morally. Whether or not something is a human being is morally irrelevant.' I do not pretend to have proved that this claim is false. But I do maintain I have shown it is certainly not uncontroversial. If

you believe already that abortion, infanticide, the elimination
of the senile and so on are all morally neutral, then the
thought-experiment about the aliens and how we settle
whether we may treat individual ones as we treat plants or
animals will indeed yield for you the conclusion that 'it is
whether or not something is a person which matters morally.
Whether or not something is a human being is morally
irrelevant.' But if you believe that abortion, infanticide, etc.
are not morally neutral but objectionable then the thought-
experiment will yield no more than the claim 'it is whether
or not something belongs to a species of persons which
matters morally'. And in this case 'whether or not something
is a human being' retains moral relevance precisely because
human beings are such a species.

And now let us return to the simple argument for abortion
on the person view, with its premise that

(2b) Killing non-persons is morally neutral.

I suggested that the argument could be attacked by rejecting
(2b) as false, and replacing it with 'the correct premise about
killing', namely:

(2c) Killing human beings is wrong

and I then considered the objection a proponent of the person
view would make to this, namely that counting *being a
human being* rather than *being a person* as morally relevant
was speciesism, and could be shown to be wrong by the
thought-experiment about aliens. I have now countered that
objection; the thought-experiment does not force anyone
who is against abortion, infanticide, etc. to give up (2c) and
replace it with (2b). What it does do is force anyone who
is not viciously speciesist to make (2c) more comprehensive;
for instance,

(2d) Killing human beings and members of any other species
       of persons is wrong.

This amendment suffices to avoid the charge of speciesism.
But it will not provide the person view with the premise it
needs to justify abortion, namely:

(2b) Killing non-persons is morally neutral.

People who believe already that abortion is morally neutral because the fœtus is not a person, and who are prepared to accept that infanticide, the elimination of the senile and severely retarded and so on are also morally neutral will accept premise (2b). But people who think otherwise have still been given no reason to do so. So the person view provides a rationally compelling argument that abortion is morally neutral or innocuous to people who believe that already, but not, so far, to anyone else.

4 TOOLEY ON ABORTION

Michael Tooley, who has published several articles[8] and, more recently, a whole book,[9] in support of abortion and infanticide, undoubtedly counts as an upholder of the person view. But he employs a rather different strategy from the one I have discussed and criticized so far, which calls for careful examination.

Tooley constructs a very complicated definition of 'person', according to which, fœtuses (and new-born infants) are not persons. Hence, by definition, he has

(D1) Fœtuses and babies are not persons.

He moves from this to

(C1) So fœtuses and babies do not have a right to life,

and from there to

(C2) So it is not wrong to kill fœtuses and babies,

i.e. killing fœtuses and babies is morally neutral (or 'morally acceptable' as he sometimes puts it).

What can be criticized here? Unlike the previous argument (p. 101) for abortion and infanticide, this argument is not formally valid. There is an obvious gap between (C1) and (C2). Traditionally, the concept of a *right* is connected with the concept of *justice*, and, if one thinks of rights in this way, the most that one will infer from (C1) is

So it is not unjust (i.e. does not violate a right) to kill fœtuses.

The fact that some action is not unjust does not mean it is morally neutral or acceptable – it still might be cruel, or callous, or wanton or selfish, for instance – so (C2) does not follow. But Tooley thinks of rights in a much more general way, and he bridges the gap between (C1) and (C2) by implicitly assuming the premise that

(P1) An action is wrong only if it is the violation of a right.

Criticism of this large theoretical assumption would take us too far afield. For the moment I will just note that, although it is far from uncontroversial, I am happy to allow it to Tooley and object to his argument on more specific grounds.

What about the move from (D1) to (C1)? As it stands, this is no argument at all, for no connection has been made between the premise and the conclusion. It needs a further premise, and Tooley uses

(P2) Only persons have the right to life.

That indeed makes the argument valid. But its conclusion, that abortion and infanticide are morally neutral, can reasonably be resisted by anyone who is prepared to reject (D1) or (P2), and this, as I shall argue, is something that anyone who is not already in favour of abortion and infanticide will be entitled to do. Tooley, in common with other upholders of the person view, thinks that anyone (rational) must accept his premises (D1) and (P2), regardless of their views on abortion. I shall argue, as I did in the preceding section, that, on the contrary, no anti-abortionist or anti-infanticidist need do so. Hence, all Tooley succeeds in doing is proving his conclusion to the people who believe it already.

Tooley needs to do two things: (a) he must get the rational anti-abortionist or anti-infanticidist to agree that only persons have a right to life; and (b) he must get them to agree to a certain definition of the concept of a person, a definition which will yield (D1).

Only persons have the right to life

Why should the anti-abortionist (I will not go on repeating 'or anti-infanticidist') agree with Tooley that only persons have a right to life? Why is this more 'rational' and less 'emotional', less of a taboo, than saying that only human beings have a right to life? The initial moves here are exactly the same as the ones we went through in the preceding section, that is, to say only human beings have a right to life is speciesism. So we should say instead that only persons have a right to life. But any anti-abortionist knows that this is usually taken to rule out the very human beings he particularly wants to include – fœtuses, infants, the very senile. And the charge of speciesism has not given him any reason for excluding them, only for including other beings as well. So, rejecting 'only persons have a right to life' he could avoid speciesism and continue to include the fœtuses, etc. by saying 'only human beings and members of relevantly similar species have a right to life'.

When I went through this flurry of moves and counter-moves earlier, it stopped there, with the anti-abortionist not having agreed to anything new at all. But Tooley apparently pushes the argument further. He claims that if, as everyone has agreed, it is wrong to kill human beings and would be wrong to kill members of certain other species, there must be an underlying basic moral principle which explains *why*.

His point here is easily illustrated. Suppose that, not being a racist, I hold that

(1) It is wrong to kill black human beings

and

(2) It is wrong to kill white human beings.

Underlying these two principles is the single principle

(3) It is wrong to kill human beings (or human beings have a right to life)

which, given the facts that black human beings and white human beings *are* human beings, explains why (1) and (2) hold. Suppose I also hold

(4) It is not wrong to kill plants.

Now (3) does not explain why that should be so. But a slightly amended version of (3), namely:

(5) It is wrong to kill any and only human beings

or, in a less barbaric phrase

All and only human beings have a right to life

explains (1), (2) and (3).

But not being speciesist, we have agreed that not only is it wrong to kill human beings but it would also be wrong to kill members of certain other species. Let us suppose one such species, the Martians, were just like us except they were a different species and looked peculiar. So we also hold

(6) It is wrong to kill Martians.

But clearly (5) cannot be the principle which underlies that because it refers only to human beings. And a reasonable anti-abortionist must surely allow Tooley to demand a principle which underlies (3) and (6). What will such a principle be like?

According to Tooley, 'such underlying moral principles will be free of reference to particular species, being formulated instead in terms of species-neutral concepts such as those of a person or a potential person'. He also says, 'The underlying principle will state that it is wrong to kill any individual, regardless of what species it belongs to, which possesses certain psychological capacities or enjoys certain psychological states.'[10]

It is these further claims about the nature or content of the underlying basic moral principles which push the argument further, for prior to Tooley producing these claims the anti-abortionist could easily meet his demand for a principle which underlies the wrongness of killing both humans and Martians. It is simply what the anti-abortionist produced before, namely:

(P) (All and) only human beings *and* relevantly similar species have a right to life

and he had still been given no reason to concede to Tooley that (all and) only persons have a right to life.

But Tooley would certainly rule out (P) because of his claims about what an underlying principle must be like. For (P) is contrary to his first requirement that the principle be 'free of reference to particular species', because it refers to human beings. But it is *not* thereby speciesist, for according to (P) it is indeed wrong to kill any individual, be it a human being or not, which ... But (P) goes on to fill in the ellipsis in terms of membership of species, human, or relevantly similar ones, whereas Tooley's second requirement is that the ellipsis should be filled in in terms of the actual possession of certain psychological capacities or states.

Is it only an irrational emotional prejudice against infanticide that would lead someone to give (P) as his underlying principle rather than giving the one that meets Tooley's two requirements? Surely not. Of course an anti-abortionist wants (P) rather than a Tooley-type principle, in part because it will explain why

It is wrong to kill fœtuses

and

It is wrong to kill infants,

whereas a Tooley-type principle will not. But conversely, Tooley wants his sort of principle because it will explain why

It is not wrong to kill fœtuses

and

It is not wrong to kill infants,

whereas (P) will not. And he has not yet given the anti-abortionists any neutral reason to concede that his position is more rational than theirs.

He clearly thinks he has given a neutral reason why the underlying principle should contain no reference to particular species – namely, to avoid speciesism, and I have argued that this is simply a mistake. Speciesism is indeed avoided by formulating the principle in terms of persons, but this is not the only way.

He also thinks that he has given a neutral reason why the principle should pick out individuals in terms of their possession of certain psychological capacities or states. It is to the discussion of this argument that I will now turn.

What sort of being can possess a right to life?

Let us suppose that Tooley concedes that the speciesism argument does not force the anti-abortionist to talk in terms of 'persons'. The next move he might make could be to suggest that we should use 'person', simply and neutrally, as shorthand for 'a being with the right to life'. If this is neutral and not question-begging what is its point? One result of it is to make (P2), 'Only persons have the right to life', equivalent to 'Only beings with the right to life have the right to life' and hence unquestionably and trivially true. But this need not beg the question against the anti-abortionists, so long as we remain clear that when 'person' is used as simply equivalent to 'being with the right to life' and not to 'being with rationality and self-consciousness', the anti-abortionists may reasonably use 'person' to apply to fœtuses and babies, and hence deny (D1), 'Fœtuses and babies are not persons'. For, using 'person' in the new way, this is equivalent to 'Fœtuses and babies do not have the right to life'. And obviously no anti-abortionist (or anti-infanticidist) is going to agree to this at the outset.

How then is Tooley to get the rational anti-abortionist to agree to (D1) 'Fœtuses and babies are not persons', supposing that 'person' is equivalent to 'being with the right to life' (and hence that (P2) 'Only persons have the right to life' gets by as trivially true)? His strategy is to raise the question 'What are the criteria for being a person?', meaning by that *not* 'What are the criteria for being rational and self-conscious?' but 'What are the criteria for having the right to life?' And he thinks that he can produce an answer to this (a) that anyone must accept, whatever their views on abortion, infanticide, etc. and (b) that rules out fœtuses and babies. I shall now consider his arguments for this.

He begins with an analysis of the meaning of '... has a right to ...'. This has gone through a number of refinements in successive versions of Tooley's views, but it would be, I think, fair to say that, whatever the details, the analysis always asserts a conceptual connection between *rights* and *desires*. The sort of being that can possess rights has to be the sort of being that can have desires. The analysis of the general 'has a right to' is then applied to the particular case of 'has a right to life'. Once again, the result of this application has, in Tooley's writings, successively more complicated upshots, but again it would be fair to say that, whatever the details, Tooley always concludes that a being has a right to life only if it possesses 'at some time' the concept of a self, or itself, a continuing subject of experiences with a past and a future.

It is not necessary to go through Tooley's writings in detail. If we look at some of the changes that he has made in his analyses and the reasons for them, we can perceive what his general method is, and thereby see how a rational anti-abortionist can continue to reject his conclusions.

He initially suggested that 'A has a right to x' is roughly synonymous with 'If A desires x then others are under a *prima facie* obligation to refrain from actions that would deprive him of it.'[11] The trouble with this, as Tooley recognizes, is that, applied to the right of life, it would produce some very odd results. What if A does not, at this moment, desire to live, because, say, he is unconscious or momentarily terribly depressed? We take as premises that unconscious and depressed people still have a right to life and therefore we amend the analysis. In his first article Tooley amended it thus: 'A has a right to x' means 'If A now desires x, or *would* desire x were it not for one of the following: (i) he is in an emotionally unbalanced state; (ii) he is temporarily unconscious; (iii) he has been conditioned to desire the absence of x, then others are under a *prima facie* obligation ... etc.'[12] (This last point is added in order to take care of another obvious counter-example, *viz.* that I might have been conditioned into being content with slavery and so not desire freedom. But I would still have a right to freedom.)

What does this amendment show about the method of producing a conceptual analysis of 'having a right [to life]'? It shows that the method involves taking as true certain sentences which employ the concept of a right (e.g. 'Unconscious people have a right to life') and as in part determining what the analysis of the concept must be. So now let us suppose that someone takes it as true that foetuses and infants have a right to life. Then they may add a fourth clause to Tooley's list of exceptions, for example, say (iv) 'He is too young'. And suppose someone takes it as true that irrevocably brain-damaged or senile people still have a right to life. They they will add a fifth clause, for example, (v) 'He is too brain-damaged, or too old'.

Tooley subsequently recognized that an analysis relying on a string of exception clauses was open to this kind of countermove.

> The clauses dealing with emotionally unbalanced individuals and with individuals who have been subjected to conditioning which has 'distorted' their desires are perhaps fair enough, for these are clearly exceptional cases, and it is not obvious exactly what account they should receive. But in the case of the temporarily unconscious individual one feels that it is an *ad hoc* modification simply to add a clause which says that an action can violate such an individual's right to something, even though he does not at the time have any desire for the thing. It would seem that a satisfactory account of rights should make clear the underlying rationale. If one fails to do this, a critic may well ask why one should make an exception of temporarily unconscious adults, but not of infants and fœtuses.[13]

In the revised version of this first article Tooley claims to provide this 'underlying rationale'. But what he in fact does is spell out four conditions under which a right is violated, conditions whose complications are specifically designed to capture just those cases he wants. So, for instance, his second condition reads:

> An action is performed at time t that prevents state of affairs S from obtaining at some later time t^*, and although individual A is not capable at time t of having a desire about S (being say brain-damaged or unconscious),
>
> (a) there was an immediately preceding time during which A did desire that S obtain at t^* and
>
> (b) it is possible that there will be some later time t' at which A would, if A were to exist at that time, desire that state of affairs S obtain at time t'^*.[14]

Of course, something as complicated as this (and it is far

from being the most complicated condition) is not intuitively true or false. One works out whether or not one believes it by working out what the bits are doing. Tooley is quite frank about this. 'Condition (2) [the one above]', he says, 'has been introduced to deal with the case of the temporarily unconscious individual.' Why is clause (b) there? 'The justification [*sic*] for clause (b) of this condition is that if, for example, a man suffers from *irreversible* brain damage . . . it would seem that one does not violate his right to life if one kills him.' Why is clause (a) there? 'Clause (a) of condition (2) is critical . . . If it were dropped, one would be forced [*sic*] to say that a human organism has a right to life even at the time it is only a fertilized egg.'[15] (I have omitted here some of Tooley's remarks which he might regard as crucial. But I will consider them shortly.)

The objections to this as a neutral analysis of the violation of a right, with which friends as well as foes of abortion will agree, are obvious.

(1) The 'underlying rationale' for adding a clause to deal with the temporarily unconscious consists of nothing but adding a condition to deal with the case which is expressed in abstract terms. So a critic might still ask why one should not add a condition, expressed in abstract terms, to deal with the case of the fœtus. Of course, this would necessitate dropping clause (a) but

(2) Clause (a) is hardly justified *to the foe* of abortion or infanticide by the fact that it is precisely the clause that rules out saying the fœtus has a right to life.

(3) Similarly, clause (b) is hardly justified to the foe of the elimination of the brain-damaged or senile by the fact that it is precisely the clause that rules out saying they have a right to life.

So, once again, it appears that someone who agrees already with Tooley that fœtuses and infants and the senile do not have a right to life will, perhaps, accept his analysis of what is involved in having a right. But if one does not already agree, one may reasonably maintain that the correct analysis has not been given.

Tooley's possibly crucial remarks that I omitted above

each concern the justification of clauses (a) and (b). In his justification of clause (b) his example is actually of someone with irreversible brain damage *that results in his being in a permanent coma*. And perhaps many people would agree that individuals who are unconscious and will never recover consciousness, like Karen Anne Quinlan, do not have a right to life, and hence no such right is violated if they are killed. But I omitted this because in fact it does not justify clause (b). It would justify something like 'it is possible that there will be a later time at which A would, if A were to exist at that time, be conscious, or have some desire that A would enjoy having satisfied'. Such a clause would rule out individuals in a permanent coma from having the right to life, but not rule out individuals who are too senile or brain-damaged ever to have again the conceptually complex desire 'to continue to exist as a subject of experiences'. There are some individuals who are infantile through senility or irreversible brain damage; they are not, and will never be, again capable of the complex desire 'to continue to exist as a subject of experiences'. But they are conscious and still may be enjoying food. But clause (b) does rule out such individuals from having the right to life. So it is not justified by the permanent coma case, which is why I omitted the details of the example above.

Tooley has two justifications of clause (a). One involves an imaginary example about putting together an adult human being in a laboratory, by combining inorganic compounds at a temperature at which the organism is frozen. We then programme in some set of beliefs, desires and personality traits. If we now thaw out this organism 'we will have a conscious human adult with beliefs, desires and a distinct personality'. If, instead of thawing this thing out, 'we grind it up for hamburgers' do we violate its right to life? Tooley thinks that most people's answer to this would be no, and says 'if this is correct then clause (a) is essential'.

Even if one allows Tooley his Frankenstein example and agrees that this construct does not have a right to life, it by no means follows that clause (a) is essential. To accept that would be to accept that anyone who agrees that the Frankenstein creation does not have a right to life must agree that fœtuses and infants do not have a right to life. A friend of abortion may be happy to do this. But a foe may reasonably maintain that clause (a) cannot be the correct way to rule out Frankenstein creations (since it rules out fœtuses and infants) and that what is essential is some quite different clause. If necessary (since we are dealing with *ad hoc* science-fiction examples) we could add an *ad hoc* further condition that Frankenstein-type creations do not have a right to life. So clause (a) is not justified by this example.

Tooley realizes that the Frankenstein example will not carry the field, and reserves his full consideration of the justification of clause (a) for the final section of his article, entitled 'Refutation of the conservative position'. Even if his argument in this final section worked (which it does not), it still would not support Tooley's claim to have provided a *neutral* analysis of having a right. On the contrary, the very fact that he admits that clause (a) needs to be justified by a refutation of the view that the fœtus has a right to life shows that the analysis is not neutral on this issue.

So I conclude that Tooley's analysis of what it is to have a right will be acceptable only to people who agree with him in advance that fœtuses and infants (and the brain-damaged and extremely senile) do not have a right to life.

Hence, only people who already agree with him about these issues will accept his definition of a *person* or *the sort of being who has a right to life*. The sort of being in question, according to Tooley, is the sort of being who actually possesses, or (reflecting clauses (a) and (b) above) did possess earlier *and* will possess again, the concept of a self, or itself – a continuing subject of experiences. So fœtuses, infants and the brain-damaged, etc. are not persons according to Tooley. Naturally not, since the analysis of what it is to have a right has been carefully constructed, clause by clause, to exclude them.

Tooley's conclusion (C1), 'Fœtuses and babies do not have a right to life', was based on the premise (P2) 'Only persons have the right to life' and the supposed definitional truth (D1) 'Fœtuses and babies are not persons'. But now it has emerged that (P2) and (D1) simply assume the truth of (C1).

5   THE PERSON VIEW AND INFANTICIDE

I conclude that we have not been given any reason to accept the person view and its argument for abortion. I shall now consider briefly the reasons we have for rejecting it, namely that it has such unacceptable consequences. But, as I mentioned at the beginning of this chapter, some supporters of the person view have tried to defend (some of) these consequences. So if we are to keep as a premise that, say, infanticide is not morally innocuous, we should look to see if their arguments cast any doubt on this.

We should begin by getting clear about what is *not* an argument. Some writers maintain that people who think infanticide is wrong are trapped in the morality of the Judæo-Christian tradition. And Tooley says:

> Infanticide is . . . of interest because of the strong emotions it arouses. The typical reaction to infanticide is like the reaction to incest or cannibalism, or the reaction of previous generations to masturbation or oral sex. The response, rather than appealing to carefully formulated moral principle, is primarily visceral. When philosophers themselves respond in this way, offering no arguments, and dismissing infanticide out of hand, it is reasonable to suspect that one is dealing with a taboo rather than with a rational prohibition.[16]

Now all of this may be true, but it does not constitute any argument against the view in question. There is nothing inherently disreputable about holding a view in common with Judæo-Christian tradition, nor even about holding a view for which one can give no argument. All argument has to start somewhere and if I take 'infanticide is wrong' as one of my premises (and am clear about the fact that I am doing so) it is no criticism of my position to say 'But you are taking it as a premise and not arguing for it'.

In fact, I need not take it as a premise but can derive it from the much more general 'Killing members of the human race and the members of any other species of persons is wrong'. Moreover, 'infanticide is wrong', *if* we take that to mean 'infanticide is never justifiable', is a much stronger premise than I need to argue that the consequences of the person view are unacceptable. All I need is 'infanticide is not morally innocuous', for the full consequence of the person view, for abortion and hence for infanticide, is that killing a non-person does not even call for any justification. The killing of a non-person is not merely *prima facie* wrong but frequently justifiable, or mildly wrong but usually justifiable – it is morally innocuous, so the question of justification does not even arise.

The full consequences of the person view in relation to infanticide have not, I think, been recognized by any of its supporters. Rather, they tend to recognize, and welcome, a few selected consequences. So, for instance, Tooley says:

> The practical importance [of the issue of infanticide] need not be laboured. Most people would prefer to raise children who do not suffer from gross deformities or from severe physical, emotional, or intellectual handicaps. If it could be shown that there is no moral objection to infanticide, the happiness of society could be significantly and justifiably increased.[17]

What sorts of cases is he envisaging here? Clearly, he intends to justify many more infanticides than could be justified as euthanasia – for instance, Down's syndrome is certainly a severe intellectual disability, but as I have pointed out, it is simply not true that if we kill a baby with such a disability we are doing it *for the sake* of the child, that death is a benefit to such a baby because its life will be a miserable burden. Tooley agrees that euthanasia should not be confused with 'quality of life' considerations; indeed, he thinks that these only become appropriate on the assumption that the infant is not a person.

> [I]f one assumes that a human infant is a person, it is only if the quality of his existence will be so bad that he will prefer death to continued existence that one can appeal to this ... sort of justification for terminating an infant's life ... The question [if one assumes that the infant is a person] is *not* whether the individual is destined to enjoy a rich and satisfying life, but whether it will at least be a life that he himself will prefer to death ... On the other hand, quality of life considerations may legitimately enter if one assumes that an infant is not a person and that infanticide does not

violate anyone's right to continued existence. For in that case one is merely deciding what potential persons should be allowed to become actual, and the rational approach would seem to be to decide on the basis of the quality of life which the potential person is likely to enjoy if allowed to develop into an actual person.[18]

So the consequence that Tooley welcomes is that infanticide will be justified in the not inconsiderable number of cases in which babies are born with severe disabilities. But he has in fact justified a great deal more than that. In the quotation above he says that what one is deciding is 'what potential persons should be allowed to become actual' and that 'the rational approach would seem to be to decide on the basis of the quality of life' which will be enjoyed by the potential person. But one might equally well say that what one is deciding is 'what sort of child do I want to raise' and that 'the rational approach would seem to be to decide on the basis of' one's personal preferences as a potential parent – as is suggested by the earlier quotation ('Most people would prefer . . .').

It is true that this quotation makes a plausible claim about what the preferences of potential parents are which would guarantee that a lot of the time the decisions were based on serious considerations about the quality of life of the potential person. But if some parents decided in favour of infanticide for reasons which had nothing to do with the quality of life of the potential person, then Tooley could have no objection to it.

Some people would prefer to be able to determine the sex of their children, and this for a variety of reasons both serious and trivial ranging from a single woman's desire for exclusively female company, to a man's desire to see himself reproduced or a couple's desire to secure an entailed inheritance. Tooley is committed to regarding infanticide as a morally acceptable or neutral way of satisfying these desires and his emphasis on the less startling cases in which the baby has severe defects makes me suspect that he has not faced up to this consequence.

Elsewhere he says (considering the question of when, in

an infant's development, it acquires the concept of a continuing self and hence becomes a person):

> Where is the line to be drawn in the case of infanticide? This is not really a troubling question, since there is no serious need to know the exact point at which a human infant acquires a right to life. For in the vast majority of cases in which infanticide is desirable due to serious defects from which the baby suffers, its desirability will be apparent at birth or within a very short time thereafter. [So] . . . infanticide will be morally permissible in the vast majority of cases in which it is, for one reason or another, desirable.[19]

It seems clear here that once again Tooley is thinking of infanticide as 'desirable' in just those cases in which the baby is born with severe defects; the 'for one reason or another' indicates only different sorts of defects. But, as many parents know, and as cases of infanticide reported in newspapers indicate, severe defects in a baby are not the only facts that can make infanticide seem 'desirable'. Some babies cry almost constantly; this is not a 'defect' apparent at birth or shortly thereafter but a maddeningly undesirable feature that emerges over a matter of weeks or even months, and sometimes it is one of the things that prompts parents to infanticide. On Tooley's principles some cases of killing a baby because its crying is driving you mad must count as 'morally acceptable'; presumably he will grant that somewhere along the line it becomes murder and hence not acceptable, but then he must also grant that there *is* a 'serious need' to know fairly exactly when an infant becomes a person and thereby acquires a right to life. So here, too, I think he has not recognized the full consequences of his position.

Finally, something needs to be said about rare cases. Consider the sort of case I discussed above (Chapter Two, Section 5) in relation to late abortions, a case in which a woman or a couple want a child but, due to a change of circumstances, change their minds: another member of the family suddenly develops an illness and will need a lot of care; she or they are suddenly faced with the prospect of being homeless. I said of these cases that infanticide would be a completely unacceptable way of alleviating such circumstances; but according to Tooley's position, it would, on the contrary, be entirely acceptable (if done early enough, raising the problem again of the 'serious need' to determine when the infant becomes a person).

Now, it might be said that, though I have a point in my other examples, this sort of example is not fair to Tooley. 'For', it may be said, 'you are right that people really do kill babies because they won't stop crying. And it is also true that babies have been killed because they were the wrong sex. But no one, or at least no one sane, would kill a baby to solve the problem of how to nurse someone who has had a stroke at the same time as looking after a baby. And no one sane would kill a baby so that they could move into "No children or pets allowed" accommodation, though people do sometimes have their pets killed for that reason. So these consequences of Tooley's position are purely theoretical.'

The standard philosophical move against this objection is to say it is simply irrelevant as it stands. The role of such examples in moral argument does not depend on their being examples of what is known to happen. But in this case there is also a particular countermove to be made. Suppose I agree that no one sane would kill a baby for such reasons. What is the explanation of that fact? I take it that the explanation is that no one sane thinks that killing their baby is a morally neutral action, but on the contrary that it is an action which is very seriously morally wrong. Hence it is the sort of action that people do only in the heat of passion or when they have become convinced, rightly or wrongly, that in *this* particular case this usually very wrong action is justifiable. But according to Tooley the belief that killing one's baby is seriously wrong is a taboo, akin in its irrational absurdity to a belief that masturbation is seriously wrong. So presumably he must think that it would be perfectly sane to kill one's baby for such reasons, once one had realized the justice of his position. So the objection can be turned into an objection to Tooley, rather than an objection to the theoretical nature of my counter-examples.

And frankly, we should not be too sanguine about the

merely theoretical nature of the counter-example. I am far from sure that babies have not been killed by sane people simply because the baby was inconvenient. Moreover, there are many eye-witness accounts of soldiers killing babies, along with women and children, when they go on the rampage through defeated towns and villages. Defending infanticide, in the way required by the person view, must involve defending the view that, although it is wrong to kill the women and children, killing the babies (as long as they are sufficiently young) is morally acceptable. And this Tooley (I am glad to say) does not attempt to do.

Tooley is quite typical of supporters of the person view in failing to mention the really challenging examples of infanticide. The few who have tried to defend the general consequence of the person view, namely that killing *any* new-born infants is morally *neutral* tend to do so, as he does, by trying to defend the much more restricted view that killing disabled new-born infants is morally justifiable in many circumstances. It is possible that this latter view is defensible, but even if it were, this would hardly count as a defence of infanticide in general.

6   THE PERSON VIEW AND OTHER ISSUES

The question of whether killing disabled new-born infants is ever morally justifiable and if so when, is obviously a question which relates to the issue of genuine euthanasia (where the human being is killed or allowed to die because she would be better off dead) and more generally to the distinct issue of killing human beings whose lives are, or are going to be, less than ideal in some way. As I have suggested above (p. 105), the usual person view tends to yield some disconcertingly ruthless conclusions on these issues too; human beings who have ceased to be rational and self-conscious may be killed, and, since this is a morally neutral act, their killing does not even call for any special justification such as 'They are in terrible pain' or 'They expressed the desire when rational not to be allowed to linger on'. Tooley's insistence that a person must have the concept of itself as a continuing subject of experiences with a past and a future (in order to have the complex desire to continue as a subject of experiences) may be even more ruthless. There are a few tragic cases recorded of people whose memory span, because of brain damage, is limited to a few minutes. They can talk and get around all right, having learnt to do so in the past and (in some sense) not forgotten; but as for having thoughts about any experience they had more than a few minutes ago, they cannot do it. It seems that their fate could hang on whether Tooley's intuitions lead him to add another *ad hoc* clause to his definition of a person or not; as the definition stands at present it is far from clear that these people are persons according to him.

However, it is possible that in many cases of killing human beings other than the new-born, the person view has some room to manœuvre, by making the standards of personhood a little less demanding. Rather than pursuing that question further, I want to consider briefly the issue concerning which no such manœuvres are possible, since it, like abortion, involves fœtuses.

Fœtal and infant experimentation

If killing fœtuses, at any stage, is morally innocuous because the fœtus is not a person, what follows about using them for research? With one important qualification about causing pain, which I shall consider below, it seems that, on the person view, any research, trivial or important, on the fœtus at any stage, early or late, must be morally innocuous too.

We should note that the 'at any stage' is crucial here. What is at issue is not merely embryonic research, of the sort tentatively approved by the 'Warnock Report'[20] (which recommends that embryos may not be used as research subjects beyond fourteen days of development after fertilization). Nine-month-old fœtuses and even new-born babies are all 'human non-persons' and so the issue is equally about using them as research material. My purpose in stressing this point is obvious. Research on six-month-old fœtuses, or premature babies, or new-born infants provides the challenging cases, the ones that show up the most obviously unacceptable consequences of the person view. Research on very early embryos, like infanticide of the very severely disabled, will be unacceptable consequences to some people, but will not prompt everyone to reject the person view automatically. The deliberations of the 'Warnock Report', and the subsequent expressions of opinion in the media, made it clear that there is widespread disagreement about early embryonic research. Some people are totally opposed to it; but many think it is justifiable in certain circumstances (if, for example, it will yield knowledge of the causes and treatment of infertility or of genetically transmitted abnormality) but would be horrified at the suggestion that embryos should be used for 'unimportant' research.[21] And some people think that, as long as we can be sure that the embryo does not suffer (which we can certainly be if it is within the 'Warnock Report' limit of fourteen days), we can use it for any research which we could use any other bit of tissue for.

But there is no indication that there is similar widespread disagreement about using six-month-old fœtuses, or premature babies, or new-born infants as research subjects. On the contrary, it is clear that most people would regard the idea that this is not only justifiable but morally neutral as a totally unacceptable consequence. If the supporters of the person view are to defend it, they must do something better than defend early embryonic research.

Moreover, the defence should do much more than argue that *some* research on nine-month-old fœtuses and babies is morally justifiable. For, as I said above, what is at issue is the consequence that any research, trivial or important, is morally innocuous, and hence does not call for any justification. So no amount of appeal to the possibility that research on premature or new-born babies might enable us to eliminate, finally, some terrible cause of suffering, such as spina bifida, would actually be to the point; all it would establish, if anything, was that some research was justifiable. But so far (to the best of my knowledge), no one arguing in defence of the person view has attempted to establish more.[22]

Causing pain

What about the qualification concerning research which causes pain? Supporters of the person view usually insert something about this, but we should pause to consider with what justification, and with what further consequences for their view, they do so.

The obvious justification for putting some qualification in is to appeal to some principle or premise about its being wrong to cause suffering. But if we take this intuitively acceptable premise all the way back to the initial arguments concerning persons, those arguments appear in a new light. We now have a new objection to the 'uncontroversial' claim that it is only whether or not a creature is a person which 'matters morally'; such an obvious objection indeed, that we should have made it straight away. Even if we agreed that the moral principle 'killing is wrong' did not apply to non-persons such as chickens and cattle, we should surely have said that 'torturing is wrong' did. Maintaining that only the suffering of human beings 'matters morally' would no doubt be viciously speciesist, but to avoid speciesism by saying that only the suffering of persons matters morally would be just as bad.

Suppose, then, that supporters of the person view agree that whether or not something is a person is not the only question that has to be settled in order to settle what counts as morally significant or morally innocuous treatment of it. What consequences does this have for their view? It certainly requires some modification of their general conclusion that abortion is morally innocuous, for some late abortions are not only killings but probably painful killings.[23]

The very fact that this would be true only of late abortions may make this seem a minor modification, unlikely to trouble any supporter of the person view. Whether or not that is so, I think a more fundamental weakness in their position has been revealed.

Their problem is this: once it is allowed that non-persons 'matter' in some ways, how are the ways to be restricted in advance? If supporters of the person view agree that the suffering of non-persons matters, how are they to guarantee in advance that the continued existence of non-persons does not matter? But if they cannot guarantee that, their insistence that all that is needed to clear the mind about the abortion issue is the recognition that the fœtus is not a *person* falls to the ground. The whole point of introducing the person/non-person distinction was to reveal that the conservatives were making a simple mistake in objecting to abortion, for in doing so they were making an issue of non-persons (who happened to be human beings), thinking about them as though they mattered; but since they are non-persons, they do not matter. Or so it was claimed. But now that is the claim which has been given up. Non-persons *do* matter, after all.

Of course, a supporter of the person view can attempt to provide a way of guaranteeing that, although the suffering of non-persons does matter, their continued existence does not. One might indeed see Tooley's suggestion that new-born kittens (non-persons) have a right not to be tortured, combined with his stipulative restriction of 'person' to 'being with the right to life', as constituting just such an attempt. But any such attempt will inevitably complicate what was, supposedly, a perfectly simple picture. It will amount to the concession that the person/non-person distinction is too crude a philosophical tool to settle the abortion issue once and for all in the way that was initially envisaged. The issue, supporters of the person view must admit, is not yet settled; something more is needed.

With hindsight, this does not seem surprising; what seems much more surprising is that anyone can ever have supposed that the abortion issue could be settled so simply, *given* its inevitable connections with other moral issues. Surely no one can have thought that the person/non-person distinction could simultaneously solve not only the abortion issue but also questions about how we should treat animals, about the use of them and embryos as research subjects, about what should, and should not, be done with, and to, the extremely senile or mentally defective, about infanticide in the cases of extreme mental or physical disability – even about surrogacy. Could anyone ever have thought that the rights and wrongs of all these extremely difficult issues could be settled by saying, 'It is persons whose lives and autonomy and rights and feelings must be treated with respect; it doesn't matter morally what is done to non-persons'? I suspect (and hope) that no one has thought that explicitly; it is, rather, the sort of position that people commit themselves to while concentrating on their favoured examples, e.g. on abortion, or on, not embryonic research in general, but early embryonic research which will yield great benefits.

If the person/non-person distinction on its own will not settle the abortion issue simply, will something else? It has seemed to many philosophers that not only the abortion issue but all other moral issues can be settled, fairly simply, by the theory of utilitarianism, supplemented perhaps by the person/non-person distinction, or a principle of autonomy. In Chapter Four I turn to a consideration of these views.

NOTES

1   Warren, Mary Anne (1973) 'On the Moral and Legal Status of Abortion', *The Monist*, vol. 57.
2   *Cf.* Tooley, Michael (1972) 'Abortion and Infanticide', *Philosophy and Public Affairs*, vol. 2, no. 1.
3   Readers familiar with the literature supporting the person view will no doubt recognize the thoughts of many authors in what follows. See, in particular, Warren, *op. cit.*, Tooley, *passim* (see note 8 below), Singer, Peter (1979) *Practical Ethics*, Cambridge University Press, Harris, John (1985) *The Value of Life*, Oxford University Press. My attack on the person view shares many points with two most instructive articles: Lomasky, Loren E. (1982) 'Being a Person – Does it Matter?', *Philosophical Topics*, vol. 12, no. 3, reprinted in Feinberg, Joel (ed.) (1984) *op. cit.*, and Teichman, Jenny (1985) 'The Definition of *Person*', *Philosophy*, vol. 60.
4   Locke, John (1690) *An Essay Concerning Human Understanding*, Book II, Chapter XXVII, Section 15.
5   *Ibid.*, Section 9.
6   See p. 104, and Chapter Six, Section 4.
7   Warren, *op. cit.*

8   Tooley's articles have gone through a confusing series of amendments and rewritings. The original one, cited in note 2, was reprinted, together with 'A Postscript', as 'Abortion and Infanticide' in Cohen, Marshall, Nagel, Thomas and Scanlon, Thomas (eds) (1974) *The Rights and Wrongs of Abortion*, Princeton University Press. A revised version, incorporating the ideas in the postscript, was then published as 'A Defense of Abortion and Infanticide' in Feinberg, Joel (ed.) (1973) *The Problem of Abortion*, Wadsworth Publishing Company. Yet another revised version subsequently appeared as 'In Defense of Abortion and Infanticide' in the second edition of Feinberg (1984) *op. cit.* His position on the killing of persons and non-persons also occurs in his article 'Decisions to Terminate Life and the Concept of a Person' in Ladd, John (ed.) (1979) *Ethical Issues Relating to Life and Death*, Oxford University Press.

9   Tooley, M. (1983) *Abortion and Infanticide*, Oxford University Press.

10   Tooley, 'Decisions to Terminate Life and the Concept of a Person'.

11   Tooley, (1972) 'Abortion and Infanticide'.

12   *Ibid.*

13   Tooley, 'A Postscript'.

14   Tooley, (1973) 'A Defense of Abortion and Infanticide'.

15   *Ibid.*

16   Tooley, (1972) 'Abortion and Infanticide'.

17   *Ibid.*

18   Tooley, 'Decisions to Terminate Life and the Concept of a Person'.

19   Tooley, (1984) 'In Defense of Abortion and Infanticide'.

20   See Appendix Four.

21   This was briefly touched on in Chapter Two, Section 4.

22   Harris, *op. cit.*, commits himself in theory to the view that new-born babies, since they are non-persons, could be used for any (painless) experimentation, no matter how trivial, if the mother did not want the baby (and perhaps if no one else did). But his arguments emphasize such facts as '. . . we know that research on the human embryo might save the lives of actual human persons, children and adults' (p. 134). (Quotations from Harris on this startling point are bound to seem less startling than they really are since, rather misleadingly, he has decided to 'use the term "embryo" to cover all stages of development from the zygote or blastocyst right through

to the end of the third trimester of pregnancy' (p. 117). The book would read rather differently if he had chosen to use the term 'baby' or 'unborn child' for the same purpose.)

23 Singer, *op. cit.*, notes that this would be a reason for 'avoiding' (p. 119) some methods of abortion.

CHAPTER FOUR

Utilitarianism: abandoning the sanctity of life

1 THE UTILITARIAN POSITION

It has seemed to some that the person view on abortion can be combined with a compassionate view on non-persons, i.e. most animals, by invoking the theory of utilitarianism. But others have applied utilitarianism to the issue of abortion directly without involving themselves particularly in the person view. In this chapter I shall discuss these two positions. We must first be clear about what utilitarianism involves, so in the first section of this chapter I give a general outline and discussion of the theory before returning specifically to the questions about abortion and animals. I will introduce utilitarianism by highlighting one of its most significant features – the abandoning of the sanctity of life.

Abandoning the sanctity of life

Throughout the preceding chapters there has been an unquestioned premise in the background – roughly, that killing is wrong, or taking life is wrong, or lives have intrinsic value which it is wrong to destroy, or life is sacred; and the belief that the premise is true is often described as the belief in 'the sanctity of life'. One obvious way in which all these different formulations of the premise are 'rough' is pinpointed by Peter Singer.

People often say that life is sacred. They almost never mean
what they say. They do not mean, as their words seem to
imply, that life itself is sacred. If they did, killing a pig or
pulling up a cabbage would be as abhorrent to them as the
murder of a human being. When people say that life is sacred,
it is human life they have in mind.[1]

This is undoubtedly true of many people who say 'I
believe that life is sacred' or 'I believe in the sanctity of life'.
It is also true that many people who express such beliefs
believe too that abortion is wrong, that infanticide is wrong,
that the killing of the extremely senile and brain-damaged
is wrong, and that their grounds for saying that any of these
other things are wrong is that in each case it is the taking
of a *human* life.

But what should be said about Tooley, for example? Does
he believe in 'the sanctity of life'? He clearly does not believe
in the sanctity of human life. But he does appear to believe
in the sanctity of *personal* life. He too believes that killing is
wrong, that taking life is wrong, that lives have intrinsic
value which it is wrong to destroy, that life is sacred – as
long as what is in question is the killing of persons, those
beings that have the right to life. This means that he is
prepared to respect the lives of any alien persons, no matter
how peculiar and inhuman they are, and the lives of, say,
chimpanzees and dolphins if they are persons. Given that he
holds all these lives to have intrinsic value, can an anti-
abortionist seriously accuse Tooley of having 'abandoned
the sanctity of life'?

Suppose that I am the bad sort of speciesist considered in
the previous chapter; that is, someone who is prepared to
say that *only* human life is sacred, and that no matter how
like us psychologically any aliens were, the fact that they
were not members of our species would license our killing
them. And I say the same about all animals, even the most
intelligent, even about the chimpanzees who communicate.
Then, if I am going to accuse Tooley of not believing in
the sanctity of life because he is pro-abortion, surely he can
accuse me of the same thing because I am anti-aliens and
pro-vivisection, even if I, unlike him, say that abortion,
infanticide, the killing of the senile, etc. is wrong.

Moreover, both of us would come off rather poorly in comparison with someone like Albert Schweitzer. Schweitzer claims that to a 'really ethical' person, 'life as such is sacred'. Such a person:

> tears no leaf from its tree, breaks off no flower, and is careful not to crush any insect as he walks. If he works by lamplight on a summer evening he prefers to keep the window shut and to breathe stifling air, rather than to see insect after insect fall on his table with singed and sinking wings.[2]

Should anyone who thinks killing plants is not wrong describe themselves as not believing that life is sacred? Surely not, if one believed that killing humans, or killing persons, or killing humans and animals, or humans and aliens and so on was wrong. The correct description is that not many people believe in the sanctity of life *to the same extent* that Schweitzer did.

The idea that one might believe in the sanctity of life 'more' or 'less' than someone else is readily comprehensible when we recognize that 'believing in the sanctity of life' actually involves having a set of beliefs, such as killing adult humans is wrong, killing animals is wrong, and so on. And, roughly, the more there is in one's set of beliefs, the more one believes in the sanctity of life. Schweitzer presumably believed all the above but also believed that killing insects and plants is wrong. Someone who believed very minimally in the sanctity of life would, perhaps, be someone who believed (something like) 'killing members of my group is wrong' and not much else. That the degree to which people believe in the sanctity of life can sometimes be compared does not mean that it can always be compared. There is no sensible way of settling whether the bad sort of speciesist described above believes in the sanctity of life more, or less, than Tooley. Given what the two of them believe, there is not enough common ground for comparison and all that can be said is that they believe in the sanctity of life *differently*.

What then is meant by 'abandoning the sanctity of life' if it is not countenancing the killing of plants (as nearly everyone does), or animals (as many of us do), or aliens (as a bad speciesist would), or fœtuses (as Tooley does)? Really abandoning the sanctity of life means giving up any belief that killing (whether it be the killing of persons, or humans or anything alive) is intrinsically wrong. And the most significant feature of utilitarianism is that according to it no killing, not even the killing of persons, necessarily counts as wrong or as an evil.

Basic utilitarianism

Utilitarianism, in its simplest statement, is the doctrine that an act is right or wrong according to whether or not it maximizes happiness or pleasure and minimizes suffering or misery.

This doctrine, popularized initially by Jeremy Bentham (1784–1832) and John Stuart Mill (1806–1873), has been much discussed ever since, and a great variety of different versions invented. To impose some order on this variety, it has become common to identify two components within utilitarian theories. Any utilitarian theory (a) identifies certain states of affairs as *good* states of affairs and then (b) claims that actions are right or wrong according to whether their *consequences* are or are not the good states of affairs, or the maximization of the good states of affairs.

Many of the different versions of utilitarianism arise from different versions of (a); so, for instance, different utilitarians have claimed that the best state of affairs is that in which there is the most pleasure (Bentham), the most happiness (Mill), the maximum satisfaction of rational desires or preferences, and so on. However, in relation to abandoning the sanctity of life, it is the second component of any utilitarian theory, its so-called 'consequentialism', which is its most significant feature.

For, according to consequentialism, no sorts of actions are intrinsically right or wrong, but individual acts are right or wrong according to their consequences, insofar as they maximize or reduce the good states of affairs. Or, to put the same point in a more accurate way: according to utilitarianism only one sort of action is intrinsically right – maximizing the good states of affairs, or producing the best state of affairs; and only one sort is intrinsically wrong – reducing it; with any other sort of action, 'it all depends'.

This feature of utilitarianism may be regarded as one of its great strengths. Singer, for instance, regards it as a strength:

> The consequences of an action vary according to the circumstances in which it is performed. Hence a utilitarian can never properly be accused of lack of realism, or of a rigid adherence to ideals in defiance of practical experience. The utilitarian will judge lying bad in some circumstances and good in others, depending on its consequences.[3]

However, the critics of utilitarianism regard this feature as one of its fundamental flaws. For the utilitarian is committed not only to judging lying to be bad in some circumstances, good in others, but also murder, torture, the exploitation of the few for the sake of the many, the abandoning of the weak and helpless, cruelty to animals, and quite generally injustice and the violation of rights. Far from being accused of a rigid adherence to ideals, the utilitarian, the critics say, cannot consistently claim to have any ideals at all – except the maximization of whatever has been identified as the good states of affairs.

Having noted this feature, someone unacquainted with philosophical writings might doubt that utilitarians had anything interesting to say about abortion, infanticide, killing animals, and other such topics at all. Is it not already obvious that they will say that abortion and so on, like lying or torture, are 'bad in some circumstances, good in others, depending on their consequences'? And it is indeed true that a lot of modern writing on utilitarianism is not directly concerned with its application to particular sorts of actions such as abortion or euthanasia or embryo research, but rather with its theory. But a number of utilitarians, leaving many of the details of refinements to the theoreticians, have applied fairly basic utilitarianism to abortion and related topics and come up with a great deal more than 'it all depends'.

Amongst the refinements put to one side by those who discuss the applications of utilitarianism rather than the theory, is the critical question of what interpretation is to be placed on 'happiness'. Some people think that until we have settled this question it is impossible to understand what utilitarianism is aiming at, and indeed, some critics of utilitarianism maintain that there is no interpretation of 'happiness' under which utilitarianism can be maintained as a plausible and coherent moral theory. If we simply take it as being something like 'pleasure', it becomes morally objectionable; if it is interpreted as an ideal notion more akin to 'true' or 'real' happiness or 'fulfilment', the doctrine ceases to be consequentialist.

However, to press this objection at the outset would seem to be putting the cart before the horse. If a discussion of the utilitarian attitude to killing is to get off the ground, its supporters must in all fairness be allowed their assumption that the difficulties inherent in defining 'happiness' will prove surmountable. After all, as Jonathan Glover says in defence of this assumption,

> most of us, whether utilitarians or not, take some account of the likely effects of our actions on people's happiness, and we should all be in a mess if there were no correspondence between trying to make someone happier and succeeding.[4]

We have a workable notion of 'happiness' and 'happier' which stands us in sufficiently good stead to understand the utilitarian attitude to killing. And, as I shall argue, there are many objections that can be made to that attitude, before we move to more general theoretical objections.

Basic utilitarianism on killing

The fundamental reason why utilitarianism has something more to say about abortion (and infanticide, killing animals, euthanasia, etc.) than 'it all depends' is that these are all cases of killing, and trying to say why killing is *ever* wrong on utilitarian grounds immediately raises problems.

Some utilitarians take it as obvious (and leave it to the theoreticians to justify) that many actions are neither right nor wrong but morally insignificant, and at least some of these involve other people – such as asking someone what the time is, or giving them change for a telephone call. But a glance back at the original specification of utilitarianism suggests that killing people might turn out to be morally insignificant as well, and this is too important an issue for the non-theoretical utilitarian to ignore.

How could killing someone turn out to be morally insignificant? Well, actions are said to be right or wrong according to whether they increase happiness or cause suffering, and the trouble is that killing someone is not, if the killing is done painlessly, causing suffering to them. It is true that, if you kill me, a whole lot of my desires will be unfulfilled. I wanted, say, to go to Venice, to see my grandchildren, to publish a book and so on, but because you have killed me, none of these desires will be satisfied. But this is not like the usual case of your doing something that prevents my desires being satisfied. If you tear up my tickets to Venice, deny me access to my grandchildren, burn my manuscript, I will suffer because my desires have been thwarted. But that requires that I am still around to suffer. If you 'thwart' my desires by killing me, I am not around to suffer – so what is wrong with killing? Apparently nothing, except indirectly.

Of course, some, probably many, individual killings would be wrong because of causing suffering to others. If you kill me painlessly, I will not suffer, but my family and friends will. An even more indirect consequence which could make some individual killings wrong is that they would cause suffering to intelligent people who want to go on living – because such people would worry about whether they were going to be killed next. That all that is wrong with your killing me at the bus stop might be that it made the other people in the queue worried about being killed seems utterly bizarre. Taking the suffering of my family and friends seriously is not quite so odd but in general, as one utilitarian has remarked, 'There is, of course, something odd about objecting to murder, not because of the wrong done to the victim, but because of the effect on others. One has to be a tough-minded classical utilitarian to be untroubled by this oddness.'[5]

This oddity can, it seems, be easily avoided. After all, utilitarianism says it is wrong not to maximize happiness or to reduce it; if you kill me you do not maximize my happiness, so, except in the rare cases where I would be better off dead, there *is* something wrong with killing – and not just indirectly. It now appears that killing is wrong insofar as it is reducing, or not maximizing, the amount of pleasure or happiness there will be in the world. If you had not killed me, the sum total would have included my enjoying Venice and seeing my grandchildren and so on.

But now a new problem arises. If what is wrong with my killing you is that if you had lived, there would have been that much more pleasure or happiness in the world (so, contrary to the utilitarian principle I have failed to maximize happiness), if that is what is wrong with my killing you, must it not be similarly wrong of me not to increase the number of those leading pleasant or happy lives? By, for instance, having lots of children, or rearing large numbers of animals? (Of course, we are supposing here that the children I produced or the animals I reared *would* have pleasant lives, just as we are supposing that my killing you was not a matter of euthanasia, i.e. you would have had a pleasant life.)

Let us for the moment concentrate on the children rather than the animals. According to the utilitarian view just outlined, killing is morally on a par with not producing children if you can, and here again one must surely be a 'tough-minded classical utilitarian' to be untroubled by the oddity of this equation. Can killing really be comparable to practising contraception,[6] or indeed, to repulsing a sexual advance? Few utilitarians are so tough-minded; the natural response is to reject this so-called 'total' view of what is meant by 'maximizing happiness or pleasure', and try to produce some other plausible interpretation.

According to the 'total' view, we are not primarily dealing with individuals and trying to increase their happiness; we are just trying to produce the biggest sum *total* of happiness possible. X billion happy people and Y billion contented mice . . . yields one total; but X billion-plus-one happy people and Y billion-plus-one contented mice would yield a bigger total, so, on the 'total' view, this is what we should be aiming at. (I shall return to the problem of over-population later.) Killing someone counts as failing to increase the total; but so does not producing more people (or failing to breed mice). It seems obvious that the way to avoid this odd conclusion is to make sure that we are dealing with individuals, not just with a sum total. Unfortunately, and to some people, surprisingly, this has proved very difficult.

Actual and future people

The first obvious move is to claim that utilitarianism applies only to people or creatures who actually exist. It tells me to make everyone or everything as happy as possible. However, though this may seem initially plausible and sensible, a little reflection shows it is not. It is not sensible because it produces another oddity, viz. that no considerations about the happiness or suffering of future generations ever count, in themselves, as morally relevant. So suppose I can greatly improve the lot of pregnant women by giving them a drug which I know will genetically affect their children in such a way that many of *those* children's offspring will die most horribly at about fifty. The only considerations that are supposed to be morally relevant here are (a) that the women might be upset if I told them that the drug will have this effect on their grandchildren at about fifty (so I ought to keep quiet about it) and (b) that some of the women might live to see their grandchildren dying horribly at fifty and suffer as a result. But the frightful suffering that the people who die will undergo, and indeed the suffering of their spouses and children – that does not count at all.

Once this sort of consequence is seen clearly, it is easy to see what is implausible about restricting utilitarianism's application to actually existing creatures. One of the things that makes utilitarianism appealing is its apparent compassion – its sensitivity to suffering. But just as this compassion extends, in principle, beyond creatures we are acquainted with because they are geographically or spatially close by, to everyone, to the suffering of the entire world, so it extends beyond creatures we are acquainted with because they are *temporally* close by. A time bias in favour of people living *now* is no more defensible than a space bias in favour of people living *here*.[7]

How, then, to include the future generations without

sliding back into the 'total' view and regarding not helping to produce a future happy creature as on a par with killing an existing one? We need to capture a moral concern about the consequences of our acts on future generations (thus ruling out the above oddity) while avoiding duties about producing the future generations.

The 'independent existence' restriction

Suppose we tried adding a different restriction. Let us say that an act is right or wrong (morally significant) only insofar as it affects a creature that already exists or will affect creatures that will exist. This makes giving the drug to the pregnant women morally significant (and with luck makes it wrong); that is, we have captured a concern about future generations. But what about the duty to produce future generations? Does (helping to) bring a child into existence count as affecting it? Did my parents do something that was going to affect me by conceiving me? I exist because of their act, and one might say, 'What bigger effect on me could they have had!' But if conceiving a child does thus count as doing something that will affect a creature that will exist, our new restriction has got us nowhere – we seem to be back with the 'total' view.

However, we could say that conceiving a child does not count as doing something that will affect someone who will exist. And this is quite reasonable. My parents did not affect me by bringing me into existence; I exist because of their act, and so their act was very significant – but its significance lies in the effect its consequences had on them, and everyone I have subsequently had anything to do with, but not in its effect on me. So we should construe that bit of the restriction which says 'will affect creatures that will exist' as not applying to the conceiving of children, or the breeding of animals. Another way to make the same point is to change the restriction itself slightly. We can say that an act is morally significant only if (a) it affects creatures that already exist or (b) will affect creatures that will exist *independently of the act*.

So although conceiving a child would affect existing people (the adults, other children) and would affect people who will exist independently of that act (the children other people will have) — they are the only ones that count. We do not have to consider the child that would result from the act when totalling up the happiness to be produced. So we are not obliged to produce children if we can, but the future generations will exist independently of my giving the drug to the pregnant women so I am obliged not to do that. And, more importantly given the context of our present discussion, we will in ordinary circumstances be obliged not to kill existing people (because of their future happiness). So killing is not on a par with using a contraceptive, or rejecting an opportunity to have sexual intercourse.

So far so good. But now a new problem arises. If it is not relevant to consider the happiness of the child I might conceive when totalling up happiness to be produced, as we just said, then it is not relevant to consider its misery either. The point of the restriction is that you don't take into account the child that would be the result of the act when considering the rightness or wrongness of the act. But this means that there is nothing intrinsically wrong with knowingly conceiving a child which, because of a genetic defect, say, will lead a life of appalling suffering.

There is an obvious utilitarian objection here, namely that, in ordinary circumstances, such an act would affect people who already exist (the parents to be, for example), making them very miserable. That conceiving a child doomed to suffer would make the people who did it very unhappy explains, a utilitarian could say, both what is wrong with doing such a thing and why no one in their right mind would do it.

But note that *what* is morally wrong with conceiving a child which will suffer, according to this view, is only the suffering of the parents (or others) themselves. This move makes explicit one of the greatest oddities of utilitarianism. This is that utilitarianism morally obliges me to promote my own happiness and avoid my own suffering just as much as (but, of course, no more than) anyone else's. To make myself happy is as morally right as to make someone else happy; and to make myself miserable is as morally wrong as to make someone else miserable. So the fact that, if I were to produce a miserable child, this would make *me* unhappy is indeed a moral reason for not doing it, according to utilitarianism.

Once again, one has to be a very 'tough-minded' utilitarian to accept that this is not only a moral reason, but the *only* moral reason for not deliberately producing a suffering child. This really does present a problem for the restriction on utilitarianism we have been considering, for whether anyone would deliberately conceive a child that was bound to suffer is beside the point; the question is, in refraining from doing so, do they refrain from doing something that they, and everyone else, think would be *wrong*? And, assuming we all would agree that it would be wrong deliberately to conceive a child that was bound to suffer, *why* would it be? A 'total' utilitarian can say what seems straightforwardly correct – it would be wrong precisely because it would be bringing it about that there was going to be a child who suffered. But the 'independent existence' utilitarian either has to say there is nothing wrong with it(!) or present things that are indirectly wrong with it, that is, considerations that do not essentially involve the suffering of the child, but do involve the parents (or others). But either response simply misses the point that we are morally concerned about the suffering child.

Other much more elaborate counter-examples to this way of restricting utilitarianism can be devised but the one above, I think, best pinpoints what this way of avoiding the 'total' view fails to achieve. Any attempt to avoid the obligation to conceive children who will be happy by saying that the child to result is not to be taken into account when considering the rightness or wrongness of conceiving, will inevitably remove the obligation *not* to conceive children who will be utterly miserable.

Does this mean a utilitarian must be driven back to the 'total' view? Not necessarily, for it is always open to someone to accept basic 'total' utilitarianism and simply add another principle or two. As I said at the beginning of this chapter, the refinements on utilitarianism are endless. But rather than embarking on an open-ended discussion of what might be done to avoid 'total' utilitarianism I shall briefly summarize the alternatives that have been considered so far, and then go on to discuss two further problems the general theory has.

We can restrict who the utilitarian doctrine applies to, either ruling out future generations entirely (discussed on p. 139) or counting them only if they will exist independently of the act in question (discussed on p. 140). This latter view, though it avoids making conceiving a child that will be happy obligatory, and does capture its being wrong to kill someone who will lead a happy life, unfortunately has to say that there is nothing wrong, except incidentally, with deliberately conceiving a child that will be utterly miserable.

We can adopt 'total' utilitarianism. This makes deliberately conceiving a child who will lead a miserable existence morally significant and wrong because of the child who will suffer. *But* it also makes deliberately not conceiving a child who will lead a happy existence morally significant, and at least as wrong as killing someone who would have continued to lead a happy existence if you had not killed them.

Both of these alternatives have other problems too. One problem has been around ever since people noticed that the original statement of utilitarianism used two superlatives, telling us to aim at the *greatest* happiness for the *greatest* number. Which superlative, in a case of conflict, is the more important? Should I aim to make already happy people even happier, and only when and if I have made their happiness as great as possible, turn to consider the plight of people who are not happy at all, aiming to increase the total happiness now by slightly increasing the number of happy people? Or should I rather aim to spread whatever happiness is already available around more and more people, and when and if I have made the number of (minimally) happy people as large as possible, then turn to consider how to increase the total happiness by slightly increasing everyone's happiness?

The 'total' utilitarian has this problem in a particularly acute form, since allowing the 'greatest number' option allows for the possibility of my being obliged to go on producing children at least until (and quite possibly after) I would literally rather die than have any more. But neither does the more restricted utilitarianism we considered avoid it. Do we allow the apparent injustice of grinding down the few in order that the many may have more and more happiness? Or do we agree that we are obliged to sacrifice a great deal of our own happiness, and indeed to force other people to sacrifice theirs, right down to the point where we only just regard our lives as worth living, if this will increase the number of happy people? Should not everyone in the developed world be forced to live at subsistence level until the people in the Third World have enough to eat? Should I not be producing a child a year, not in order to increase the population but to put them out for adoption and increase the number of happy parents?

Utilitarianism and involuntary euthanasia

Another well-known problem for utilitarianism concerns the killing of someone whose future life is going to be more miserable than happy. On any version of utilitarianism we have considered so far this is not wrong, indeed, it is positively obligatory *even if* the person does not want to die, and you kill him against his will.

This is the problem of involuntary euthanasia.[8] If someone can express their preferences about whether or not they want to go on living, surely these should count for something. But, on any version of utilitarianism discussed so far, whether or not I want to go on living is entirely irrelevant to whether or not you ought to kill me. All that matters is whether my continued existence will be more miserable than happy.

If we were all perfectly rational (and omniscient) perhaps this would not matter. If I really would be better off dying within the next week than continuing to live, and know this, then *if* I were perfectly rational I would (other things being equal) prefer to die. But the trouble is that I might not know that I would be better off dead, and even if I did know, I still might, irrationally, prefer not to die. I can go on irrationally hoping; even if I do not do that, I can be (as surely many people are) just plain afraid of dying.

What this situation encapsulates is the fact that *what is in my own interests* – what will benefit me, or make me better off or happier – is not necessarily the same as what I want or prefer. And since utilitarianism, as discussed so far, directs us to maximize what is in people's interests, what will make them better off or happier irrespective of those people's wishes, it is, unless qualified in some way, unavoidably paternalistic.

People's views about the extent to which paternalistic action is permissible (if at all) or indeed required, vary over a wide spectrum. At one extreme, defenders of the right to freedom or liberty insist that everyone must be allowed to go to hell in their own way if they so choose – and some even extend this claim to children, saying that it is wrong to force them to go to the dentist, or to school or stay out of pubs, for their own good, and against their wishes. At the other end of the spectrum stand, theoretically at least, the 'tough-minded classical utilitarians'. They admit the relevance of what people want only insofar as this does coincide with what is in their interests or (as usual) in the form of side-effects. So involuntary euthanasia, like voluntary euthanasia, will, in ordinary circumstances, be a positive duty.

Preference utilitarianism

There is a version of utilitarianism which supposedly avoids this problem, called 'preference utilitarianism'. According to preference utilitarianism we should aim to maximize the satisfaction of people's preferences, or minimize the thwarting of their preferences. Killing a person who prefers to continue living is therefore wrong, other things being equal. (The 'other things being equal' is the clause that any utilitarian always has to put in, in virtue of the doctrine being consequentialist. On *any* version of utilitarianism the wrong done to anyone killed is merely one factor to be taken into account. In the case of preference utilitarianism the preference of the victim could be outweighed by the preferences of others.) Involuntary euthanasia, like every other sort of action is, according to utilitarianism, bad in some circumstances, good in others, according to the consequences. But at least preference utilitarianism has managed to give a reason why it might be bad in some circumstances *because* the victim wanted to go on living. Without that, it seems that it could only be bad in the most accidental way – say, that if the victim dies now her fortune will go to someone who will waste it, whereas if her death is postponed for a week it will go to a charitable institution.

'Preference utilitarianism', as thus defined, constitutes a move away from what I have been calling 'basic' utilitarianism, since it is an attempt to specify exactly what good states of affairs utilitarianism would have us maximize (*cf.* p. 134). The problems which prompt its invention, and the new problems it creates in its turn, reflect the fact that the problem of specifying what we are supposed to maximize (what is meant by 'happiness' in basic utilitarianism) cannot be postponed for long.

For suppose we take people's 'preferences' to be just what they say, sincerely, they prefer. Then we may indeed avoid paternalism – but we do so at the cost of giving up on trying to prevent suffering. The Savage in Huxley's *Brave New World* demanded the right to suffer and preferred whipping himself to joining in the fun the New World offered. Many of the slaves in the South fought on their master's side in the American Civil War, preferring continued oppression to change. Many heroin addicts prefer to stay on heroin. Moreover, people's preferences embrace bringing death or suffering on others. The combined preferences of the family that the old man should die so that they can have his money will outweigh his preference for continued life; the combined preferences of thousands of women that rapists should be castrated will outweigh the preferences of the small number of rapists.

Suppose on the other hand that we try to take people's preferences to be (something like) what they *would* prefer if they were perfectly rational, and knew all the relevant facts. Then we may be justified (as utilitarians) in preventing the suffering of the Savage, the slaves and the heroin addicts. But, by the same token, we are once again justified, indeed obliged, to practise involuntary euthanasia on occasion. For involuntary euthanasia arises as a problem precisely because we are *not* perfectly rational and, not being omniscient, frequently do not know all the relevant facts. So this form of preference utilitarianism is a return to paternalism. Nor will this version of preference utilitarianism necessarily avoid the problem created by people having wicked or vicious preferences, unless we can show that these are intrinsically irrational.

Without discussing any further versions of utilitarianism, we shall turn to consider the effects of applying it to various issues, beginning with the question of our treatment of animals, left uncriticized in the preceding chapter.

2   UTILITARIANISM AND ANIMALS

As described so far, basic utilitarianism remains uncommitted as to whose happiness and suffering is at issue. One could, in theory, be a speciesist utilitarian, and maintain that actions are right or wrong solely according to whether or not they maximize *human* happiness or minimize *human* misery. Or, moving from basic utilitarianism to some form of preference utilitarianism one could be what might be called an 'elitist' utilitarian, maintaining that what was to be maximized was the satisfaction of *rational* preferences. Only rational creatures can have rational preferences, so on this version of utilitarianism, the suffering of non-rational creatures would not count.

But if one does not want to be speciesist or elitist it seems that a compassionate concern to reduce suffering should embrace any creature that *can* suffer, as indeed Bentham maintained it should:

> The day *may* come when the rest of animal creation may acquire those rights which never could have been witholden from them but by the hand of tyranny. The French have already discovered that the blackness of the skin is no reason why a human being should be abandoned without redress to the caprice of a tormentor. It may one day come to be recognized that the number of legs, the villosity of the skin, or the termination of the *os sacrum*, are reason equally insufficient for abandoning a sensitive being to the same fate. What else is it that should trace the insuperable line? . . . The

question is not, Can they reason? nor Can they *talk*? but, *Can they suffer?*[9]

We should note now a point I shall be discussing at greater length later, namely that one does not have to be a utilitarian to agree with Bentham here. Indeed, as I shall argue shortly, if one wants to champion the cause of animals, utilitarianism is not at all the theory one should be appealing to. However, interpreted as being concerned quite generally with maximizing the happiness and minimizing the suffering of any creatures, utilitarianism certainly looks as though it provides compelling grounds for arguing that much, if not most, of our present treatment of animals is morally indefensible – our factory farming, the ways in which we slaughter them in agony and fear, the cruel and unnecessary experiments we perform on them and so on. But what, given its general deliverance on 'the sanctity of life', can utilitarianism yield about killing animals?

Killing animals

As we saw above (p. 138) according to basic utilitarianism, killing a creature is wrong only insofar as doing so reduces the total amount of pleasure or happiness there would have been if it had not been killed. If, by killing it, the total amount of pleasure or happiness could be increased (or the total amount of misery be reduced) then this would be morally right. If, in killing it, somehow as much happiness would be produced as was being lost, then the reduction and production would cancel each other out, and the action would be morally insignificant. On this view, it has been said, 'it is as if sentient beings are receptacles of something valuable and it does not matter if a receptacle gets broken, so long as there is another receptacle to which the contents can be transferred without any getting spilt'.[10]

Now a number of utilitarians accept that individual creatures are indeed to be regarded as 'receptacles' for happiness in this way. And they conclude from this that the wrong done by killing an individual, i.e. reducing the quantity of happiness in the universe (when this is the result), can be counter-balanced by bringing into existence a similar individual who will lead an equally happy life, i.e. by replacing one receptacle with another. Hence the name 'the replaceability argument'.

This argument is usually used to justify abortion and infanticide in the case of disability. The killing of the fœtus or baby is wrong insofar as its life would have contributed some happiness to the sum total; but if one kills it, and conceives and produces another with no disability, then the sum total will be increased by at least the same amount, and probably more. But before considering this application of the argument, let us consider it in relation to killing animals.

So far the argument has assumed, not quite the unsatisfactory view that two wrongs make a right, but an almost equally unsatisfactory view, namely that by doing something you should have done anyhow, you can somehow make up for having done something wrong. For so far, the position is as follows. I am supposed to be maximizing happiness; I kill a chicken and thereby (other things being equal) do wrong by reducing the total happiness. Then, instead of eating a fertilized hen's egg, I arrange for it to be hatched, thereby counter-balancing the earlier reduction. But, given that I am supposed to be maximizing happiness, why do I not arrange for the egg to be hatched *and* refrain from killing the first chicken? I ought to be arranging for eggs to be hatched anyhow – how can my doing so make up for my having wrongly killed the chicken? It is as if my kicking a child were made up for by my giving her a kiss. Why not just give her kisses instead of kicks?

The standard way around this problem is to restrict the application of the replaceability argument to the cases in which the replacement occurs 'as a result' of the killing. What is meant by this?

The idea, roughly, seems to be as follows. There is obviously some limit to the number of chickens, fish, mice, etc. we can breed without killing and using them. And the available food supply sets some limit on the number of wild animals there can be. Suppose the limit has been reached. Then (and only then) to kill an existing animal is, so to speak, to make space for a new one. If we did not kill the existing one, no new one could be born or, at least, survive. But if we do kill this one, a new one will occur 'as a result': '. . . the killing of one animal makes possible its replacement by another who would not otherwise have lived' as one of the proponents of this argument has put it.[11]

I think that this does not make sense, for I cannot work out what individuals are supposed to be doing. As a town dweller, should I be breeding mice? Or/and cats? Should I have chickens in my small backyard, and, given that it is small, will this mean I can kill a chicken rather than taking an egg whenever the yard becomes too full to support the chickens happily? This sounds like cheating, but am I supposed to spend my time finding the surplus chickens other good homes? These rather trivial questions reflect, I think, a much deeper problem about utilitarianism which I shall return to later. For the moment, let us suppose that the application of the replaceability argument to animals does make sense and that the upshot is as follows:

> One possible case would be raising chickens for their meat not in factory farm conditions but roaming freely around a farmyard . . . Assume . . . that for economic reasons we could not rear the birds if we did not eat them. Then the replaceability argument will justify killing the birds, because depriving them of the pleasure of their existence can be offset against the pleasures of chickens who do not yet exist, and will exist only if existing chickens are killed. It is important to realize how limited this point is in its application. It cannot justify factory farming, where animals do not have pleasant lives. Nor does it normally justify the killing of wild animals. A duck shot by a hunter has probably had a pleasant life, but the shooting of a duck does not lead to its replacement by another. Unless the duck population is at a maximum that can be sustained by the available food supply, the killing of a duck ends a pleasant life without starting another, and is for that reason wrong on straightforward utilitarian grounds. The only exception would be if there were overriding utilitarian reasons for the killing, if, for instance, killing was the only way to obtain food. So although there are situations in which it is wrong to kill animals, these situations are special ones, and do not cover very many of the billions

of premature deaths humans inflict, year after year, on nonhumans.[12]

If this is right, basic utilitarianism provides very stringent limits on the permissibility of killing animals. What then happens when the same argument is applied to fœtuses?

Killing fœtuses

Killing a fœtus is reducing the amount of happiness there would have been if I had not killed it, and is thereby (other things being equal) wrong. Can this wrong be counter-balanced by my subsequently bringing another child into existence? Not even then, because, if I am supposed to be maximizing happiness, this is something I should do anyhow (cf. hatching the hen's egg above). The only way the wrong done by killing a fœtus can be counter-balanced is by producing another child 'as a result' of killing the fœtus.

Whatever this means, it certainly will not justify abortion in the standard liberal cases. Abortion for pregnancy due to rape will not be justified by it, nor abortion to preserve the mother's health, nor abortion to limit the size of her family, unless the existing children are on the verge of starvation. Nor will it justify the abortion of fœtuses which, if not aborted, will develop into babies with disabilities – unless the disability is great enough to guarantee a life in which there is more misery than happiness. For in none of these cases will it be the case that another child would survive or be produced 'as a result' of killing the fœtus.

The only case of abortion this replaceability argument could justify is, I think, one in which a woman is absolutely determined to have a child within the next year, because she knows that then she is going to die. She gets pregnant, and discovers that the child will, or might, be disabled. Knowing she will be dead in eleven months she cannot, as someone aiming at maximizing happiness, plan to have this child and then another. But she can plan to replace this one with another which would not be conceived if the first were not aborted; i.e. the killing of the first will 'make possible' its replacement by another who would not otherwise have lived. But nearly all other abortions would be wrong.

One might think that, on a utilitarian basis, many abortions would be justified because they spared the woman suffering or unhappiness. But it is noteworthy that in nothing that has been said so far have we considered explicitly the possibility that the wrong done in killing one creature might be counter-balanced by the increased happiness (or reduced suffering), as a result of the killing, of other creatures. The only possible counter-balance so far allowed is replacement by a *similar being*.

It is immediately obvious that if we allowed the other sort of counter-balance this argument against the killing of animals would hardly get off the ground. The duck shooter can, not implausibly, claim that the amount of pleasure he gets from hunting, killing, eating and boasting about the duck, is as great as, or greater than, the amount of pleasure the duck would have had if it had not been killed. The meat eaters can cite the pleasures of eating and cooking, and add in the enjoyment of domestic dogs and cats who share the treats. The fur coat wearers can hymn the joys of seal and sable. And so on.

What this shows is that the replaceability argument is not in fact part of utilitarianism. This becomes clear if we look back at the original analogy of receptacles (p. 148). The point of regarding individuals as mere receptacles of something valuable is that the receptacle itself is of no intrinsic value – which is just what one might expect to be the upshot of a doctrine which has abandoned any version of the sanctity of life. What is of value are its 'contents' – the amount of happiness which will be added to the sum total. So, as the analogy says, it does not matter if we lose the receptacle, as long as we do not lose the amount of happiness. But there is no reason why we have to make a point of creating a *new* receptacle (let alone one of the same sort) to contain the contents of any destroyed receptacle as long as there are other receptacles around. To make a special point of creating a new one would be to admit that the receptacles themselves have some sort of value. But the utilitarian assumption is that they do not.

A utilitarian who wishes to champion the cause of animals

may, of course, simply add the replacement view as an extra premise. He can, if he wishes, say that the only thing that can make up for the wrong done by killing an animal is its resulting replacement by another animal of the same sort. But once it is recognized that this is an extra premise which has nothing to do with utilitarianism, its extraordinarily arbitrary nature becomes manifest. *Why* can the sort of reduction of happiness in the universe that results from killing an animal *only* be counter-balanced by bringing another animal into existence? And why does the other animal have to be of the same sort – even to the point, apparently, where only a duck can replace a duck?

Moreover, as we have just noted, the replacement view yields a very restrictive view on abortion, a view that seems positively anti-utilitarian in some of its results. Let us return to the example of a woman who has, we might say, already done utilitarian duty in producing several children and does not want any more because she, and the existing ones, will suffer (though not to the point where they would be better off dead) if she does. And let us leave to one side for the moment the persisting problem of 'total' utilitarianism, namely that it apparently commits her to breeding children (and mice and whatever) to increase the total sum of happiness as much as possible. So she is not obliged to get pregnant. But unfortunately she does. So now what is at issue is killing. And what the replacement view says about killing something, and thereby reducing the total amount of happiness there would have been if you had not killed it, is that this can only be counter-balanced by another creature of the same sort coming into existence as a result. And clearly, that is not going to happen. So she must not have an abortion.

Conclusions

What the replaceability argument does, in effect, is to cancel the usual utilitarian 'other things being equal' clause. And, as I suggested above, something like this *has* to be introduced if the cause of animals is to be championed in the teeth of the selfishness, greed, vanity and folly of many, if not most, human beings. For there is no room in utilitarianism, with its 'realistic' eschewal of ideals, for the idea that some sorts of pleasure or enjoyment are wrong in themselves. Since bullfighting gives pleasure to thousands at the relatively small cost of a few hours of terror and pain for the bull a utilitarian should, in theory, be in favour of it for the Spaniards – pending their coming to find some other form of sport, which causes less suffering, more enjoyable. Fox-hunting gives pleasure to fewer, but some of the literature on it leads one to think that the pleasure deriving from the practice is sufficient to inform a whole life, whereas the fox does not suffer for very long. It is worth repeating – being cruel, like killing, lying, stealing and so on, is, according to utilitarianism, bad in some circumstances, good in others, depending on its consequences.

Having recalled this aspect of utilitarianism, we should look back again at the suggestion that utilitarianism provides compelling grounds for objecting to much of our present treatment of animals – amongst other things, the 'cruel and unnecessary' experiments we perform on them (*cf.* p. 148). Now amongst 'cruel and unnecessary' experiments on animals, many people would include the experiments we do on them which enable us to indulge in trivial or vain or unnecessary pleasures without suffering as a consequence. Perhaps the most well-known example, which has given rise to the 'beauty without cruelty' campaign, is our using animals to test new cosmetics. Another fairly familiar one is our forcing animals to inhale various things in the pursuit of some form of cigarette which will not cause lung cancer. If we describe these experiments as 'cruel and unnecessary' we are not necessarily denying that they do or would, on balance, have good consequences for happiness and suffering. Rather, we are saying that the sort of pleasure or happiness derived from vanity or smoking is too trivial or self-indulgent to be worth causing suffering for.

This same thought too forms the basis of many people's vegetarianism. Some people actually do not enjoy eating meat, but many vegetarians do not deny that they loved it, and still miss it, that a great source of pleasure has gone out of their lives. But for most non-utilitarians, this fact is neither here nor there; the pleasure was simply of a trivial sort, not worth killing animals for. In the special case of smoking, there also seems to be the thought that, since we are free to choose not to smoke, people who do bring their suffering on themselves. Few people would be so vindictive as to say that smokers deserve their lung cancer, but without being vindictive one can say, 'If anyone has to suffer because people smoke, let it be the people who are self-indulgent and silly enough to smoke, not anyone – or any thing – else. Why should any other human or animal suffer because of their folly?' But once again, there is no room within utilitarianism for the thought that there might be something unfair in making an innocent creature suffer in order to avert the suffering that I am bringing on my own head. All that is at issue is how to minimize the suffering.

I conclude that, if one wants to champion the cause of animals, utilitarianism is not the theory one should be appealing to. If one adds to it the entire arbitrary and non-utilitarian 'other things being equal' clause), one manages, perhaps, to make a better job of defending animals' lives, but still leaves them at the mercy of much 'unnecessary' experimentation. Adding the replacement view also leads to a most restrictive position on abortion, a point which has been overlooked by one of its most well-known proponents, Peter Singer.

Singer on persons and non-persons

Singer's earlier writings[13] are exclusively concerned with arguing against our treatment of animals, but in his widely read *Practical Ethics* he discusses not only that, but abortion, infanticide and euthanasia too. In this book he has two distinct aims, which are, on the face of it, entirely independent. He wants to 'elevate the status of animals'; he also wants to defend a very permissive view of abortion and infanticide (and indeed euthanasia).

Anyone unacquainted with current philosophical literature might reasonably think that this was a very odd position to take up. Would one not expect someone arguing against the way we slaughter animals to be rather 'pro-life' in general, and hence against abortion and infanticide? Would the obvious argument against the way we kill animals not be something to the effect that there was no good reason for restricting the claim that killing is wrong to human beings; that animals' lives are sacred, or have intrinsic value, or should be respected as well as ours? However, by *Practical Ethics* Singer has explicitly abandoned the sanctity of life and espoused utilitarianism. He has, moreover, made two of the mistakes I discussed in the preceding chapter, namely (a) he has succumbed to the idea that the *only* way of avoiding vicious speciesism is to talk in terms of persons and non-persons, and (b) he has also succumbed to the idea that, once we are clear about the fact that the fœtus or new-born infant, though a human being, is not a *person*, the abortion issue is 'transformed'. And it appears that he expects this introduction of the term 'person' to provide the insight which yokes his two apparently disparate aims together: we elevate the status of animals by repudiating speciesism, and we license abortion and infanticide by recognizing that fœtuses and babies are non-persons.

Non-speciesist utilitarianism does something (though, as I have argued, not enough) to elevate the status of animals to the point where we take serious account of their suffering, and, since it 'realistically' abandons the sanctity of life, it opens the door to licensing abortion and infanticide. So far, Singer's two aims are satisfied. He also offers a couple of arguments from within utilitarianism in defence of the idea that it is more wrong to kill a person than non-person (other things being equal). If they worked, these arguments would, in accordance with his first aim, elevate the status of quite a lot of animals, since Singer thinks that not only apes, whales and dolphins but also monkeys, dogs, cats, pigs, seals and bears are persons. Moreover, they would weigh against fœtuses and babies as non-persons, thus lending implicit support to the second aim.

But whether or not these arguments work will not affect the main problem with Singer's position, which is that he cannot simultaneously elevate the status of non-persons (mice, hens, etc.) and license their killing (abortion and infanticide). If we are to abandon the sanctity of life (to let in abortion), then we let in killing the animals. If we appeal to special arguments about killing persons to block that, we are still left with the slaughter of the mice, hens, ducks, sheep and new-born baby seals. And any arguments against killing them that we claim to find in utilitarianism will apply to fœtuses and babies too. Hence, as I argued above, the replaceability argument applied to abortion yields a particularly restrictive policy.

Singer overlooks this fact for the simple reason that he does not apply the argument to abortion, i.e. to the killing of very young, non-person, human animals. Instead, in a form of reverse speciesism, he gives the very young of the human species individual treatment. In the case of every other sort of non-person animal we say, 'The killing of a non-person is wrong insofar as one reduces the amount of happiness there *will be* in the universe; this can only be counter-balanced by replacing the "receptacle" of that amount by a similar receptacle, etc.' But uniquely in the case of the young human non-person, we do not consider how much happiness *will* be lost if we kill one now, instead of letting it live on for the next seventy years or so. Instead, we are asked to compare the fœtus at a particular stage of its existence with creatures with 'similar characteristics'. This leads to the conclusion that a fœtus of less than three months compares unfavourably with 'a fish, or even a prawn' in terms of consciousness. Indeed, the further conclusion is that, since fœtuses of less than eighteen weeks are, Singer thinks, probably incapable of feeling anything at all, abortion up to this point 'terminates an existence that is of no intrinsic value at all'.[14] But it is supposed to be agreed ground, given that we are relying on utilitarianism, that there is *no* creature whose existence or life has intrinsic value. The continued existence of something has value only insofar as it *will* increase the amount of future happiness; on this criterion, the average human fœtus completely outranks any prawn. The fact that the fœtus in its early stages is 'incapable of feeling anything at all' is no more relevant than that a person under an anaesthetic is similarly incapable, or that hibernating bears apparently cannot feel much. The fœtus, the anaesthetized person, the hibernating bear, though indeed their existence has no intrinsic value, are all beings likely to have a happy future and hence (other things being equal) are all creatures it would be wrong to kill, on straightforward utilitarian grounds.

3   MODIFYING UTILITARIANISM

Another writer who has made a point of applying utilitarianism to the abortion issue, with the aim of arguing for a liberal position on abortion (and infanticide) on fairly plausible grounds is Jonathan Glover.[15] Starting with 'total' utilitarianism he adds two non-utilitarian principles intended to modify its most implausible and unacceptable consequences. However, it is questionable whether these principles succeed in making his position on abortion plausible, as I shall now argue.

The autonomy principle

As we noted above (p. 144), one of the most startling consequences of utilitarianism is that it not only licenses but actually requires us to practise involuntary euthanasia (other things being equal), i.e. to kill someone who would be better off dead, even if he says he wants to go on living. Glover's way of avoiding this unacceptable consequence is to introduce a principle of autonomy, according to which (roughly) it is wrong not to respect people's autonomy or personal freedom. Once again roughly, this on its own amounts to claiming that it is intrinsically wrong to prevent someone from doing or having what he wants, *regardless of the consequences*.

Glover does not believe in giving respect for autonomy the absolute priority guaranteed by that italicized phrase. He thinks, for instance, that a utilitarian consideration of your interests should override respect for your autonomy when what is in question is, say, your becoming a heroin addict, or committing suicide when momentarily depressed about a failed love affair or exam. But he notes one important difference between paternalistic killing (i.e. involuntary euthanasia – killing you for your own good, against your wishes) on the one hand, and paternalistic prevention of heroin addiction or suicide on the other, namely 'the finality of an act of killing'. When I paternalistically prevent you from starting to take heroin or committing suicide I do so in the belief that you will be glad later that I did. If I am wrong, it is still open to you have another go. 'But', he says, 'if I kill you, this is final. You will not have second thoughts, and mine will come too late.'[16]

So, according to Glover, utilitarianism sometimes overrides the autonomy principle. But if there is any point to introducing it, it must sometimes override utilitarianism. We might say that, at least when killing is in question, it always overrides utilitarianism. But Glover finds this implausible.

> It does not seem plausible to say that there is no *conceivable* amount of future misery that would justify killing someone against his will. If I had been a Jew in Nazi Germany, I would have considered very seriously killing myself and my family, if there was no other escape from the camps. And, if someone in that position felt that his family did not understand what the future would feel like and so killed them against their wishes, I at least am not sure that this decision would be wrong.[17]

So, rather than saying that someone's desire to go on living always overrides the utilitarian consideration that she would be better off dead, Glover formulates the following principle:

> Except in the most extreme circumstances, it is directly wrong to kill someone who wants to go on living, even if there is reason to think this desire not in his own interests.[18]

Of course, it must be remembered that this principle still carries an implicit 'other things being equal' clause. All Glover is concerned with here is 'direct' objections to killing someone who would be better off dead, i.e. objections that relate solely to the person killed, independently of side-effects, or consequences that relate to other people. The autonomy principle gives a reason, as preference utilitarianism tried to, why involuntary euthanasia might be wrong because the victim wanted to go on living, even though (a) it is agreed that she would be better off dead (i.e. that this is a case for euthanasia) and (b) no one else would be worse off (i.e. it is not wrong because of side-effects). It is brought in to correct an admitted defect of utilitarianism, namely, that the only *direct* objection it can make to killing is that killing is (usually) a case of reducing the amount of worthwhile or happy life. This objection does not apply in the case of euthanasia, hence the need for the autonomy principle.

But this leaves it entirely open that side-effects can not only justify, but require killing. Suppose that by killing one person I can save two others from great misery. Admittedly it may often be doubtful that the amount of misery caused by refraining would outweigh the amount of happiness lost if the one person's life is cut short, but (assuming with Glover that we often can make these sorts of calculations) there will be other cases where it is clear that killing the one will result in a net increase in happiness. Well, utilitarianism then *requires* me to kill.

It might be thought that the final formulation of the autonomy principle rules this out. After all, it says that '*except in the most extreme circumstances*, it is directly wrong to kill someone who wants to go on living'. Perhaps saving only two people from great misery is not 'extreme' enough? Perhaps killing someone who wants to go on living is justifiable only if refraining will have extremely bad consequences, for example, hundreds of people will suffer or die?

But Glover's discussion of the concentration camp example makes it clear that the 'extreme circumstances' are not side-effects. They refer, as he makes clear later when explicitly discussing involuntary euthanasia, to the cases in which the future life of the victim is going to be extremely hellish, and (or?) of an awfulness that the victim cannot grasp. So the autonomy principle applied to killing, in the form in which Glover accepts it, does nothing to qualify the basic utilitarian position that killing people is right in some circumstances, wrong in others, depending on the consequences. So, for instance, killing a patient who would be better off dead, be it involuntary euthanasia or not, would be right if it spared the victim's relatives great suffering, or released a hospital bed that someone with better prospects needed.

Abandoning the right to life

Bearing this in mind, we should turn to consider what Glover says about the right to life. He begins by pointing out correctly that one motivation for saying that we have a right to life is 'to take questions of life and death out of the realm of calculation of consequences'. That is, one reason for saying there is a right to life is the belief that, contrary to the claims of utilitarianism, it may be neither justifiable nor required to kill one person to save two others misery, but that, on the contrary, this would be wrong because it violated the right to life.

Glover distinguishes two versions of the claim that there is a right to life. One is the claim that there is an absolute right to life, i.e. the claim that 'to say that people have a right to life is to say that it is *never* morally justifiable to kill them'.[19] The second, weaker version is that there is a *prima facie* right to life, which allows that killing can be justified by its consequences 'in exceptional circumstances'. He dismisses this latter view as being not significantly different from his own. He goes on to discuss the more usual version of the 'absolute' view, which, allowing for the possibility of conflicting rights (e.g. my right to life against your right to self defence) says that it is never morally justifiable to kill someone *except* in the exercise or defence of another right. This he also dismisses on the grounds that if we introduce the right to happiness, the 'absolute' version collapses into something once again insignificantly different from his own position. An absolute version that has any substance and differs significantly from his position must, he thinks, be one which makes killing overridingly wrong or else makes its wrongness independent of people's desires or their likely future experiences. The objection to this is, presumably, that making killing overridingly wrong commits us to absolute pacifism in the face of no matter how much evil (it would be wrong to kill a tyrant who could only thus be prevented from inflicting torture on hundreds of children), and making the wrongness independent of people's desires and their likely future experiences rules out voluntary euthanasia.

Is Glover correct in saying that appeals to the right to life either do not 'significantly differ' from his own view or amount to these extreme positions? In several important respects this is certainly not so. Believing in 'the right to life' is similar to believing in 'the sanctity of life'. It involves, at least, believing that various sorts of killing are wrong; it also involves beliefs about the bearers of rights, about what can justify killing, and about the forfeiting and waiving of rights. So, for instance, it has been traditional to believe that, in violating someone else's right to life, one forfeits one's own; the murderer of the innocent may hence be killed without his right to life being violated. (I am not supporting this view, merely using it to illustrate how one might believe in the right to life without believing that killing was overridingly wrong.) It is also possible to believe that one's right to life can be waived; if you say sincerely that you want me to kill you then my killing you may be justified or even required – when, for instance, your future prospects are frightful and you would be better off dead (voluntary euthanasia). This still allows the possibility that my killing you might be wrong even if you have waived your right, since it might be wrong for other reasons. If your future prospects are not so bad then my killing you might well be wrong, despite its not being in violation of your (waived) right.

Believing in the right to life standardly involves believing that if you say you want to go on living, my killing you cannot be justified, let alone required, by appeal to the fact that you would be better off dead (involuntary euthanasia). And, quite generally, it involves rejecting any number of justifications of killing in terms of the beneficial consequences the killings would have. So for instance, someone who believes in the right to life will undoubtedly believe that killing one person in hospital in order to use their organs to save the lives, or spare the misery, of five others would be clearly wrong. But, believing this, I might still believe that there could be some cases in which someone innocent had to be killed because the consequences of not killing them would be so frightful for others. I need not, that is, believe that the single notion of the right to life gives me a cut and dried way of solving all the agonizing life and death problems. I may not be sure in advance exactly what these problem cases are like, or what should be said about them, but I may be sure that, whatever they are like, the decision is not going to be easy, and that the killing will count as an evil, albeit a necessary one.

Now none of these beliefs amounts to either of the extreme positions Glover outlines. But they all express positions which are a far cry from his own utilitarianism, even when it is modified by the autonomy principle. As we noted above, the autonomy principle does not even rule out involuntary euthanasia as such (p. 161), and it certainly does little to block the usual utilitarian head-counting calculation of killing one to save or aid some larger number.[20]

But it is in relation to claims about the bearers of the right to life that Glover's autonomy principle is particularly revealed as falling far short of what many people find acceptable. For on close inspection it turns out to rely on a covert appeal to the person/non-person distinction, and its upshot is that the principle applies only to persons. Now although Tooley may be happy to say that only persons have the right to life, many other people who believe in 'the right to life' appeal to it most particularly in relation to certain non-persons – notably foetuses and infants. But Glover's autonomy principle is designedly formulated in such a way as not to apply to foetuses and infants. How does this come about?

The principle is formulated, in the context of the discussion of involuntary euthanasia, as: it is directly wrong to kill someone *who wants to go on living*. Now let us recall Tooley's arguments about the desires of foetuses and babies. Foetuses and babies, do not, of course, have sophisticated concepts, such as those of *life* (or of *their own continued existence*) and of *death*. And desires, according to Tooley, presuppose the possession of the relevant concepts. So foetuses and babies (and infants up to some rather vague stage, and, presumably, people in a similarly vague state of senility and some mental defectives) do not desire or *want to go on living*. (Of course, neither can they want or desire to die, which is equally impossible for the same reasons.) Since fœtuses and babies (and the brain-damaged, the senile, etc.) do not *want to go on living*, the autonomy principle does not apply to them.

But, *pace* Tooley, there is no immediate block to saying that fœtuses, babies, infants, mental defectives, etc. have a right to life, and this is just what many people who believe in the right to life want to say.

So Glover is mistaken in claiming that moderate appeals to the right to life do not differ significantly from his own view. For granting not only rational adults but also fœtuses, babies, etc. a right to life does not make killing overridingly wrong; in particular, it does not rule out voluntary euthanasia, for then the right is explicitly waived. But it does uphold the view that killing fœtuses, babies, etc. is wrong in the same way as killing a rational adult. And this is very different from Glover's view.

Conclusions

Although Glover explicitly repudiates any belief in the sanctity of life, and defends abortion and infanticide, he also maintains that he is defending the view that 'in general there is a very strong presumption that killing someone is wrong'.[21] But this is highly questionable. The simple fact is that, since utilitarianism has abandoned the sanctity of life and replaced it by the idea that killing is right in some circumstances, wrong in others, depending on its consequences for maximizing happiness, it cannot be used to defend the view that killing is particularly wrong. This feature of utilitarianism is *not* seriously modified by the introduction of the autonomy principle, as I noted above (p. 161). All that the autonomy principle does is provide a second 'direct' objection (except in the most extreme circumstances) to killing, and direct objections are ever prone to be overruled by side-effects, i.e. effects on people other than the one killed. The autonomy principle does nothing to take questions of killing out of the realm of the calculation of consequences in general. It takes the question of killing an individual just one step beyond calculating the consequences for *him* to considering *his* wishes. But, when it comes to settling whether killing is wrong in a particular case, utilitarianism always takes the question of killing an individual beyond the direct objections which relate solely to the person killed. Whether an actual killing is (or would be) wrong is, of course, not settled by the circumstances solely relating to the victim, but by the consequences for happiness and misery in general. It is natural for us to think of the autonomy principle as ruling out cold-blooded calculations about killing one person to provide essential spare organs for others. But that is because we are thinking of the principle as operating like the right to life, whereas it is nothing like as strong as that.

Killing and not producing

Another point which may count against Glover's claim that he is defending the view that there is a strong presumption that killing is wrong is that he is happy to embrace one of the most implausible consequences of 'total' utilitarianism, namely that killing is morally on a par with not producing as many happy children as one can (*cf.* p. 138 above). Now, if we assume that there is nothing (or nothing much) wrong with practising contraception, or rebuffing sexual advances (which seems entirely reasonable), then Glover's view is that, except for the extra weight provided by the autonomy principle, there is nothing (or nothing much) wrong with killing – which hardly squares with his claim about defending the strong presumption.

But on the other hand, perhaps Glover does think there is something very wrong with practising contraception and rebuffing sexual advances. These alternatives suggest that he can be presented with a dilemma.

According to the 'total' utilitarianism which he accepts, the only direct objection to killing is that it reduces the amount of happy life there would have been if the killing had not been done. But the same is true of deliberately failing to produce a child; here too one has failed to maximize happiness – 'in either case the result is one less such person [one who would, *ex hypothesi*, have enjoyed more happiness than misery] than there might have been'.[22] When this total utilitarianism is modified by the autonomy principle, the killing of foetuses *and* infants remains unaffected by it. So, assuming that infanticide is very wrong (while leaving the seriousness of abortion as an open question), and that refusing to produce as many children as one can is not, we can present Glover with the following dilemma.

(1)   Given that there is nothing, or nothing much, wrong with not producing as many happy children as one can, his claim is that there is nothing, or nothing much, wrong with infanticide – and this is unacceptable.

Or

(2)   We could say that, given that infanticide is certainly very wrong, his claim is that not producing as many happy children as one can is very wrong – and this is unacceptable.

Glover's response to this objection is, as far as I can see, to claim (unacceptably, according to (2)) that abortion, infanticide and not producing as many happy children as one can are directly wrong in theory, other things being equal, but that, since other things are not equal, in practice it basically turns out (unacceptably, according to (1)) that there is nothing much wrong with abortion and infanticide and not producing *unwanted* children.

The significant change in that last clause is 'unwanted' for 'happy'. Glover remains committed to the wrongness of not producing happy children (or rather, children who will lead 'thoroughly worthwhile lives'[23]). What makes the difference in practice is that if we produced as many children as we could, many of them would be unwanted.

No unwanted children

Addressing the question 'How wrong is deliberate non-conception?'[24] Glover discusses two facts that in practice would make non-conception permissible or even obligatory.

One is over-population, the other is that a child may be unwanted. 'An unwanted child', Glover says,

> is likely to place a great extra strain on both parents, and especially on the mother. Any other children in the family are also likely to suffer from this additional member, either through shortage of space or through the psychological pressures on their parents. An unwanted child is also less likely to have a thoroughly worth-while life than a wanted child. It is also likely that the most anti-social adults are often those who have not been loved enough as children.[25]

These considerations lead Glover to add a second, apparently substantial, qualification to his total utilitarianism, *viz.* the principle that *there should be as few unwanted children as possible.*

Now this seemingly innocuous principle calls for very careful interpretation for, as with his autonomy principle, it is easy to interpret it as much more anti-utilitarian, and in accordance with conventional morality, than it actually is. It is natural to interpret it as saying that people should not go in for intercourse thoughtlessly; that if neither partner is prepared to welcome a resulting child then they should be careful to use contraception, or other ways of avoiding pregnancy, including abstention. It might also be interpreted as saying that, rather than producing as many children as one wants, one should, ideally, adopt existing unwanted children and failing that, produce fewer than one wants and adopt the remainder. Here too, it would be about the point of trying to limit the number of children one produced.

But Glover's principle is quite different. It is not intended to point out cases in which intercourse, or failing to use a contraceptive, would be irresponsible and wrong; for producing any children (except appallingly disabled ones), wanted or unwanted, is increasing the number of people with worthwhile lives and hence responsible and morally right according to his utilitarianism. Glover's principle is intended to justify or excuse my not doing this right thing on lots of occasions. Other things being equal I ought to have produced a child every year since I was sixteen; however, it was morally justifiable of me not to do so because the children would have been unwanted. Note that this does *not* mean 'it's all right not to have children if you don't want them – i.e. all right to be celibate or practise contraception if you want to'. It means 'it's all right to prevent there being unwanted children' – not obligatory, just all right.

One way to prevent there being unwanted children is, given you don't want them, to make sure you don't conceive or inseminate. But another way is, having conceived one, to abort. And another is, having given birth to one, to kill it. In all these cases the 'total' view says that the right thing to do would be to maximize the number of worthwhile lives – by conceiving (or inseminating) in the first case, by carrying the fœtus to term in the second, by not killing the baby in the third – but the principle that there should be as few unwanted children as possible justifies my not conceiving, or my aborting, or my killing, when I do not want the (or a) child. So although in theory not producing as many happy children as possible, abortion, and infanticide are all directly wrong, in practice they would turn out to be wrong only when the (or a) child was wanted.

'Unwanted by whom?' one might ask. This is a point on which Glover is confused. When he first introduces his principle about unwanted children he seems to envisage it as playing the strong role of protecting a new sort of personal autonomy. If *I* do not want a child, if that is, any child I conceived would be unwanted by *me*, then I am justified in not conceiving and producing. (Or, if a man does not want a child, if any child he generated would be unwanted by *him*, then he is justified in being celibate or using contraception.)

This would accord well with what many people find absurd about the 'total' view, namely the idea that one could be *obliged* to produce children, especially if one does not want them, and perhaps even more especially if one wants to lead a celibate life. This is quite consistent with thinking that someone who does not want children is missing out on something very important in life. One might even think that if someone does not want children that shows that they are cold or unloving or selfish or egoistic in some way – and these are all ways one should not be. But this is to think that not wanting children of one's own is wrong, or a mistake of some sort, which is still a far cry from thinking that people ought to produce children even if they do not want them. The point here seems to be that *not* producing children is something over which we have a right; it is open to each one of us to choose not to if we want. Of course, as with any rights, there could be occasions on which it was wrong to exercise it – perhaps it would be wrong to allow the human race to die out if one could help to get it going again.[26] And it is hardly necessary to point out that, as with other rights, this one can be waived, or waived in respect of just one other person, so that many couples would think themselves entitled to refuse to contribute to producing any child outside their marriage, but not entitled to refuse within it. But aside from the special case of preserving the human race, and outside family relationships, we think a woman has a right to decide not to be a mother, and a man a right to choose not to be a father.

Here is the passage in which Glover appears to be defending such a right:

> . . . *there should be as few unwanted children as possible.* The only exception to this would be in the extreme case where a population was so dangerously small that desperate measures were necessary to avoid extinction. This is a case which for practical purposes we can ignore at present. We can take it that, when we consider all relevant factors, including side-effects, it is morally justifiable deliberately to prevent conception of a child *one does not want.*[27]

As stated, this does amount to a principle about a right, for it makes it morally justifiable for someone to decide not to be a mother or a father *regardless of the consequences for happiness and suffering.* Suppose some man is making me very unhappy by refusing to let me have his child; this is morally justifiable if he does not want a child. Suppose I could make an infertile couple immensely happy by producing a child for them; given that I would then have increased their happiness (and the worthwhileness of their lives) and, moreover, have increased the number of worthwhile lives, am I morally justified in refusing? Yes, if I do not want a child.

But to introduce rights is to abandon utilitarianism, i.e. to take, as the above examples show, questions about what is right or wrong out of the realm of calculation of consequences (as is done when we assert there is a right to life – see p. 161). But Glover does not take himself to be abandoning utilitarianism, only modifying it slightly, and the way in which he states his view above is clearly just a mistake. What he should have said is something like 'We can take it that . . . it is morally justifiable deliberately to prevent conception of a child one does not want *and which will not be wanted.*' But when the principle is expressed that way, the absurdity of the 'total' view is hardly avoided, for all we have to do is bring in other people who want children and we are back with the obligation to produce them.

In the context, not of deliberate non-conception, but of abortion, Glover acknowledges one aspect of this problem, admitting that 'the possibility of providing children for those who want them' is 'not something simply to dismiss'.[28] However, he evades the problem here by confusing the question of 'forcing women to bear children they do not themselves want' with the question at issue, *viz.* whether women have a moral duty to bear children when they do not want to (and indeed whether men have a duty to father children when they do not want to). Of course, a utilitarian can reasonably maintain that forcing people who do not want to produce children to do so would (except in the most extreme circumstances, e.g. when the human race is facing extinction) have consequences of misery and frustration that would be bound to outweigh the desirable consequences of increasing the number of worthwhile lives and of there being a few people with children they otherwise would not have had. But no utilitarian can reasonably deny that people who are not being forced *ought* to produce children for the sake of others if they can, unless it is going to lead to enormous misery and suffering for them. So no man should deny me his child – even if he finds the thought of being in any way associated with me and my life repellent. And, unless pregnancy and child-bearing will affect my life very much for the worse, making it not worth living, I should refuse a child to no man, and to no couple, if, for whatever reason, they very much want one, and are likely to give it a worthwhile life.

So I conclude that Glover is committed to the view that in those cases in which someone wants a child that another person can father or conceive and bear, the second person is morally obliged to produce it (unless the bad consequences for them of their doing so outweigh the overall benefit).

Conclusions

Far from mitigating the difficulties of the 'total' view, Glover's principle of 'there should be as few unwanted children as possible' preserves or aggravates them. On the one hand, as I argued above, it leaves unaffected what many people find absurd in the 'total' view, namely the idea that in quite ordinary circumstances one may be morally obliged to father, or to conceive and bear, children, even if one simply does not want to, or one does not want to for or with the person in question. The contemporary question of fœtal research adds an even more startling dimension to this difficulty. The original idea was that one was obliged to produce children in order to increase the number of people leading worthwhile lives (hence, increasing total happiness). This was then modified to the idea that one was obliged to produce wanted children in order to increase the happiness of already existing people and increase the number of people leading worthwhile lives (hence, increasing the total). Some scientists now maintain that if they had enough fœtuses available they could do research which would spare future and perhaps even already existing couples the misery of being unable to have a child and lead to a reduction of people born with congenital defects. So on the total view it seems we would be obliged to produce a suitable number of fœtuses, thus sparing future and perhaps existing people great suffering, and leading to the eventual production of more people leading worthwhile lives.

Surrogacy too acquires a new twist. At present, the debate is about whether it is wrong for women to act as surrogate mothers, and in particular whether it is wrong of them to act as commercial surrogates. On Glover's view, surrogacy (other things being equal) would be a duty, as would sperm donation by particularly desirable fathers.

Not only does Glover's theory impose all these obligations where many people would want to say there is none, it also releases us from a number of obligations many people would say we have. Suppose that I have conceived and borne a child and, having produced it, find I do not want it. Maybe I never wanted it in the first place, but disliked contraception and was scared of abortion, or maybe I thought I did want a child but have now changed my mind. And let us suppose that it is a far from perfect child and that it is unlikely that it will be adopted. There is no question but that it could have a worthwhile life; we need only imagine that it has the kind of defect or disability that makes couples unenthusiastic about adoption. (It is a sad but understandable fact that couples seeking to adopt want 'perfect' babies, and indeed that many want to be in a position to know that the baby's parents are of their own race, or even their own social class.) So it is a paradigm case of an unwanted child. And on Glover's theory I am not obliged to keep it and bring it up, not obliged to try to love it, not even obliged to place it in a foster home – on the contrary, I am morally justified in killing it. For on the total view the direct objection to infanticide is the same as the direct objection to not producing a child (not increasing the total number of worthwhile lives);[29] and on the total view modified by the principle of the fewest possible unwanted children this is morally justified when the child will not be wanted.[30]

4 THE ROLE OF SIDE-EFFECTS: A SIDE ISSUE

Much of the defence of 'permissive' views on abortion, and, even more frequently, infanticide, rests on the appeal to 'side-effects'. This is not peculiar to utilitarians. So, for example, Mary Anne Warren argues for the permissibility of abortion under any circumstances, for any reason, including vain or trivial ones, in terms of rights. However, she produces 'side-effect' arguments to explain why infanticide is usually wrong, and that is basically the utilitarian consideration that the 'needless destruction of a viable infant inevitably deprives some person or persons of a source of great pleasure and satisfaction, perhaps severely impoverishing their lives'.[31]

The appeal to side-effects has two characteristic weaknesses. The first is that it explains the wrongness of an action in what many people find ludicrously inappropriate terms. Thus, for example, Glover, discussing a (hypothetical) case in which a woman decides to abort a six or seven-month-old fœtus in order to take advantage of a chance for a holiday abroad, claims that the side-effects of abortion explain the wrongness here. But when we turn to his list of side-effects these turn out to be (a) the fact that late abortions can be dangerous and upsetting for the woman, and (b) the fact that they can upset the doctors and nurses involved. So if we disapprove of someone for having a late abortion to go on holiday our grounds are supposed to be (a) that we think she is being a bit reckless with her own health and (b) that we think she is being rather inconsiderate to the doctors and nurses. But to many people this would seem obviously false; if we disapprove we do so not for those reasons, but because we think the action is shockingly callous and inhumane.

Glover admits that his side-effects do not provide 'the central ground' for our disapproval. The central ground, he says, is that we feel that 'a woman who cares more about a holiday abroad than about killing her potential child should not have got pregnant or should have had an abortion at once'.[32] So, he says, we can criticize the woman's action without giving up the view that it is always morally justifiable (other things being equal) to abort a child you do not want. But this is surely a muddle. Probably many of us do think that someone so callous should not have got pregnant, or should have had an abortion at once, just as we feel that she should not have the late one in order to go on holiday, even if she is fighting fit and has found a surgeon who does not mind doing it. But many people who think this will not be the ones who agree with Glover's line on abortion, namely that it is morally on a par with contraception or celibacy. Contrariwise, how can Glover maintain that this woman should not have got pregnant or should have had an earlier abortion? After all, *he said* that there is no intrinsic moral difference between not getting pregnant, and having an abortion at any stage, and infanticide.

The second weakness of the appeal to side-effects is that they can very rarely, if ever, be relied on to guarantee the wrongness of whatever is in question. Even supposing that abortion cannot in general be regarded as 'an equally acceptable alternative to contraception' because of its side-effects, there will always be the occasional cases – for instance, the one I sketched above – in which the normally present side-effects do not occur. And then *that* abortion will count as an acceptable alternative to contraception. Similarly for infanticide, and similarly too for compelling women to conceive and bear children when they do not want to, and compelling them to have abortions when they do not want to. Glover says that 'the horrors' of a *system* which compelled women to accept abortion against their will would 'seem to outweigh the likely advantages of such a policy'.[33] But he remains discreetly silent about the obvious possibility that in a particular case the woman's suffering might be outweighed by the resulting benefits and hence that a compelled abortion might be not only permissible but morally required on utilitarian grounds.

Appeal to side-effects has the same weaknesses when used to defend the view that the production of more people with worthwhile lives is a duty. It may well be the case that there are too many people around already, but it would appear ludicrously inappropriate to many people to say that this fact *justifies* my rejecting an opportunity for intercourse. In most circumstances my rejection does not call for a justification. And, as before, the appeal to side-effects is not reliable. New Zealand has a small population for its size, and a declining birthrate. We can easily imagine a case in which childless New Zealand couples want children and cannot afford to travel to overcrowded places on the globe to acquire them. And then the normally present side-effects which protect the claim that non-production is as much a duty as refraining from murder from its blatant implausibility will lapse – and the utilitarian is left with the claim that not to provide a child for such couples is as bad as killing someone who leads a solitary life.

The upshot of all this is more radical than is suggested by the slogan 'actions are right in some circumstances, wrong in others, according to the consequences', for many if not most people would say that abortion and infanticide are right in *some* circumstances – where, for instance, if the child is allowed to live, it will suffer horribly and inevitably die within a few months despite intensive medical intervention. But here something more than consequences is at issue; there is also the reason for which the action is done. If the fœtus or the baby is killed in these circumstances, it is killed for its own sake, not because it does not matter what you do as long as the consequences are for the best. But the 'sometimes right, sometimes wrong' aspect of utilitarianism covers not only sorts of actions described as, for example, 'abortion', 'infanticide', 'lying', etc. but also descriptions that build in the reasons for which the actions are done. So 'being callous' is sometimes right, sometimes wrong, according to the consequences, and so are 'being cruel', 'being unjust', 'being self-indulgent', 'being selfish', and so on. No doubt the immediate consequences of such actions will very often be bad; very often the side-effects will too, but sometimes they will not – and the utilitarian is then committed to saying that these actions are not wrong in any way at all.

NOTES

1 Singer, Peter (1979) *Practical Ethics*, Cambridge University Press, p. 72.
2 Schweitzer, Albert (1961) *Civilization and Ethics*, Allen & Unwin.
3 Singer, *op. cit.*, p. 3.
4 Glover, Jonathan (1977) *Causing Death and Saving Lives*, Penguin Books, p. 63.
5 Singer, *op. cit.*, p. 79.
6 *Cf.* Glover, *op. cit.*, p. 65.
7 Glover, *ibid.*, p. 66.
8 'Involuntary' is contrasted with 'voluntary' and 'non-voluntary'.

Voluntary euthanasia is euthanasia known to be in accordance with the wishes of the one who is killed; *involuntary euthanasia* is euthanasia known to be contrary to the wishes of the one who is killed; *non-voluntary euthanasia* is euthanasia where the wishes of the one who is killed are not, and perhaps could not be, known. *Cf.* Foot, Philippa (1977) 'Euthanasia', *Philosophy and Public Affairs*, vol. 6, no. 2.

9 Bentham, Jeremy (1789) *Introduction to the Principles of Morals and Legislation*, Chapter 17.

10 Singer, *op. cit.*, p. 100.

11 *Ibid.*, p. 104.

12 *Ibid.*, pp. 104–5.

13 See, for example, 'Animal Liberation', *The New York Review of Books*, 5 April 1973 and 'All Animals Are Equal', reprinted in Singer, P. (ed.) (1986), *Applied Ethics*, Oxford University Press. Both of these articles concentrate on the suffering we inflict on animals rather than on our killing them and neither is avowedly utilitarian. The latter notably distinguishes between 'important interests' and 'trivial' ones such as 'pleasing our palate' as opposed to 'satisfying nutritional needs'.

14 Singer, *Practical Ethics*, p. 118.

15 Glover, *op. cit.*

16 *Ibid.*, p. 76.

17 *Ibid.*, p. 82.

18 *Ibid.*, p. 83.

19 *Ibid.*, my italics.

20 Indeed, since Glover thinks there is no difference between killing and (deliberately) allowing to die, the latter will also violate the autonomy of anyone who wants to go on living. So the autonomy principle will actually require my killing one to provide needed spare organs for two who will otherwise die, if those two want to go on living.

21 Glover, *op. cit.*, p. 83.

22 *Ibid.*, p. 138.

23 *Ibid.*, p. 141.

24 *Ibid.*, p. 140–2.

25 *Ibid.*, p. 141.

26 *Cf.* Glover, *op. cit.*, pp. 69 and 142.

27 *Ibid.*, p. 142, my italics.

28 *Ibid.*, p. 144.

29 *Ibid.*, pp. 162–3.

30 *Ibid.*, p. 142, as corrected by me.

31 Mary Anne Warren, in the 'Postscript on Infanticide, February 26, 1982' to 'On the Moral and Legal Status of Abortion', in Feinberg, 2nd edn, *op. cit.*

32 Glover, *op. cit.*, p. 145.

33 *Ibid.*, p. 246.

CHAPTER FIVE

Women's rights and wrongs

1 INTRODUCTION

In the last two chapters I have been discussing the two prevailing radical lines of argument concerning abortion. As I said in Chapter One, I think it is worth subjecting widely read expressions of these views to very detailed criticism, in part because they are so prevalent. But only a purist would think that their prevalence mattered a great deal if they were wrong only in detail. Naturally, my objection to them is that I think they are not only wrong in detail but fundamentally wrong. It is now time to stand back a little and to pick out rather general features the two views share to which one might object.

A very general objection would be that both positions are over-simple in their deliverance of cut and dried answers. Restated in slightly more specific terms, the objection is that both positions grossly underestimate the range of considerations that are relevant to the morality of an action.

Suppose that I am trying to decide what to do on some particular occasion, and suppose also that I am a conscientious person who wants to do what is right or, at least, avoid doing what is wrong. Then, when what is at issue is killing something human, almost the *only* consideration the person view bids me take account of is 'Shall I be killing a person?' and if the answer to that is 'No', I need hardly consider anything further. Whether or not I am killing a baby, or my mother, or a fœtus I deliberately conceived and have carried for six months, none of these is relevant. I do not even need to consider the question 'Shall I be killing a non-person who would otherwise have many happy years of life?' I might need to consider whether or not a non-person is due to suffer very greatly, for perhaps in that case I must kill it. But if I am in any doubt then I might just as well kill it – there is no need to worry about whether, for instance, the life of a baby born with Down's syndrome will, or will not, be happy or worthwhile. I should not worry about whether my killing of *this* non-person is justifiable in *these* circumstances, because the killing of a non-person does not, as such, call for any justification.

Utilitarianism bids me consider only the question 'What will be the consequences for happiness and misery in general?' So, when what is at issue is my killing something human, it does not even count the fact that the action will be a *killing* as relevant. It also rules out, as irrelevant, any considerations which look back, rather than forward to consequences, such as my having promised someone to preserve his life, or my having become pregnant deliberately rather than through having been raped. It also rules out, in being impartial, any individual relationships, or the lack of them, as irrelevant, such as the fact that the human being in question is my mother, or someone else's child. And all these remain irrelevant even in a modified utilitarianism which allows that 'Does she want to die?' can be a consideration in addition to consequences.

This very general feature of the two positions underlies a number of other objectionable features they have. It is because they treat so little as relevant to the morality of an action that they have such far-reaching consequences concerning other cases of killing – our killing of animals, euthanasia (voluntary or involuntary), the killing of the extremely mentally damaged or senile, and most particularly, infanticide – many of which are unacceptable to ordinary morality. The very terms in which ordinary morality objects to the consequences are the ones that have been dismissed. So, for instance, if someone coolly proposed an act of casual infanticide (as in, say, 'We can't take Laura on holiday, why don't we drown her') one would want to say, 'But that would be *killing* a *baby*!' But utilitarianism takes no special account of the former (the fact that it would be killing), and the person view takes no account of the latter (the fact that what would be killed is a human baby).

Their treating so very little as relevant underlies another objectionable feature the two positions share, namely the fact that they both deliver such black and white answers to so many cases that are not black or white – abortion and infanticide in cases of predictable or actual severe disability, non-voluntary euthanasia; it is neither an accident nor a mistake that people agonize over what should be done in such cases. The decisions are very difficult precisely because different relevant considerations pull in different directions. But if only one or two considerations are brought in, inevitably fewer dilemmas remain. (It is interesting to note that as soon as Glover does introduce his autonomy principle, we lose the clear black/white solution to involuntary euthanasia. For 'He doesn't want to die' then pulls one way while 'He would be much better off dead' pulls the other and it is obviously impossible that there should always be a single balance to be struck.)

Another upshot of the positions' treating so little as relevant is that neither takes any account of what is special about, or peculiar to, abortion as a form of killing, namely that it is the termination of a pregnancy, something that essentially involves a woman's body. Once this point has been made, one might be struck (if one had not been already) by a remarkably odd feature of the two views I have been discussing, namely this: one could read the texts which expound them without ever picking up on the facts of human reproduction at all. Imagine that one was an alien, extra-terrestrial, anthropologist who did not know (a) that the human race was roughly fifty-fifty female and male and (b) that only the females get pregnant and bear children and (c) that pregnancy lasts for nine months by the end of which time the fœtus is quite large and (d) that giving birth is painful and dangerous. If one were not already familiar with these basic facts, is there anything in the texts expounding the person and utilitarian lines of argument on abortion which would suggest them? Is there anything in those texts which would be mysterious or incomprehensible if one did not know these facts?

It is, of course, always hard to read something pretending one does not know what one knows very well, but, as far as I can tell, it would be possible to understand most of what Tooley, Singer, Glover and many like-minded writers say about abortion even if, like the imaginary alien, one knew nothing about human reproduction. Moreover, one would learn very few facts about it by reading what they say.[1]

And one might say, this is a fundamental flaw. It is absurd to discuss abortion in such abstract terms that its circumstances are never mentioned or even presupposed. One cannot discuss abortion as though a woman's having an abortion were just like any other case of killing a human being or a non-person or whatever. It is unique as a case of killing, and importantly so.

All these faults – and surely they are faults – are to a certain extent avoided in the well-known article, 'A Defense of Abortion',[2] by Judith Jarvis Thomson. She explicitly takes account of the fact that abortion is the termination of a pregnancy by discussing it in terms of the exercise of one's right to determine what happens in or to one's own body – the aspect of abortion which feminists have always emphasized. No other real case of killing involves the exercise of this right (though Thomson considers some imaginary ones); abortion does and is thereby unique.

One particularly important consequence of actually bringing in the fact that abortion arises in relation to pregnancy and is thereby unique is that quite a lot can be said in defence of abortion *without* wholesale commitment to other sorts of killing. Although Thomson allows, for the sake of the argument, the most conservative premise about the moral status of the fœtus (that it is morally on a par with an adult human being or a person), and argues for a fairly permissive position on abortion, she does not thereby commit herself to any correspondingly permissive line on infanticide, or murder, in general, as supporters of utilitarianism and the person view do.

This is not to say that she entirely avoids committal to, what I would say are, unacceptable consequences, nor, as I shall try to show, does she entirely avoid the fault of inappropriate black and white deliverances. She still has not brought in a large enough range of considerations as relevant. Nevertheless, her arguments represent a 'quantum jump' in their level of sophistication when compared to those we have been considering, and for this reason I take the article as worth going through very carefully.

Before embarking on this detailed discussion, I should mention the article's most salient characteristics.

(1) Without herself believing it, Thomson allows the conservative opponents of abortion their premise that the foetus is a human being or a person[3] from the moment of conception. She argues that, even granting this premise, abortion is permissible in a large number of cases.

(2) She explicitly does not attempt to argue that abortion is always permissible. On the contrary, she maintains that abortion is sometimes permissible, sometimes not – not 'according to the consequences' as utilitarianism says, but 'according to the circumstances' as all but the most 'conservative' opponent of abortion say. (Few non-Catholics subscribe to the view that abortion to save the mother's life is impermissible even when, without the abortion, both mother and child will die. In those circumstances, at least, abortion is justifiable.)

(3) As I mentioned above, she takes account of what is special about, or peculiar to, abortion as a form of killing, by discussing it in terms of the exercise of a right over one's own body.

(4) She allows that actions can be wrong *in different ways*. They can be wrong in being unjust, when they violate a right, but they can also be wrong because they are callous, cruel, selfish and so on.

2 THOMSON'S ARGUMENTS

Thomson begins by laying out what she takes the conservative argument against abortion to be.

Every person has a right to life. So the fœtus has a right to life. No doubt the mother has a right to decide what shall happen in and to her body; everyone would grant that. But surely a person's right to life is stronger and more stringent than the mother's right to decide what happens in and to her body, and so outweighs it. So the fœtus may not be killed; an abortion may not be performed.[4]

Agreeing that it sounds plausible, she goes on to describe an imaginary case which, she says, 'suggests that something really is wrong with that plausible-sounding argument'. The imaginary case is one in which I wake up one morning to find that a kidney patient has been attached to my kidneys. If we stay thus attached then in nine months he will be cured of his fatal ailment and able to survive independently. But he will die if I detach myself before then, because, until he is cured he needs to be attached to someone else's kidneys and I alone have the right blood group to help. This case makes Thomson suspect something is wrong with the plausible-sounding argument for the following reason. Like the fœtus case, it is a conflict between the right to life and the right to decide what happens to and in your body. But in this case it is not obvious that the right to life completely overrides the right to decide what happens to one's body – that, morally speaking, I simply have to put up with it and stay plugged in to this man. After all, what if he needs not nine months, but nine years? Or the rest of my life?

Thomson concludes that it would be 'outrageous' to suppose that I would be morally obliged to spend the rest of my life attached to this man. (For no relevant reason, he is a violinist, so the example is always referred to as 'the violinist case'.) But if I am not morally obliged to do so, something must be wrong – there must at least be some premises missing – in the plausible-sounding conservative argument.

To some people this sort of far-fetched example (which is but the first of many in Thomson's article) seems simply irrelevant. It may be that this reaction, though ill-grounded as it stands, can eventually be argued for (see below, p. 206). But until it is argued for, we should accept the relevance of the role such examples play in argument – if I say such and such in one case (that the right to life overrides), I must agree that the same is true in another case *or* point to the morally relevant difference between the two cases. Of course, many morally relevant differences between pregnancy and finding that someone has attached my kidneys to a kidney patient immediately leap to mind, but many of these are discussed by Thomson later in the article. So far, all the example is supposed to have shown is that it is not obvious that the conservative premise about the fœtus's right to life is going to guarantee, without further assumptions, that abortion is impermissible in many cases. It suggests that the standard liberal premise about the woman's right to decide what happens to her body might, with some further assumptions, guarantee that abortion was permissible in many cases.

Conflicts between rights to life

Thomson opens her attack by discussing, not the generality of cases, but the small number where what is at issue is the conflict between the fœtus's and the mother's right to life, and she justifies a woman's performing an abortion on herself in such cases by appeal to the right of self defence.

In discussing this justification in Chapter Two (Section 2) I claimed that it was not clear that 'if my choice lies between my life or an infant's it is straightforwardly permissible for me to kill the infant'. But according to Thomson this *is* clear; if I kill an innocent person to save my life, whether this be by infanticide or abortion or unplugging myself from the violinist, it is clear if anything is that I do *not* do what is impermissible. This is close to being a rock-bottom disagreement (though see below p. 200) between Thomson and me so I shall leave it aside for the moment.

Suppose Thomson is right on this point, and hence that, even supposing the fœtus to have as much right to life as any child or adult, abortion by the mother to save her life is permissible. Does it follow that abortion to save the mother's life is permissible when performed by a third party? It clearly does not *follow*, for the reasons I gave in Chapter Two: the third party is not killing the fœtus in *self* defence but in defence of the mother, and nothing said so far has justified a third party's supporting the mother's right to life rather than the fœtus's. Indeed, it might be said that no third party is justified in taking it upon themselves to choose who will live and who will die when two lives are in conflict.

But Thomson argues that choosing, as a third party, between the mother's life and the fœtus's (or the mother's right to life and the fœtus's) is not a case of choosing between people with equal rights. The fœtus and the mother have an equal right to life, that is true, but the mother also has a right to decide what happens to her body, because she owns it, it is hers, not the fœtus's.

Criticizing this argument, Glover remarks (a) that it is inappropriate to describe someone's body as their property, as if it were their house or coat and (b) that even if this were allowed, property rights do not have the moral weight that Thomson is giving them here.[5] If I am on a river bank and see two drowning people reaching for the only life-belt, it is surely not true that I ought to intervene and make sure its owner is the one who survives. Actually, Thomson cautiously says that she is arguing only that a doctor *may* perform an abortion (when the mother's life is at stake) not that the doctor ought to. But the criticism still applies. Is it even morally permissible to intervene and choose which life to secure solely on grounds of property? Is it morally permissible for me to choose to take the life support machine from one person and attach it to someone else who will die without it, solely on the grounds that she is very rich and owns it? I do not think so.

However, although Thomson herself uses the analogy of the house and coat, I think that these examples are neither necessary nor appropriate, and betray a misunderstanding of the concept of the right over one's own body. This is a 'property right' in the old sense of 'property' according to which it covers not only external goods, but anything which is one's own, and which one has a right to or in. When the concept of a natural right was really flourishing (in the seventeenth and eighteenth centuries) the favoured examples of things that were one's own 'property' were one's life, limbs, body and actions and it would have been odder to describe something morally insignificant, like a coat or life-belt, as someone's property. So what we need, as the parallel case, is one in which two people with an equal right to life differ in that if a third party intervenes to save one he or she will also be protecting some further serious natural right of that person. Perhaps while they are both alive, one is, innocently, causing the other one great agony. To kill the first is both to protect the right to life of the second and also, say, to protect that person's right not to be subjected to unnecessary suffering (supposing that that is a natural right). This is not an ideal parallel case, because, at the opposite extreme from coats, preventable great agony is perhaps too morally significant. It may have much more weight than the right to decide what happens to one's body in the case of abortion. But – and this is probably significant – I cannot think of any other.

Violating the right to life

The opening moves in Thomson's argument are fairly self-contained; they could indeed be regarded as a mini-article about 'Conflicts between rights to life'. But from now on the argument takes a much more radical turn, to consider cases in which the mother's life is not at risk. Since 'the right to life' is, in such cases, not something that weighs on both sides and cancels out, it becomes necessary to consider what it amounts to, and hence what counts as violating it.

Does it, for instance, include the right to be given the bare minimum one needs to survive? One might think it was bound to (and traditionally it has been taken to include the basic necessities of food, drink and shelter). But Thomson argues that it does not, since something an individual needs to survive might not be anything that he had a right to be given by anyone. Suppose that what I need in order to get over an operation is a pint of your blood. Do I have a right to it? Thomson thinks not – it would be kind of you to give it to me but you are not obliged by justice to do so. In terms of the virtues, it would be an act of charity (of loving kindness or benevolence) to do so, but you would not act unjustly in refusing. Thomson's reason for saying that I do not have a right to a pint of your blood would be, once again, that it is *yours* not mine.

The point of this argument is to show that the fœtus's right to life does not include the right to be given the use of the mother's body, despite needing this to survive. And since depriving the fœtus of the use of the mother's body is, as things are, killing it, it turns out the fœtus's right to life does not include the right not to be killed – or at least, it does not include the right not to be killed by the mother. So she does not violate its right to life by killing it.

One might think that if the right to life did not amount at least to the right not to be killed then it did not amount to anything at all. But in the next move in her argument Thomson suggests that the right to life consists in the right not to be killed *unjustly*. What she means by this in general is left unspecified, but she does give us one sort of example. I would be killing someone unjustly (a) trivially, if I killed them without their actual or presumed consent, and (b) by depriving them of something they had a right to. The clause (b) gives the backing to the killing's being unjust – it is unjust because it is a violation of a right.

So let us take a case in which someone does have a right to the use of my body to survive precisely because I have given them that right; I say, 'It's yours, to use as you need for the next (say) nine months.' If, having given them the right to use my body in this way, I then deprive them of its use and thereby kill them, this, in Thomson's view, is an unjust killing, and thereby a violation of the right to life.

Thomson already holds that the fœtus does not have a right to the use of the mother's body *which follows from*, or is included in, its right to life. But now the question arises, does it have the right, or could it acquire it, in some other way? It might for instance be said that a woman gives the fœtus that right by becoming pregnant. If that were so then abortions would turn out to be unjust killings and hence violations of the right to life after all.

Against this Thomson asserts it as a premise that a woman cannot be said to have given the fœtus the right to use her body if she is pregnant because of rape. Plausibly the pregnancy must result from voluntary intercourse. (Plausibly

too, though Thomson does not mention this, the woman –
or perhaps girl in this context – must know that intercourse
may result in pregnancy: the innocent or mentally deficient
who have intercourse without realizing that this is how
pregnancy comes about cannot be regarded as having given
the fœtus the right to use their bodies.) However, this still
leaves a very large number of cases; does Thomson agree
that in all cases of pregnancy due to voluntary intercourse
in full knowledge of the facts of life the mother could be
said to have given the fœtus the right to use her body – that
the intercourse as it were amounts to an offer to have one's
body thus used?

She clearly does not, but her argument at this point
depends on two rather unsatisfactory analogies. In one she
imagines that children come about by people-seeds taking
root in one's carpet; this may happen even if one has gone
to great trouble to try to prevent it by putting fine mesh
screens over one's windows. In the other analogy, she does
not consider children, but how people might acquire a right
to use my house, and says it would be absurd to suppose
that someone had acquired it by just blundering in, through
a window I had happened to open, behind bars I had installed
to keep people out which happened to have a defect. In each
case I go to some trouble to try to keep people-seeds or
people out; in each case there is supposed to be a way that
would guarantee keeping them out, say with sealed windows,
but it cannot be said that I am responsible for their being in
my house and that hence they have a right to it simply
because I do not go in for this extreme measure.

These analogies are obviously supposed to be with contraception; despite the woman's efforts not to become pregnant,
she does. Given that she was trying not to, her voluntary
intercourse cannot count as an offer, conferring a right, to
have her body used by the fœtus. But the difficulty with
the people-seed analogy is that, because it is so far-fetched,
it lacks all the background that enables one (sometimes) to
make up one's mind. Do these people-seeds just root for
nine months? What are the available alternatives to uprooting
and killing them – can they be transplanted, can you swap
your house for nine months with someone who wants

children . . .? The difficulty with the other analogy is that it misses out the crucial aspect of the fœtus being dependent on the use of the woman's body for its survival. The analogy that is needed would be a case in which, somehow, by opening the window I ran a (small but recognizable) risk of someone's coming in whose survival depended on his staying.

Suppose I am living in a house in France in 1944. As I happen to know, its earlier occupiers had run it as a link in a chain smuggling Jews out of Germany, and – as I happen to know – the simple signal they use to show that the hiding places were free was to leave a window open. If all the windows were shut it meant 'Danger, keep away'. The chain was broken years ago; I kept all the windows shut throughout the first summer just in case but heard not even a rumour of any Jew trying to hide anywhere in the village. By the second summer, the risk seemed negligible, so I allowed myself to open the occasional window when it was very hot. Suppose one night a Jewish refugee climbs in, not having heard the chain was broken, and interpreting the open window in the way I knew there was the possibility someone might. His survival depends on my sheltering him, as I knew the survival of anyone who interpreted the open window in the old way would. Can I now say that I am not responsible for his being in my house and dependent for his survival on me? If not, then it may well be that Thomson's analogy lacks the very feature which is relevant, *viz.* that someone's survival hangs on what is done. (If someone thinks it is essential that this case should provide some parallel with care about contraception, which I in fact do not, it can be read in. This case can be seen as analogous to one in which a woman becomes pregnant after she had good reason to suppose she was past the age of conceiving. For the first year she uses contraception, by the second year, the risk seems negligible, so she stops.)

The point of this section of the argument is to show that the fœtus may be killed without its right to life being violated in all those cases in which the woman has not given the fœtus the right to use her body. It is taken as a premise that the woman has obviously not given the fœtus such a right in the case of pregnancy due to rape, and argued that she has not done so in (any?) cases in which she has become pregnant despite practising contraception. So, Thomson concludes, the best that the conservative argument can establish is that there are *some* cases in which abortions are unjust killings and hence violations of the right to life – say, when a woman tries to get pregnant, and succeeds and then changes her mind for some reason – and this is a far weaker position than the conservative view is standardly content with.

There is a regrettably loose use of the term 'right', Thomson says, according to which it is said to follow from the fact that I ought to do something to or for someone that they have a right that I do so. Someone who used the term in this loose way might argue against Thomson in the following way. 'Rights do not arise only because someone has voluntarily assumed responsibility. Take pregnancy arising from rape. I agree that the woman has not *given* the fœtus the right to use her body. Nevertheless, as things have unfortunately turned out, the fœtus (who, remember, we are assuming is to be regarded as morally on a par with any other person) is dependent for its survival on the use of her body. So obviously she ought to allow it to use her body. So in that sense, the fœtus has a right to the use of her body.'

Thomson's major objection to this use of the term 'right' is that it obliterates the real distinctions there are to be drawn between acting unjustly (violating someone's right) and acting wrongly in other ways – greedily, callously, cruelly and so on. Acting in the latter ways is no less wrong than acting unjustly, but the ways are different. These distinctions have already been prefigured in the discussion above. To give a pint of blood when this involves trouble and perhaps serious risk on my part would be an act of charity or kindness; to refuse to give a pint of blood when I am on the spot and can thereby save someone's life, without trouble or risk, would be callous. But it would not be unjust.

However, in the context of this particular argument about abortion, Thomson sees no need to insist on this point – as long as the people who are using 'right' in the loose way do not get confused about what is 'morally required'. They may say that I 'have a right to' everything that you ought to do for me, as long as they grant that, even in this sense of 'right', I do *not* have a right that anyone should 'make large sacrifices, of health, of all other interests and concerns, of all other duties and commitments, for nine years, or even for nine months' in order to keep me alive. That is, no one is morally required to keep me alive at such a cost – unless someone has given me a (real) right, and then *he* is morally required even at such a cost.

The point of this section of the argument is twofold. It identifies a muddleheaded way in which someone might object to Thomson's argument so far (by relying, without realizing it, on the loose sense of 'have a right'). Once it is clear that what is really at issue, whether described in terms of 'having a right' or not, is whether one person is *morally required* to do or undergo certain things in order to save another's life, we are ready to go on to recognize the difference between the Minimally Decent Samaritan and the Good Samaritan.

The Samaritans

In the Bible story of the Good Samaritan (Luke 10: 30–5) there are at least two people, the priest and the Levite, who act wrongly or 'indecently' in Thomson's terminology; they see a naked wounded man lying half dead by the side of the road, and, turning a blind eye on this person who obviously is in desperate need of help, each one 'passed by on the other side'. These two, in Thomson's terminology, fail to act as even Minimally Decent Samaritans. The third man, the Good Samaritan, acts very well – kindly, compassionately, generously; he stops, binds up the man's wounds, puts him on his own beast and takes him to an inn, and further, takes care of him until the next day, and further, before he leaves, he asks the innkeeper to go on looking after the man, and further, he pays for some of this care in advance and further he promises to pay whatever else the care costs next time he comes.

If that is the sort of thing that a Good Samaritan does,

what would a Minimally Decent Samaritan do? Well, not as much as the Good Samaritan and not as little as the two people who act so callously and selfishly. The Minimally Decent Samaritan at least stops to see if there is something fairly trouble-free he could do to help; he can surely spare something to put on the worst of the wounds and the time to take the wounded man to the nearest inn even if at that point he seizes the opportunity to shift the responsibility on to someone else and hurry away. There is room for some disagreement here; some people might say that all that decency required was stopping and doing what one could in a few minutes before hurrying on. On the other side, some people might say decency requires not just shuffling the responsibility off when you get to the inn, but making sure someone else, e.g. the innkeeper, has taken over. Still, these are disagreements within a framework of agreement – that there is acting as a Minimally Decent Samaritan and there is acting better than that, as a Good Samaritan.

The point of this distinction is that we are, Thomson thinks, morally required to be Minimally Decent Samaritans, but we are not morally required to be Good Samaritans. And the point of claiming this in the context of abortion is that Thomson thinks that in many cases of carrying a child to term, the woman is being, not just a Minimally Decent but a Good Samaritan to the unborn person inside her.

She then returns again to the question of third party intervention. Earlier, she had concluded that the fœtus's right to life did not include the right not to be killed *by the mother*, for *she* might refuse the fœtus the use of her body, and be within her rights to do so. But this left open the question of whether a third party, i.e. the doctor who performs the abortion, was entitled to intervene and protect her right in this way. But now we can consider the question in a new version. Suppose that someone has somehow got themselves into a situation in which they are being compelled to act as a Good Samaritan would, but against their own wishes. Since they are not morally required to act as a Good Samaritan, it seems that, without being indecent, they can try to extricate themselves from this predicament, and one way of trying would be to ask a third party to get them out. Can a third person do so with minimal decency? According to Thomson, intervention in some cases would not simply be an act of minimal decency, but what a Good Samaritan would do. (I must confess I cannot see why she says it is what a Good Samaritan would do.) So where a woman, in being pregnant, is being compelled to act as a Good Samaritan, a doctor may extricate her from this situation by performing an abortion for her, and herself act as a Good Samaritan in so doing.

Conclusions

Of course, all this is consistent with there being some cases in which carrying the child to term calls for only minimal decency. Thomson leaves unspecified what these might be, but she does assert that it would be positively indecent for a woman to request (and for a doctor to perform) an abortion at seven months for a trivial reason, such as to avoid the nuisance of postponing a leisure trip abroad. She claims it as a merit of her account that it does not yield a general yes or a general no on the question of whether abortion is permissible or impermissible, but rather supports the view that some abortions are and some are not. Moreover (though she does not mention this point), this view that some abortions are impermissible (e.g. the sort just mentioned) whereas others are obviously permissible (e.g. a sick and terrified fourteen-year-old, pregnant due to rape) is not essentially dependent upon an appeal to the varying status of the fœtus, as in the mixed strategy, for the argument throughout has been allowing the conservative premise that the fœtus is a person from the moment of conception. Late abortions due to changes of mind for trivial reasons will be indecent not essentially because the fœtus has become a person, but rather because, assuming it to have been a person from the moment of conception, the mother assumes responsibility for it and thereby gives it rights if she knowingly allows it to use her body to survive for several months. Once she has done this, she cannot (with minimal decency) change her mind for trivial reasons. We may compare this with another example Thomson gives: a couple might decide to have a child they have conceived adopted, simply because they do not want children. If they had taken all reasonable precautions against conception, and had non-trivial reasons against having an abortion, then, Thomson thinks, this would be all right, because the child does not have a right to them as (acting) parents just in virtue of their biological relationships.

But if they try to conceive the child, and then do not put it out for adoption but take it home with them – then they have given the child rights, and they cannot now (with minimal decency) arrange to have the child adopted because they have changed their minds and decided they do not want children at the moment after all.

3   DISCUSSION AND FURTHER CRITICISMS

Thomson's article raises a number of particularly interesting and difficult issues. I shall concentrate on one central criticism, namely that her concentration on the single consideration of *rights* leads her to overlook the force of the other considerations which she has, very properly, introduced. Briefly, I shall argue that the most her arguments could hope to establish is that abortion (assuming the fœtus is a human being or a person) is frequently not unjust (the violation of a right), leaving it open whether abortion is usually, in her own words, 'self-centred, callous [or] indecent' and hence impermissible for these reasons. It is to her credit that, instead of restricting herself to the blanket descriptions 'right/wrong' or 'permissible/impermissible/required', she has introduced into the discussion the more complex con-siderations of justice, callousness and self-centredness, and indeed the distinction between the minimally decent and the very good. But she mostly overlooks the force of these, concentrating almost exclusively instead on justice, in the form of questions about rights.

The preoccupation with rights shows up in two ways:

(1) In relation to the only form of the conservative argument that she considers seriously.

(2) In relation to two assumptions which dominate much of her discussion.

The conservative argument

John Finnis,[6] in an article written in response to Thomson's, criticized her concentration on rights, and in her reply Thomson said:

> ... his main complaint against me in the part of his paper which deals with rights is that I was wrong to discuss them at all – my doing so 'needlessly complicates and confuses the issue.' I find this puzzling. My aim was to raise doubts about the argument that abortion is impermissible because the fœtus is a person and all persons have a right to life; and how is one to do that without attending to rights?[7]

Now it is true that Thomson does begin the original article by saying that she is going to raise doubts about this argument:

> Opponents of abortion commonly spend most of their time establishing that the fœtus is a person, and hardly any time explaining the step from there to the impermissibility of abortion ... I suggest that the step they take is neither easy nor obvious, that it calls for closer examination than it is commonly given, and that when we do give it this closer examination we shall feel inclined to reject it. I propose, then, that we grant that the fœtus is a person from the moment of conception. How does the argument go from here? Something like this, I take it. Every person has a right to life. So the fœtus has a right to life. No doubt the mother has a right to decide what shall happen in and to her body; everyone would grant that. But surely a person's right to life is stronger and more stringent than the mother's right to decide what happens in and to her body, and so outweighs it. So the fœtus may not be killed; an abortion may not be performed.[8]

And that argument is indeed the one she goes on to 'raise doubts about' in some detail, as we have seen.

But, having raised these doubts, she is entitled to conclude only that *this* version of the argument does not establish that, if the fœtus is a person, abortion is impermissible. If what you have done is show that a particular argument does not work, then that is *all* you have shown – you have not shown that its conclusion is false. But by the end of the article she is claiming that this is what she has argued: 'I *do* argue that abortion is not impermissible', 'I *am* arguing for the permissibility of abortion in some cases' (my italics).

The end of the article would be, if not justified, at least not a *non sequitur* if she had maintained that *the* argument had to take the form she imposes on it. But it would have been most implausible of her to maintain this, for the following reason. As she herself notes there are other versions of 'the' argument which do not mention the right to life; for example, the fœtus is a person, the fœtus is an innocent person, 'directly' killing an innocent person is impermissible, so abortion is impermissible. One may read Thomson as dismissing this, and similar versions of 'the' argument on the grounds (a) that they all make killing in self defence impermissible (and indeed they do), and (b) that this is plainly false – killing in self defence is not impermissible. Now I would not criticize her for simply assuming (b) with no argument – she has to be allowed some premises. But as versions of a conservative argument against most abortions, these cannot be dismissed so readily. Suppose they were each amended – as some people do amend them – to rule out all direct killing of the innocent *except* in self defence. Then they are still arguments against a third party saving the mother's life at the expense of the fœtus (which she discusses only in terms of the right to life version) and they are still arguments against abortion on any other grounds[9] – which she also discusses only in terms of her version.

Two assumptions

It may be that Thomson overlooks the possibility that other versions of the conservative argument might prove challenging because of her reliance on the first of the two assumptions I mentioned above. These, as I said, reflect her obsession with rights, and shape much of her discussion. They are:

Assumption 1 The only thing I am morally required to do is *not violate other people's rights*.

Assumption 2 Other people have a right 'against' me (i.e. I have a moral duty or requirement in relation to them) only if I have voluntarily assumed a special responsibility for them.

These two assumptions (or something remarkably close to them) can be seen at work on the several occasions on which Thomson argues that I may (I am not morally required not to) deprive someone of, or deny them, something they need for survival *because* they do not have a right to it (Assumption 1); where the reason why they don't have a right to it is that I have not given them that right by voluntarily assuming a special responsibility for them (Assumption 2). Someone might summarize her article as follows:

> 'Even supposing the fœtus to be a person from the moment of conception, it is in only a few cases that a woman has a duty, or is morally required, to carry a child to term rather than have an abortion. For she is morally required to do this only if having an abortion would be violating a right of the fœtus and hence an unjust killing (Assumption 1). But the fœtus has a right to the continued use of her body only if she has voluntarily assumed a special responsibility for it (Assumption 2).
>
> 'This is clearly shown by the case of the violinist, who (by Assumption 2) has no right to the use of my body. I would be being a Good rather than a Minimally Decent Samaritan if I stayed hooked up to him, because I am not morally required to stay hooked up; and I am not required to stay hooked up because he does not have that right (Assumption 1).'

It was within the assumptions of this argument that I produced the example about living in the house which used to be a refuge for Jews escaping from the Nazis. Leaving the argument itself uncriticized I produced the example to suggest that contrary to the implication of Thomson's analogies, a woman who had voluntary intercourse, even with contraception, could be regarded as thereby assuming a special responsibility towards any fœtus that resulted.

But now let us criticize the assumptions themselves. Consider Assumption 2: why should it be so confidently assumed that I can land myself with responsibilities only through my own voluntary actions, rather than get saddled with them by accident? Suppose someone abandons a baby on my doorstep. If I do not realize this has happened, and the baby dies of exposure during the night, this could not in any way be said to be my fault. The baby is not my responsibility – I did not even know it was there. But suppose I find the baby there when I am putting the milk out. Can I just shut the door again, saying 'No responsibility of mine'? It seems to me that I cannot. By sheer bad luck I have been saddled with the responsibilty of this baby simply because whoever abandoned it picked my doorstep and I happened to open the door. And it will remain my responsibility until I can find someone else, or some institution, to take it on. (In many countries this will not be too difficult; I can take it to the police and then it becomes their responsibility.)

'But', it might be said, 'even if you can acquire a special responsibility for this baby just through the accident of its being on your doorstep and your opening the door, that doesn't mean it has thereby acquired a right in relation to you. To assume it has a right that you take it in just because you ought to take it in is to use "has a right" in exactly the loose extended sense that Thomson discusses.'

This response is justified with respect to the question of *what establishes rights*. But in connection with Thomson, all it does is direct one's attention to the first assumption. Let us accept that the baby does not have a right 'against' me that I bring it in. But if it is also granted that I cannot just shut the door on it, that it is morally incumbent on me to bring it in, then here is something that I am morally required to do for someone which is not a case of their having the right against me that I do it. So the first assumption is false.

Although it is, I think, clear that much of what Thomson says involves Assumptions 1 and 2, other things she says seem obviously inconsistent with them. For one thing, she could hardly make Assumption 2 without making the so-called 'right to life' no right at all. But (although she severely limits what the right to life involves) she agreed that everyone has the right to life; and this cannot possibly be because each one of us has voluntarily assumed a special responsibility to everyone else.

But the really interesting inconsistency lies in the fact that the baby on the doorstep example I used above to disprove Assumption 1 is simply a variation on the Samaritan story. It is indecent simply to turn a blind eye on someone who is in need of help you can give if they are not to die; a minimally decent person does not simply shut the door or pass by on the other side. And though we are not morally required to act as Good Samaritans, we are morally required to act as minimally decent ones. And if Thomson herself says this, how can she be supposed to make Assumption 1?

I think this is a point on which she is confused, and the confusion occurs at a pivotal point in the argument. Assumption 1 (that the only moral requirement is not to be unjust, i.e. we are not, in effect, morally required to act as Minimally Decent Samaritans) is operating until the distinction between the two sorts of Samaritan is implicitly introduced. That is, the earlier moves fail to anticipate what a big difference the introduction of considerations about callousness, self-centredness, or indecency, is going to make. Up until this point, the only question allowed is 'Would it be unjust of me to unhook myself from the violinist?'

Once these considerations *are* introduced, the all-important question becomes 'Would it be callous, self-centred or indecent of me in some other way, to unhook myself from the violinist?' But Thomson does not explicitly address herself to that question. Instead she says that 'nobody is morally *required*' to stay hooked up 'for nine years or even nine months' in order to keep another person alive – except that is, in the cases where the other person has a right to demand it.

But this is a fatal equivocation. If by 'nobody is morally required to', Thomson means 'no one would be unjust who refused to' then she has indeed argued for this – but its (putative) truth has nothing to do with the question 'Would someone be callous, etc. if they refused to?' If, on the other hand, by 'nobody is morally required to' she really does mean 'no one would be callous, self-centred or indecent who refused to' then she has indeed answered the all-important question – but she has answered it with only the barest unargued assertion.

That 'Would it be callous, etc.?' is the 'all-important question', and hence the one for which argument rather than bare assertion is crucial, can easily be shown.

According to Thomson herself, being callous, self-centred or indecent is 'no less grave' than being unjust; we are morally required not to do it. And although not being indecent is a far cry from being a Good Samaritan, it is frequently being a minimally decent one. So we are morally required to be Minimally Decent Samaritans. Now let us take this point back to the beginning of the article and 'the' conservative argument against abortion.

The claim that we are all morally required to act as Minimally Decent Samaritans immediately yields a new version of the argument. Something like this: there are ways of treating people which are morally indecent (for instance, arranging their death when they need only nine months effort from you to survive), the foetus is a person and needs its mother's body for only nine months to survive, so most abortions are morally indecent. So no Minimally Decent Samaritan would have one (in most cases). So they are impermissible (one is morally required not to have them, or perform them) in most cases.

Of course, Thomson could, and undoubtedly would, reject *this* instance of what is morally indecent, since she takes it as an assumption that someone who stays hooked up to the violinist for nine months is not just a Minimally Decent but a Good Samaritan. But *that* is the very assumption which has not been argued for at all.

Refusing to sustain

Now that we are clear about the way in which the violinist case is central, let us look at it again. The fundamental claim is that, in the violinist case, I am not morally required to stay hooked up to him for nine months – it would not be callous, or selfish, or self-centred, or indecent in some other way of me to unhook myself and let him die.

My difficulty here really is over allowing the argument to get started. I agreed with Thomson that the violinist does not *have a right* that I stay hooked up to him. I also agree with her that I would not be acting indecently if I refused to stay hooked up to him, in bed, for the rest of my life; and that I would be acting indecently if all he needed was one hour's use of my kidneys to survive and I refused him that. But I do not share her confidence that, between this great spread of a lifetime, or even nine years, which cannot be required of one, and an hour, which can, the nine months so certainly belongs on the nine years/lifetime side. I wonder how far Thomson is prepared to extend the one hour side. Suppose he needs a day? A week? A month? Would it still be callous to refuse?

In the attempt to get clearer about what to think about the violinist case we might turn to consider what we would say about other cases in which sheer chance lands one in the position of choosing between letting a stranger die or giving up some substantial amount of one's time and effort to enable them to survive. There are not, I think, many such cases. One, which was standard fare in fiction until the establishment of the telephone, is that of the wanderer who arrives sick unto death on my doorstep and has to be very carefully nursed for weeks or even months until he recovers. At least traditionally it is always assumed in such cases, I think, that the stranger *cannot* be left to die, that we are morally required to take him in, even in the full knowledge that he will, say, be on our hands for the next four months or so (because of the snows or the rains). Closely related examples still occur at sea: if we find someone adrift we are morally required to pick him up and not leave him to die, even in the full knowledge that he will make life in the boat physically miserable (because of shortage of food and space) and that we shall not be able to contact another boat to take him on board for months.

A different sort of case has resulted from recent developments in information processing. Leukaemia victims can sometimes be saved by bone-marrow transplants, but at present it is often difficult if not impossible to find suitable bone-marrow. A patient's closest relatives are the best bet, but if their marrow is not suitable, or if the patient has no close relatives then usually there is nothing further that can be done. But in the United States they have started putting information about people's marrow type on computer and centralizing all this information. Recently a search through the listings yielded just one person whose marrow could save the life of a particular young man dying of leukaemia. The hospital wrote to the person telling them about this and asking for their help (of course all the expenses were to be paid). And the person refused.

The hospital did not divulge the reasons for refusing – perhaps indeed they were not given – and perhaps the person had reasons which would justify the refusal. But, personally, reading about it, I was shocked. I agree it is quite something suddenly to drop everything one is doing, fly from one side of America to the other, have an operation surrounded by strangers, and be in some pain. I can see how someone might find the prospect frightening and upsetting and want to put it off, or, failing that, avoid it completely. But – to save someone's life? You cannot refuse to do something just because it is frightening and unpleasant and a bit painful when it is a matter of someone else's life, can you? As I say, I thought not, and that, though it was indeed 'tough luck' in Thomson's words on the person to find themselves landed in this position, there was only one morally decent way out of it – to try to save the patient's life.

These cases lead me to conclude that a significant amount of time and trouble, worry and risk, may be morally required of one, to save someone's life even when only chance has brought about a circumstance in which one's choice lies between giving that time and trouble, or letting someone die.

It is true that the preceding cases are not just like Thomson's violinist case. But then it in turn is not just like pregnancy. In her case I am (a) bed-ridden, (b) in enforced communicating company with a stranger, and (c) like that for a whole nine months. It is presumably the fact that I am bed-ridden which licenses her describing the case (by implication) as one in which I have to sacrifice my other duties and commitments and that fact plus the presence of this stranger which makes it one in which I have to sacrifice many of my other interests and concerns. I cannot do my job, I cannot visit my sick mother, I cannot go to my sister's wedding, I cannot go to the films, I cannot go swimming, I cannot read (well, perhaps the violinist is a great talker), I cannot have a confidential conversation with anyone and I cannot make love. And all of this for a whole nine months. But the usual pregnancy does not make one bed-ridden, and even when it does, very rarely for nine months; nor is the fœtus, even assuming it to be a person, someone whose presence rules out reading, private conversations, and sex.

Now *if* what I had to do to save someone's life was spend nine whole months bed-ridden, in their constant company, with all that that entailed, then that, one might say, demands a great deal more than either nine months of nursing (when I still have some time to myself, and I am on my feet and have some private life) or a day or so bed-ridden, surrounded by strangers, preparing for and recovering from an operation (which is only a day or so, not nine months). So someone might agree with my judgement about the other cases, but agree with Thomson's about the violinist. But then most cases of pregnancy are more like the other cases than they are like that of the violinist. I am not sure what I think about the violinist case, but I am sure that the more I make it akin to the average pregnancy (I am not bed-ridden, can lead my normal life for a lot of the nine months, etc.) the more certain I become that anyone who finds themselves in the violinist situation *is* morally required to put up with it; that it would be callous, or cowardly, or self-indulgent or self-centred to refuse cold-bloodedly. (I say 'cold-bloodedly' because if you had to decide quickly whether to put up with it or not you might panic about the responsibility and refuse or pull out the plug without really thinking. And then it would not be true that, in full knowledge of what you were doing, you had deliberately chosen to let someone die rather than endure whatever was needed, and hence not true that you had made a callous or cowardly or self-indulgent or whatever choice.)

So I conclude that Thomson does not manage to establish that abortion is, in many cases, permissible, while granting that the fœtus is a person. *If* it were granted that the fœtus is a person most pregnancies would be most similar to cases in which someone faced with a choice between letting someone die and putting up with what was needed to save them would be morally required to endure it; to refuse would be callous or cowardly or self-indulgent, etc. So, *if* the fœtus is a person many abortions would be callous or cowardly or self-indulgent, etc. – and impermissible.

4   ABORTION AS SPECIAL

Three features

That Thomson should fail to establish the permissibility of abortion, in almost any case but self defence, is not particularly surprising, given that she began by conceding to the conservatives their premise that the fœtus is a person, even in the earliest stages of pregnancy. In doing so, one might say, she set herself an impossible task, and can hardly be criticized for failing to achieve it.

But one might well criticize her for believing that she could succeed. Believing she could succeed amounts to believing that the feminists' appeal to the right over one's own body is enough to meet head on the most conservative position over the status of the fœtus, without the need to appeal to anything that is special about abortion. And that, I would maintain, is a mistake.

At the beginning of this chapter, I criticized the exponents of the person view and utilitarianism for failing to take account of the important uniqueness of abortion as a case of killing. Thomson's article, I said, avoids this fault 'to a certain extent', by discussing abortion in terms of the right to determine what happens in or to one's own body. No other real case of killing involves the exercise of this right; abortion does and is thereby unique. However, that abortion, as a case of killing, uniquely involves the exercise of the right is far from being its only special feature, and I would maintain that the fundamental flaw in Thomson's article is that this is the only special feature she clearly recognizes. This flaw underlies her singular concentration on rights which I criticized in the preceding section, but it shows up in many other ways too.

As I said above, it shows up in the very task the article sets itself. The very idea that one could show that in many cases of abortion, other than abortion to save the mother's life, the only relevant consideration was the woman's right to do as she chose with her own body – that the status of the fœtus and whether or not it was a person was not relevant – is a mistake.

Abortion has not just one, but several special features, and it is a mistake to ignore any of them. One is indeed the one Thomson brings out – that it is the exercise of one's (putative) right to determine what happens in and to one's own body. But another is that the fœtus is not a person – not like the violinist or any ordinary average adult one might find oneself involved with. Notwithstanding my wholesale attack on the person view, I have never attempted to deny that obvious truth, and it is noteworthy that Thomson's article becomes particularly implausible at just the point at which she has to maintain that unhooking oneself from the violinist, when one's own life is not at stake, is morally permissible. Coldbloodedly causing the death of another adult, communicating, conscious human being with, it is reasonable to suppose, his own family and friends, interests, hopes and plans, just because you have a (putative) right to do so, is bound to be shockingly callous, and it is important that causing the death of a fœtus, particularly in its early stages, is not *just* like that. As I indicated in the second chapter, my own view on the moral status of the fœtus is that, as a potential human being, it is morally unique, and hence that abortion is, as it were, especially special, in being the killing of such a being. But whatever view one holds about the status of the fœtus, it remains true that abortion is not *just* like killing an average adult human, with his own complicated involvement in an ongoing life.

But these two features (that abortion is the exercise of one's right over one's body, and that it is not just like the killing of an ordinary adult) are not the only two ways in which abortion is special as a form of killing. Its third extremely important feature is that it is the termination of a pregnancy and there are many morally relevant differences between pregnancy and the violinist case. These, put at their simplest, are (a) that their effects or upshots are very different, and (b) that their causes are very different.

The difference between the effects of staying hooked up to the violinist on the one hand, and going through with a pregnancy on the other, is huge. The issue, in the violinist case, is always, and only, my present physical condition. Putting aside again the self defence case, the only question is, can I stand remaining in this condition for the next nine months for his sake? I do not have any worries at all about the future beyond these nine months. But (putting aside again the case of abortion to save the woman's life) very few abortions are sought because the pregnant woman is concerned solely about her present physical condition in itself, with no worries about the future beyond the next nine (or rather, eight or seven) months. If I do not unhook myself from the violinist then the upshot after nine months is that some adult human being, with whom I can shake hands and bid goodbye, survives. If I do not have an abortion, then after nine months the upshot is that there will be a *child*, a new person in the world, and moreover, that child will be mine – I shall have become a mother, and in one sense will remain one for the rest of my life.

Such a child will be, not only my child, but the child of its father. The fact that pregnancy is (standardly) caused by a single act of sexual intercourse and that the male partner in that act is the father of any child that results, once again makes for a huge difference between pregnancy and the violinist case.

A critic of Thomson's has said that in the case of rape, the woman's situation is 'adequately analogous to the violinist case for our intuitions about the latter to transfer convincingly' but that in all other cases this is not so since

in the normal case [of unwanted pregnancy] we cannot claim that the woman is in no way responsible for her predicament; she could have remained chaste, or taken her pills more faithfully, or abstained on dangerous days and so on. If, on the other hand you are kidnapped by strangers and hooked up to a strange violinist, then you are free of any shred of responsibility for the situation, on the basis of which it could be argued that you are obligated to keep the violinist alive.[10]

This criticism of Thomson is stated within the terms of accepting that I cannot acquire responsibilities through sheer bad luck. But, putting any criticism of that point to one side, we should still be struck by how very unlike the violinist situation and even pregnancy due to rape are. For wanting to terminate a pregnancy caused by rape is particularly a response to its cause, to the knowledge that what is growing inside one is in some sense *his*, the rapist's, and will become a child which is one's own and *his*, if one does not have an abortion. But the knowledge that one has been kidnapped to sustain the violinist does not make him a constant reminder of something terrifying and disgusting, nor invest one's present situation with any particular horror, nor give one reason to dread the future.

That pregnancy is utterly unlike the violinist situation in these different ways is, of course, perfectly obvious, though all too easily forgotten in the context of abstract philosophy. What is not so obvious is why they are morally relevant. They are relevant because abortions are sought for reasons which connect with these facts.

It is a notable aspect of Thomson's article that very little is said about women's reasons for wanting abortions. The only two cases that are mentioned (apart from abortion to preserve one's own life) are the desperately frightened fourteen-year-old girl pregnant due to rape and the woman who, for once, *is* concerned only with her present physical condition and wants to terminte her seven-month pregnancy so that she can have a holiday abroad. Now this is once again the result of the preoccupation with rights and hence with acts which are unjust; for the injustice of an act is largely determined by whether or not it violates rights, independently of the agent's reasons for acting so. But Thomson herself has introduced callousness, self-centredness and other moral faults onto the board, and once this is done, we must consider the particular sorts of reasons women have for wanting abortions. For it is the reasons people have for doing things that reveal them as callous, self-centred and so on, or not. But as soon as we do discuss the reasons women have for wanting and seeking abortions and the sorts of considerations that come up, the many ways in which abortion is utterly unlike the violinist case immediately become apparent.

Reminding ourselves of how varied the reasons can be makes particularly vivid two points of Thomson's which we may rather have lost sight of. I noted, at the beginning of this chapter, that she maintains (a) not that abortion is always permissible, but that it is sometimes permissible, sometimes not, according to the circumstances, and (b) that, when it is wrong, it can be wrong in different ways – sometimes unjust, sometimes callous and so on. Precisely which circumstances make a relevant difference, and precisely how many different ways there are for abortion to be wrong, is probably impossible to determine. But in the remainder of this chapter I shall discuss briefly some of the considerations that come up when one is trying to determine whether it would be wrong for *this* woman (or girl) to have an abortion in *these* circumstances, and what sort of person would do so for *those* reasons, by way of illustration of how various the decisions can be.

My discussion will be limited by the premise that, since abortion is the killing of something, and something human at that, it is, contrary to utilitarianism and the person view, intrinsically a morally serious matter. Naturally, I do not pretend to have proved that abortion, as the killing of something human, is thereby a morally serious matter. I have done my best to undermine the arguments purporting to show that it is not, and would claim that these suffice to shift the burden of proof, but I can do no more.

Reasons for abortions

Let us begin by briefly considering the cases which are most akin to the violinist one, in that the woman wants an abortion for reasons that are at least mostly connected with the physical condition of pregnancy and the prospect of the seven or eight months to come. When women are in very poor physical health, or worn out by child-bearing, or forced to do physically very demanding jobs, then they cannot be described as self-indulgent, or callous or irresponsible, if they seek abortions. To go through with a pregnancy when one is utterly exhausted, or when one's job consists of crawling along tunnels hauling coal, as many women in the nineteenth century did perforce, is heroic but people are not to be blamed for not achieving heroism. That they can view the pregnancy only as eight months of misery, followed by hours if not days of agony and exhaustion, and abortion only as the blessed escape from this prospect is entirely understandable, and does not manifest any lack of serious respect for human life.

These cases contrast sharply with others which are connected with the physical condition of pregnancy, such as Thomson's paradigm example of an indecent reason for seeking an abortion. To regard pregnancy, especially in its more advanced stages, as nothing but a tiresome and pleasure-inhibiting physical condition, as an adolescent regards a pimple before a date, is startlingly self-centred, callous, insensitive, and does manifest a lack of serious respect for life. Indeed, it could truly be described *as* childish or adolescent, though this sounds like an understatement. It may be taken as less of an understatement if we remember that a degree of absorption in one's own pleasures and pursuits, and lack of thought for others, which is quite natural in children, amounts to cruelty, callousness and wickedness in adults. A twelve-year-old who hits her baby brother because he will not stop crying and puts him in the bottom drawer and goes out to play is one thing; a twenty-five-year-old who does the same is quite different. We do not expect children to 'know what life's about', to appreciate what is serious. But adults are supposed to, and when they do not, and continue to live as though all that mattered in life were their own immediate pleasures, they tend to do particularly frightful things.

Abortions are more usually sought for reasons that connect with the fact that pregnancy produces, not just *a* child but, the woman's child. She does not want to have any more children, or she does not want to have children at all, or she does not want to have one now; and so she wants to terminate the pregnancy.

But the 'and so' is too swift. For if what she wants is not to increase her family, or not have a family at all, or not start a family now, then *those* wants could be satisfied by continuing with the pregnancy and having the baby adopted. Utilitarianism apparently commits healthy women of child-bearing age to the self-sacrificial duty of producing babies for couples who want them, and though one can reject this as an outrageous demand, it usefully serves to remind us of how desperately unhappy childless couples can be, and how their whole lives can be transformed by being able to adopt. In countries where there is a shortage of babies for adoption, this seems to be a consideration which a generous and thoughtful woman would take into account. To throw away the opportunity to bring so much happiness into other people's lives, to destroy the very thing they value so much because you don't value it, described that way, abortion to avoid having to bring up a child seems self-centred, callous and wanton.

However, this judgement would, in its turn, be too swift. It is not clear that we would admire a woman, who went through a pregnancy with a view to having the baby adopted by strangers, as particularly generous and thoughtful. She might, on the contrary, seem rather cold-blooded. This, I take it, is a reflection of the fact that we expect women to become deeply emotionally involved with the children they bear; a woman who can contemplate the idea of giving her child to strangers without pain seems oddly detached in a way that is not admirable.

Indeed, it seems that many woman who opt for abortion rather than pregnancy followed by adoption, despite believing that abortion is wrong, do so because they cannot contemplate the idea without pain. Some say that if they had the baby they know they could not bring themselves to have it adopted, so their choice has to lie between abortion and having a child that they bring up. Others say that if they had the baby and had it adopted they would always worry about how it was getting on, and what had become of it. But at the end of her article Thomson raises a telling point in relation to this:

> ... while I am arguing for the permissibility of abortion in some cases, I am not arguing for the right to secure the death of the unborn child. It is easy to confuse these two things in that up to a certain point in the life of the fœtus it is not able to survive outside the mother's body; hence removing it from her body guarantees its death. But they are importantly different. I have argued that you are not morally required to spend nine months in bed, sustaining the life of that violinist; but to say this is by no means to say that if, when you unplug yourself, there is a miracle and he survives, you then have a right to turn round and slit his throat. You may detach yourself even if this costs him his life; you have no right to be guaranteed his death, by some other means, if unplugging yourself does not kill him. There are some people who will feel dissatisfied by this feature of my argument. A woman may be utterly devastated by the thought of a child, a bit of herself put out for adoption and never seen or heard of again. She may therefore want not merely that the child be detached from her, but more, that it die. Some opponents of abortion are inclined to regard this as beneath contempt – thereby showing insensitivity to what is surely a powerful source of despair. All the same, I agree that the desire for the child's death is not one that anybody may gratify, should it turn out to be possible to detach the child alive.[11]

Having said this much, Thomson reminds us that she has been talking throughout *as if* the fœtus is a human being, like the violinist, but that it is not. 'A very early abortion', she says, 'is surely not the killing of a person, and so is not dealt with by anything I have said here.' But this at best leaves it as an open question what Thomson thinks about 'the right' or the decency of securing the death of the fœtus, as an alternative to suffering with the knowledge that one's child is somewhere out in the world, unseen and unheard of. Suppose that medical technology had advanced to the point where fœtuses, or even embryos, could be extracted from the womb alive and undamaged, and develop into normal healthy babies in laboratory conditions. Would we think then that a woman had a right to say whether her fœtus was to be aborted dead or live, on the grounds that she would be devastated by feeling responsible for it for the rest of her life? And if she had such a right, that it was all right for her to exercise it?

One possible case might be conception due to rape, where the woman could not face the thought of a child who literally embodies a combination of herself and the man who did this terrible thing to her. But in any other case, for a woman, who has successfully terminated her pregnancy, and who is not prepared to bring up the child herself, to insist that the fœtus be killed, because she cannot bear the thought of *her* child growing up somewhere unseen and unheard of, does seem selfish, self-indulgent and even greedy in some way. What would childless couples desperate to take the fœtus over say about her decision? She has something they want terribly; she does not want it, but she does not want them to have it either.

As things are at present, a woman who opted for adoption despite the devastation she expected it to cause her, would also have to be someone who opted for carrying the child to term and bearing it. And refusing to do that, one might say, is nothing like as selfish or self-indulgent as simply insisting that an extracted fœtus or embryo be killed. Nevertheless, there may be something selfish and self-indulgent in taking abortion as the easy way out of avoiding either the guilt of adoption or the responsibility of bringing up the child oneself. It may also be simply thoughtless – if the woman does not even get round to considering adoption as a possibility – or cowardly. For another salient feature of pregnancy is that, in its later stages, it *shows*. If one carries a child to term, everyone will know, and lots of people will say things to one in the expectation that (of course) you are going to keep it – and to many of them you will have to say blatantly, 'Oh no, I've arranged to have it adopted'. And one might simply cringe at the thought of having to go through that, especially if one's reasons for not wanting to bring the child up oneself were rather selfish or self-indulgent.

I have not yet mentioned one of the distinguishing features of pregnancy, namely the fact that, outside of cases of rape, pregnancy is standardly caused by voluntary intercourse with some man, who is thereby the father of the child. This brings him and his rights, interests and feelings into the picture in a way that no third party with whom *I* have some special connection is bound to be brought into the picture in the violinist case. In a decision to terminate a pregnancy which resulted from a casual night with a stranger, consideration of his rights and feelings is not called for. But if the decision amounts to killing what would be not only *my* child, but the child of someone with whom I have bonds of respect and trust, friendship if not love, then what *he* thinks and wants must be a consideration to be taken into account if I am not to be callous, irresponsible, arrogant and insensitive.

This would be particularly so if he were the father of a child conceived within a marriage, or similar partnership. For marriage seriously thought of, as a partnership of mutual love, involves at least a mutual interest in the results of sexual intercourse within that marriage, and commitment to a shared future. If I do not want us to have children, or not yet, and my partner does want us to have children, right now, I can expect him to consider my wishes with sympathy and respect but must consider his the same way.

Finally, I must briefly mention the reason for seeking abortion which connects not so much with the fact that a woman's pregnancy results in her, and the father's, child, as with the fact that it results in *a* child, a new life. It is particularly in connection with this fact that abortions are sought to avoid bringing a disabled child into the world. For many women, and couples, who wonder whether to opt for abortion this decision is by far the most painful and difficult, and in probably most cases, it is agonized over in entirely unselfish terms. No doubt some women or couples think 'I can't face how much *I* shall suffer' but it is, I think, unduly cynical to suppose that this is common. What is usually dreaded is how much the child might suffer or how narrow its life might be.

Since it is a decision that usually involves such unhappiness I am unwilling to devote much abstract discussion to it. People who are philosophers by profession can often bring their philosophy to bear on the most painful episodes in their lives, or indeed on its end, with no sense of oddity or strain, but it is at best pretentious and at worst cruel to thrust it at most people who are suffering or have suffered. So I should like even the brief discussion below to be taken as addressed to those of us who have been fortunate enough not to be faced with such decisions, not as criticizing anyone who is or has been.

My criticism is directed against those who describe or think of the decision to have an abortion in such cases in a certain way. It is often described as though disabled people ought not to be born or allowed to live; indeed in an intemperate article in the *Guardian*, Polly Toynbee maintained that it was a 'scandal' that so many disabled babies were born, when 'almost all these births are now preventable'. The outraged response that her article, and similar articles and TV programmes, provoke from disabled people themselves, and from their parents, shows immediately what is wrong with this way of talking. The decision to have an abortion in the case of actual or suspected disability cannot be justified in terms of its being better that such people are not born or by saying that it is 'more humane' to kill them, or that their lives would not be worth living, without manifesting the most callous insensitivity to the obvious value of the lives of many already existing people.

No doubt this callousness is usually the result of people not thinking carefully enough about what their words mean; they do not really intend to say, of various people with various disabilities, that all these people would be better off dead, and that it would be 'more humane' to kill them *now*. But one rather wonders about the woman who wrote to *The Times* saying that she considers it 'anti-social' for pictures of thalidomide children laughing to be shown in newspapers or on television. And even if those who say that the lives of the disabled are not worth living do not really mean it, many disabled people, and parents of disabled children, find its being said, understandably, enraging, insulting, hurtful, devastating – and threatening. A blind woman who is actually pro 'abortion on demand' reported being in a group listening to other women discussing disablement as a justification for late abortions; she said, 'Their relationship to me and the way they were talking about it was really very bad. It actually negates my whole purpose in this life. I felt totally intimidated. I just sat and sort of cried inside.' Another blind woman followed up this remark by saying, 'The really awful thing is that they talk about abortion and disabled children as if you weren't there ... I do feel sometimes they are talking about *me*. I think that generally people do think disabled people shouldn't be allowed to exist.'

One would hope that very few people really do think that disabled people should be killed against their will. But it is true that, when discussing the killing of new-born babies with disabilities, or even more, the aborting of babies with actual or possible disabilities, people without disabilities do talk as though people with them did not exist. And I think disabled people, and indeed any people who care about the morality of our society, are right to see this as threatening and dangerous.

One way in which it is dangerous is that it fosters a lot of false beliefs. Until I read a letter from a woman with severe spina bifida (in response to a 'put them out of their misery' article on infanticide) I had been conned by the media into believing that the lives of spina bifida babies were entirely wretched and that in any case they never survived to grow up. I also for many years had a set of entirely inadequate beliefs about babies born with Down's syndrome (Mongolism), thinking that they rarely if ever developed beyond the mental age of a toddler. This lamentable ignorance on my part, which I assume is not rare, is in part the result of a sort of conspiracy of silence that exists in our society about the disabled, a silence which makes their lives and the lives of their families even more difficult in many ways.

The way in which their lives are actually coming under threat is, I think, as follows. It is said that in many cases, abortion or infanticide is the only humane thing to do, since the alternative is a miserable life neglected in an unfeeling and understaffed institution. Now in an individual case this will, not invariably but usually, be simply false. Unless the mother or parents are literally unable to look after a child with the anticipated disability, and everyone is unwilling to adopt a baby with disabilities, it is simply false that '*the* alternative' to being killed is a miserable life in an institution and correspondingly false that 'the *only*' humane thing to do is to abort the fœtus or kill the baby.

Conclusion

The above brief review, schematic as it has been, should serve to remind us of how very complicated an issue 'the' abortion issue is. A variety of women, ranging from twelve-year-olds to fifty-year-olds, seek a variety of abortions, from early to late, in a variety of circumstances, from the most comfortable or fortunate to the most exacting or difficult, for a variety of reasons, from the callous and selfish to the sensitive and unselfish. Small wonder that people say 'every woman's experience of abortion is different'. Small wonder if moral philosophy cannot come up with the cut and dried answer to the question of whether abortion is always wrong or not. And small wonder if people think that moral philosophy could not offer any systematic or theoretical way of thinking about this rich complexity.

But in fact, the terms in which the last part of the discussion has been couched form the iceberg tip of a large system in moral philosophy, to an exposition of which I now turn.

NOTES

1 One might eventually gather that women find bearing children rather arduous from Glover's appeal to side-effects (Glover, *op. cit.*, p. 145).
2 Thomson, Judith Jarvis (1971) 'A Defense of Abortion', *Philosophy and Public Affairs*, vol. 1, no. 1. Reprinted in many places, including Singer, Peter (1986) *Applied Ethics*, Oxford University Press.
3 We shall not now be drawing any distinction between these two.
4 Thomson, *ibid*.
5 Glover, *op. cit.*, pp. 131–2, quoting Warren (1973) *op. cit.*

6 Finnis, John (1973) 'The Rights and Wrongs of Abortion', *Philosophy and Public Affairs*, vol. 2, no. 2.

7 Thomson, Judith Jarvis (1973), 'Rights and Deaths', *Philosophy and Public Affairs*, vol. 2, no. 2.

8 Thomson, 'A Defense of Abortion'.

9 See Chapter Two, Section 2, 'The conservative view', p. 41.

10 Warren, *op. cit.*

11 Thompson, *op. cit.*

CHAPTER SIX

Neo-Aristotelianism

1 INTRODUCTION

The aim of the last four chapters has been, one might say, basically destructive. In the second chapter I tried to show that it was not possible to settle the abortion issue in isolation simply by settling the moral status of the fœtus; any view about the latter involved committal on other issues. In the third and fourth chapters I tried to show what was wrong with trying to think about these issues – abortion, fœtal research, our treatment of animals, euthanasia, infanticide, etc. – in the crass terms of the person/non-person distinction, or in terms of utilitarianism. In the last chapter I was less critical of Thomson's general approach, but there too I attacked her arguments concerning killing or refusing to save, maintaining that simply thinking in terms of one's rights was insufficient. 'Well,' one might say, 'if we are not to think about these issues in terms of the person/non-person distinction, or utilitarianism, or rights, how *are* we to think about them?' This reasonable question is one to which I shall now try to provide an answer. The time has come to try to offer an alternative; a way of thinking ethically which, if it does not deliver simple good answers, at least does not deliver simplistic bad ones. So this whole chapter is devoted to moral theory; in it I outline and discuss a theory which, in my view, has the sort of richness and complexity which is needed for thinking about these issues.

In order not to arouse expectations that will not be fulfilled I should stress two points at the outset. One is that I am merely offering the theory; I do not argue for it, nor do I spend much time defending it against certain well-known objections. Just as the utilitarians, knowing that their theory has various problems, believe that these can eventually be overcome, so I and other supporters of this theory believe the same of ours. I do not expect my reader to find it beyond question or criticism; what I hope, is that it shall be found interesting and worthy of further consideration. The second point to be stressed is that I do not use the theory to provide the answers to our moral problems; indeed, as will emerge, it is built into the theory that I am not in a position to do so. I claim that the theory gives us the right way of thinking about the issues; I do not claim that, thinking in this way, I have yet managed to come up with the right thoughts.

Many modern moral theorists do moral philosophy in terms of a very limited vocabulary. Acts may be 'right' or 'wrong' or 'morally neutral/innocuous' (neither right nor wrong) and that is about it; this is the position in, for instance, Tooley's, Singer's and Glover's discussions. According to a different but equally limited vocabulary, acts may be 'obligatory' or 'impermissible' or 'permissible' and that is about it. (I more or less stayed within the confines of this vocabulary while outlining the various positions of the status of the fœtus in the second chapter.) Very often the moral character of agents rather than their acts is not mentioned at all; when it is, the descriptions tend to be limited to 'good person' and 'wicked person'.

Thomson's article nicely illustrates how this thin vocabulary might begin to be enriched and how important distinctions and points can be made thereby. For instance, rather than allowing only the blanket description 'wrong', she uses 'unjust', 'callous', 'selfish', etc. She is thereby able to say something much more substantial than that 'abortion is sometimes wrong and sometimes not'; she can say that sometimes it is unjust, sometimes callous, sometimes selfish ... and sometimes none of these things. Her distinction between the Minimally Decent and the Good Samaritan is clearly an advance on being limited to describing people as 'good' or 'wicked'.

However, Thomson's enrichment is only the beginning.

We have, in fact, an enormous vocabulary with which to describe people and their actions in ways relevant to morality. We may describe them, for instance, as courageous, honest, public-spirited, kind, fair, loyal, responsible ... and conversely as cowardly, dishonest, mean, anti-social, cruel, disloyal, feckless and so on. There is a particular way of doing moral philosophy which exploits this rich vocabulary and our familiarity with it, namely an approach that takes as basic the idea of *the virtues* (courage, honesty, generosity, justice, public-spiritedness, kindness, etc.), the agent who has some or all of the virtues (*the virtuous person* who is courageous, honest, generous, etc.), and the way she acts (*virtuously*, i.e. courageously, honestly, etc.). It also uses, unselfconsciously and without special inverted commas, the concept of *the worthwhile*, assuming – as any of us do when we use it in serious moral conversation – that, difficult as it may be to define, it has at least some straightforward applications.

This way of doing moral philosophy derives from the ancient Greek philosophers Plato and Aristotle, most particularly from the latter. It might seem incredible that ancient Greek moral philosophy could have any useful application to our modern age; must it not be even more remote from us, even more outdated, than ancient Greek science? But, surprising as it may be, this is not so. It is true that one needs to adapt, to supplement, and to depart from, what Aristotle says to a certain extent; hence the 'neo-' in the title of this chapter. It is also true that the ancient Greek view of ethics differs in certain important respects from our modern one, and contains at least one concept which it is very difficult to translate. So understanding neo-Aristotelian theory requires a slight shift of focus and a little patience.

2 THE THEORY OUTLINED

In order to give the theory a chance of appearing plausible I need space in which to set it out. So the next section of the chapter is devoted exclusively to introducing it, and I would ask my reader, for the moment, simply to forget about the issues with which we have been concerned, and concentrate only on the theory.

The later sections of this chapter, and the next chapter, are also theoretical in that they involve reflecting neo-Aristotelianism back on the theories of the person view and utilitarianism. Although I have criticized these two positions so unsympathetically, it is no part of my project to deny that they have something in them – if they had not, presumably not so many people would have found them plausible. There is, we might suppose, something significant in the person/non-person distinction. After all, the initial argument for it looked plausible. Similarly, there is surely *some* form of speciesism which is wrong, and, just as surely, something right about utilitarianism. If neo-Aristotelianism is as good a theory as I claim it is, it must be able to accommodate those good aspects of the inferior theories while remaining free of their errors and limitations. In the later sections of this chapter, and in the next, I try to show that the theory can indeed do this. This also serves the purpose of allowing for further exposition and explanation of the theory. But now let me introduce it.

I said above that the ancient Greek view of ethics differs in certain important respects from our modern one, and hence that understanding it requires a slight shift of focus. One difference emerges at the very outset.

We are accustomed to thinking about ethics or moral philosophy as concerned with the rightness and wrongness of actions. Is (all) abortion wrong? Would it be right to abort a fœtus that was going to become a baby who suffered very greatly? Is (all) infanticide wrong? These are the sorts of questions to which ethics or moral philosophy is supposed to provide answers. But the ancient Greeks start with a totally different sort of question; ethics is supposed to answer, for each one of us, the question 'How am I to live well?' What this question means and does not mean calls for some discussion.

'How am I to live well?'

This question can be expressed in a variety of ways; none is perfect, but one comes to understand it in grasping the variety.

How should/ought/must I live in order to live the best life/ flourish/be successful?

The first comment that needs to be made is that one should not be misled by the presence of so-called 'value' words ('well', 'should', 'best', 'must', 'ought') into thinking that these are specifically *moral* words. For then one will under-stand the question as 'How am I to live *morally* well?' 'What is the *morally* best life?' 'How should I live from the *moral* point of view?' And although, as we shall see, one would not be entirely wrong to do so, it is not the proper understanding of the question. We should/must/ought not read in a 'morally' qualification, any more than we would at the beginning of this sentence, or in such questions as 'How am I to do well in the exam?' 'How should/must/ ought I get to the station from here?' We would not take the latter, for instance, to mean 'How should I get to the station from here from the moral point of view?' or 'What is the moral way of getting to the station from here?' Similarly, we should not take any of the given versions of the ancient Greek question as having this sort of qualification either. This point shows up particularly clearly in any versions involving 'flourish' and 'be successful' – compare 'How should . . . etc. this plant be treated in order that it will flourish?' and 'How ought I to study if I am to be a successful student?' where once again we would not think for a moment that these were moral 'shoulds' or 'oughts'.

The next comment that needs to be made is also about these versions, about what is meant by 'flourish' and 'successful'. 'Flourishing' is one of the standard translations of the Greek word *eudaimonia*, and this is the concept that I said was very difficult to translate. It is used in ways which lead us to translate it (when it is an abstract noun) as 'good fortune', 'happiness', 'prosperity', 'flourishing', 'success', 'the best/good life'; where it is an adjective applied to a person it is translated as 'fortunate', 'happy', 'prospering', 'flourishing', 'successful', 'living well'.[1] The extent to which any one of these is and is not an adequate translation can be seen by comparing what we say about them and what

Aristotle says about *eudaimonia*. For a start, he tells us that it is what we all want to get in life (or get out of it); what we are all aiming at, ultimately; the way we all want to be. And, he says, we all agree in one sense about what it consists in, namely, living well or faring well. But another truth about it is that we can disagree about what it consists in too, to the point where some of us can say it consists in wealth, others that it consists in pleasure or enjoyment and others that it consists of honour or virtue.

What do we say about success and prospering? Well, 'successful' and 'prosperous' have a materialistic sense in which they connote wealth and power; when we use them in this way it is obvious to us (a) that one can be happy and count oneself as fortunate without them and (b) that they do not necessarily bring with them happiness and the good fortune of loyal friends, loving relationships, the joys of art and learning and so on. So many of us will say that (material) success and prosperity are not what we want; that having them does not amount to faring well. But 'success' has a non-materialistic sense as well. Someone who possesses wealth and power may yet count her life to be not a success but a failure, perhaps because she finds herself to be unhappy and lonely and lacking the conviction that anything she does is worthwhile. Similarly, someone who lacks wealth and power may still count their lives to be a success – 'I am rich in the things that matter', one says, 'My children, my friends, my books, my memories, my job . . .' And it is the possibility of this non-material sense of 'success' which makes it a suitable translation of '*eudaimonia*'. Perhaps nowadays 'prosperous' can have only the materialistic sense, but the non-materialistic one still lurks in 'May you prosper', the wishes for a prosperous New Year, and indeed in the non-materialistic use of 'rich' I just exploited above.

My discussion here of two different senses should not be taken to imply that the word 'success' is literally ambiguous. In describing the lives of many people as successful one will not necessarily be meaning 'successful in one sense rather than another'. For it is no accident that the word has these different senses, since so many people believe that wealth and power are things that matter, are things one is fortunate in having, because they bring happiness. Hence too, the materialistic interpretation that can be given to 'the good life' or 'being well (or better) off'. This was as true of the ancient Greeks as it is of us; which is why some people say that *eudaimonia* consists in having wealth.

I said above that one of the truths that determines the concept of *eudaimonia* is that it is something everyone wants, the way everyone wants to be. Someone who said that she did not want to be *eudaimon* would be incomprehensible. Some philosophers, for instance John Stuart Mill, have maintained that this is true of happiness, and 'happiness' is certainly the most common translation that has been given. 'True (or real) happiness' would be better, since we tend to say that someone may be happy (though not truly happy) if they are living in a fool's paradise, or engaged in what we know is a fruitless activity, or brain-damaged and leading the life of a happy child; whereas such people are not flourishing or leading successful lives and none of us would want to be that way.

But even 'true (or real) happiness' is not obviously something everyone wants – unless, as I am sure was true of Mill, one is already thinking of 'true happiness' as *eudaimonia*. For, thinking of (true) happiness as something like (well-founded) contentment or satisfaction or enjoyment, one might intelligibly deny that one wanted to be happy. For surely one can think that happiness is not the most important thing in life; 'We're not put on this earth to enjoy ourselves' people say. I might want not just to be happy, but to do great deeds, discover great truths, change the world for the better, no matter what it cost me in terms of happiness.

Of course, rather than saying, 'No matter what it cost me in terms of happiness', I might say instead, 'Then I would die happy' or 'Then I would count myself as happy or content, no matter what it cost me'. This, I think, shows that 'happiness' does not have to connote bovine contentment or a life full of pleasure and free from striving and suffering; and as above, it is the possibility of this second sense – happiness despite a lot of striving, effort and suffering – which makes it a suitable translation of '*eudaimonia*'. Once again, as with 'success', the word 'happiness' is not ambiguous. It is no accident that it has these different senses since so many people do want contentment and a life that is pleasurable and enjoyable without cost.

Bearing all these points in mind, let us return to our question 'How am I to live well?' and its various versions 'How should/ought/must I live in order to flourish/be happy/successful?' We have seen that when 'success', etc. are construed in the intended way, this is a question that any one of us is bound to be interested in because we all want to flourish/be happy/successful; the very idea that someone interested in life should not want to 'make a go of it' in this way is deeply puzzling.[2] This, one might say, contrasts with wanting to be *morally* successful or wanting to lead a *morally* good life – there is nothing puzzling about someone who does not want to do that. As we noted above, the 'should/ought/must' in the various versions of the question should not be given a particularly moral reading; any more than they would be in 'How should/ought/must I live in order to be healthy?'

So much for the discussion of what the question means. But now we are clear about that, a new difficulty arises. How can the question, understood in the right way, possibly have anything to do with ethics or moral philosophy? If we understand it as asking 'How am I to live morally well?' we can see why it counts as a question for ethics to (try to) answer. But this interpretation is the one that has just been carefully ruled out. It now seems to be an entirely self-seeking or egoistic question which has nothing to do with ethics.

Another obstacle we have in understanding the ancient Greek view of ethics is that it does not embody the contrast, between the moral on the one hand and the self-seeking or egoistic on the other, which this new difficulty relies on. But the obstacle may be surmounted by looking carefully at the answer Aristotle gives to this question that apparently has nothing to do with ethics.

His answer is: 'If you want to flourish/be happy/successful you should acquire and practise the virtues – courage, justice, benevolence or charity, honesty, fidelity (in the sense of being true to one's word or promise), generosity, kindness, compassion, friendship . . .', i.e. as we might say 'You should be a morally virtuous person'.[3]

'Be a morally virtuous person'

With this answer we are clearly back in the business of doing ethics, but how could this have come about when we started with the self-seeking or egoistic question?

The claim that is basic to this Aristotelian view is that it comes about because, as human beings, we naturally have certain emotions and tendencies, and that it is simply a brute fact (made up of a vastly complex set of other facts) that *given* that we are as we naturally are, we can only flourish/ be happy/successful by developing those character traits that are called the virtues – courage, justice, benevolence and so on. This has to be argued for each character trait that is said to be a virtue and all I can do here is illustrate briefly and roughly how the argument goes and what sorts of facts are appealed to.

Consider one of the simplest cases – generosity. Here are some of the relevant facts. We are naturally sociable creatures who like to have friends and want to be loved by friends and family. We also like and love people who do things for us rather than always putting themselves first. We also (and this is important) are not merely sympathetic but empathetic; the distress of others may distress us and their pleasure may be pleasurable to us. Given that this is how we are, someone who is mean and selfish is unlikely to be liked and loved and hence likely to be lonely and unhappy; someone who is generous is likely to enjoy the benefits of being liked and loved and moreover, in the exercise of their generosity will derive much added enjoyment, for the pleasures of those they benefit will be pleasures to them.

Consider another case – honesty. Amongst the relevant facts here are some that are similar to the preceding ones – that we want friends, want them to be trustworthy, want them to trust us – and some that are rather different, for instance, that there are likely to be occasions in our lives when we need to be believed (as the many fables on the theme of too often crying 'wolf!' illustrate). Folk wisdom also contains the adage that 'honesty is the best policy' and the conviction that 'the truth will out' to the discomfort of those who have lied. The exercise of this virtue is not as immediately enjoyable as the exercise of generosity so often is, but the honest person has the advantage of not having to keep a constant guard on her tongue and has peace of mind thereby. One should also note that the honest person can tell the truth effortlessly in circumstances where it would be embarrassing, frightening, unpleasant or unfortunately impossible for the person who does not have the virtue. Literature abounds with scenes in which a character desperately needs to tell the truth, for if she does not, a profound relationship in her life is going to be destroyed – she will lose her lover, or her closest friend will feel betrayed, or her son will turn in bitterness from her, or she will put herself in the hands of the blackmailer or ... to her subsequent irremediable regret and misery. But the truth in question is one of those truths it is hard to own up to – and she cannot bring herself to do so. But had she armed herself with the virtue of honesty she would have been able to. Much more could be said here too about the harm one does oneself through self-deception and how difficult it is to be simultaneously ruthlessly honest with oneself but dishonest to other people.

Even more than honesty, courage is a character trait one needs to arm oneself with, given that we are as we are – subject to death and pain and frightened of them. It is not so much that we need courage to endure pain and face death as ends in themselves, but that we are likely to have to face the threat of pain or danger for the sake of some good which we shall otherwise lose. One might imagine that someone in the position of the person I mentioned in the last chapter, who had the opportunity to save someone's life by donating their bone marrow and did not do it, was someone who saw this as a wonderful opportunity to do good but lacked the courage to do it. This might well be a source of deep regret, and how much more bitter the regret would be if one's cowardice led to the death of someone one loved. If I have managed to make myself courageous I am ready to

save my child from the burning house or car at whatever
risk to myself, to stand up to the terrorists who threaten
my friends' lives and to my racist neighbours who are trying
to hound me and my family from our home. In a society
in which cancer has become one of the commonest ways to
die we also need courage to enable us to die well, not only
so that we may not waste the last years or months of our
lives but also for the sake of the people we love who love
us.

Now all the above is schematic. I do not pretend to have
shown conclusively that generosity, honesty and courage
are necessary if one is to flourish/be (truly) happy/successful,
and of course much of what I have said is open to detailed
disagreement. I cannot go through many of the details here,
but I will discuss one pair of objections that spring very
naturally to mind, since the responses to them form part of
the further exposition.

Two objections

The two objections one might want to make are that,
contrary to what has been claimed, the virtues are surely
neither (a) necessary nor (b) sufficient for flourishing/being
(truly) happy or successful. Not necessary because, as we
all know, the wicked may flourish like the green bay tree;
not sufficient because my generosity, honesty and courage,
for example, might, any one of them, lead to my being
harmed or indeed to my whole life being ruined or ended.

How, to take the latter objection first, do we envisage
that my virtue might lead to my downfall? It is not quite
right to say that it is obviously the case that, having the
virtue of generosity, I might fall foul of a lot of people who
exploit me and rip me off, or find myself poverty-stricken.
For built into each concept of a virtue is the idea of getting
things *right*: in the case of generosity giving the *right* amount
of things for the *right* reasons on the *right* occasions to the
right people. 'The right amount' in many cases is 'the amount
I can afford' or 'the amount I can give without depriving
someone else'. So, for instance, I do not count as mean, nor
even as ungenerous when, being relatively poor, or fairly

well off but with a large and demanding family, I do not give lavish presents to richer friends at Christmas. Nor do I count as mean or even ungenerous if I refuse to let people exploit me; generosity does not require me to help support someone who is simply bone idle, nor to finance the self-indulgence of a spendthrift. Any virtue may contrast with several vices or failings and generosity is to be contrasted not only with meanness or selfishness but also with being prodigal, too open-handed, a sucker.

Once this point is borne in mind, examples in which I may suffer because of my virtue are considerably less easy to find. Nevertheless, there are some; sudden financial disaster might befall many of us, leaving the generous in dire straits where the mean do much better. Just as, in the past, people have been burnt at the stake for refusing to lie about what they believed, so now, under some regimes people are shut in asylums, and subjected to enforced drugging for the same reason, while the hypocrites remain free. My courage may lead me to go to the defence of someone being attacked in the street but to no avail and with the result that I am killed or maimed for life while the coward goes through her life unscathed. Given these possibilities, how can anyone claim that the question 'How am I to flourish?' is to be honestly answered by saying 'Be virtuous'?

There are two possible responses to this. One response is to grit one's teeth and deny that the virtuous person can be harmed by her possession of virtue. To be virtuous *is* to flourish, to be (truly) happy or successful; nothing counts as being harmed except doing evil and nothing counts as a genuine advantage, or being better off, than doing what is right. There is more than a grain of truth in this view, to which I shall return in a minute, but, on the face of it, it is, as a response to the sorts of examples we have envisaged, simply absurd. As Aristotle says, 'Those who maintain that, provided he is good, a man is happy (*eudaimon*) on the rack or when fallen among great misfortunes are talking nonsense . . .' (The point of these examples is that I become unable to exercise virtue either because I am dead, or because I have become physically, mentally or materially incapable of doing so.)

The second response is to deny that the answer to the question was ever supposed to offer a guarantee. If I ask my doctor 'How am I to flourish physically/be healthy?' she gives me the right answer when she says 'Give up smoking, don't work with asbestos, lose weight, take some exercise . . .' Even if, despite following her advice, I subsequently develop lung cancer or heart disease, this does not impugn its correctness; I cannot go back to her and say 'You were wrong to tell me I should give up smoking, etc.' She and I both know that doing as she says does not guarantee perfect health; nevertheless, if perfect health is what I want, the only thing I can do to achieve it is follow her advice. Continuing to smoke, work with asbestos, etc. is asking for trouble – even though, it is agreed, I may be lucky and live to be ninety.

Similarly, the claim is not that being virtuous guarantees that one will flourish. It is, rather, probabilistic – 'true for the most part', as Aristotle says. Virtue is the only reliable bet; it will probably bring flourishing – though, it is agreed, I might be very unlucky and because of my virtue, wind up on the rack. So virtue is not being made out to be guaranteed sufficient for flourishing.

But now we return to the first objection. Is virtue not being made out to be necessary? It was just said to be the *only* reliable bet, as if, as in the medical case, making no effort to acquire the virtues was asking for trouble. But don't the wicked, as we said above (p. 228), flourish? In which case virtue cannot be necessary.

The two possible responses to this objection are elaborations on the two that were given to the other. The first denies that the wicked ever do flourish, for nothing counts as having an advantage or being well off or . . . except doing what is right. The second, continuing to pursue the medical analogy, still insists that virtue is the only reliable bet and, agreeing that *sometimes* the non-virtuous flourish, maintains that this is, like fat smokers living to be ninety, rare and a matter of luck. So, for instance, it is usually true that people who are entirely selfish and inconsiderate miss out on being loved, but such a person might be lucky enough to be blessed with particular beauty or charm of manner, or by lucky chance come across someone else very loving who fell for them completely in the mysterious way that sometimes happens. But, the claim is, we can all recognize that this *is* a matter of luck – one could never rely on it.

However, many people may feel that this response is implausible. 'It is not simply by pure chance and luck that non-virtuous people flourish', it might be said. 'Power is just as good a bet as virtue, if not a better one, for flourishing. If you have power, people will, as a matter of fact, love you for that; you will be respected and honoured – and all despite the fact that in order to get and maintain power you will undoubtedly have to be selfish, dishonest, unjust, callous ... to a certain extent. So the answer to "How am I to flourish?" should not be "Acquire virtue" but "Acquire power".'

This objection can be seen as a form of one of the oldest, and still current, debates in moral philosophy. In Plato's *Republic* it takes on a form specifically related to the virtue of justice: if injustice is more profitable than justice to the man of strength, then practising injustice is surely the best way of life for the strong. Its most modern version is entirely general: 'What reason have I to be moral?' One very important question it raises is whether morality, or moral judgements, provide reasons for everyone for acting. If some action is wrong, ought not to be done (because, say, it is dishonest or unjust), does this mean that everyone has a reason not to do it, or is it open to the powerful to say truly that there is no reason for them to refrain?

What, then, should be said about this old, but still hotly debated issue? When we were considering how 'success' could work as a translation of '*eudaimonia*' we noted that one could be successful in a material sense – wealthy and powerful – while still counting one's life not a success but a failure, because, say, one felt lonely and unfulfilled. Now consider someone who is (a) successful in the materialistic sense, (b) non-virtuous – they have acquired their power by cheating and lying, ruthlessly sacrificing people when it suited them, but (c) perfectly happy – they do not feel guilty, or lonely, or unfulfilled or that their life is a failure in any way. The question we then ask ourselves is: do we find this person's life enviable or desirable? And the 'grain of truth' I said was contained in the view that nothing counts as a genuine advantage or being better off than doing what is right is that many of us are going to say 'No'. We may be hard put to explain *why* we say 'No'; perhaps we cannot say anything more than that we could not live like that, or that we would not want to have cheated our friends or to have let our parents or children down. But our inability to say more than this does not matter; all that matters is that we can view a life containing every apparent benefit and advantage as one that we do not want because it contains having acted wrongly in various ways.

To anyone who thinks this way, Aristotle's answer to 'How am I to flourish?' is going to emerge as the only possible answer. 'Acquire power' was, in any case, an answer that could only recommend itself to the minority who thought they could achieve this, and it now appears that even if I count myself as part of this minority, I may still not regard the acquisition of power as something that will give me the life I want.

The limitations of the answer

Aristotle's view allows that his answer will not work for everyone. It fails for two different sorts of people. One is the sort of person who has been sufficiently corrupted by their upbringing not to be able to see anything amiss in the life of the person who is 'successfully' non-virtuous. It is an important part of his view, and of neo-Aristotelianism generally, that there really is something amiss to be seen; it is not just that those of us who find the life unenviable see things one way and those who find it enviable see things differently. And I should mention here that this is one area of neo-Aristotelianism which is well-known to be problematic. Opponents of the theory insist that the admission that the answer fails in this way is fatal, and commits neo-Aristotelianism to denying that there is any truth or objectivity in claims about what counts as a flourishing or successful human life. Once it is admitted that people who are not intellectually lacking may see things differently from the upholders of virtue, and admitted further that no process of rational argument will get them to see things any other way, once these two points are admitted, it is clear that there can be no truth about the matter. It is not that the upholders of virtue are seeing things correctly, as they really are, while the corrupted are making mistakes. There is no question here of 'correctness' or 'mistakes' or 'how things really are', just two different attitudes, or sets of reactions or preferences, or ways of seeing the world, neither of which can lay claim to being the correct one.

Supporters of the theory maintain that this objection relies on an inappropriate conception of truth, objectivity and reality, a conception which works well enough when applied to physics but won't work when applied to either morals or human psychology. To say even that much is, I hope, to show that there is no point in my pretending to settle this issue here. It is currently one of the major disputes in philosophy, with ramifications in the philosophy of language and of mind as well as in moral philosophy. I believe that 'our side' is going to win; but I would not want to conceal the fact that there is a large question mark here.

The other sort of person for whom Aristotle's answer may not work would be an 'unnatural' human being, an exception that brings us back to the beginning of the discussion of how 'You should acquire and practise the virtues' could be an answer to 'How should I live in order to flourish?'

I said that this came about because, *qua* human beings, we naturally have certain emotions and tendencies such that, as a matter of brute fact, we can only flourish by developing those character traits that are called the virtues. We are, for example, naturally sociable creatures who . . . and so on. But facts about what is natural to a species are only ever facts about what is true of most of their members. As a species we are sighted, but some people are born blind; as a species we are five-fingered and five-toed, but some people are born with extra (or fewer) fingers or toes. As a species we are sociable, but this does not rule out the possibility that some of us may be born solitary types – 'natural' hermits, and thereby 'unnatural' human beings. If there are people who by nature do not enjoy the company of others and feel out of place sharing our communal life (it is thought possible that (some) psychopaths are such people) then the Aristotelian answer may fail in such a case, precisely because it fails to connect with what such a person wants. However, it is worth noting that, even in this case, it may well be that the Aristotelian answer is better than any other for such a person, for it may be that he wants other things that necessitate his associating with other people. Suppose, for instance, that he prefers solitude to company but also desires knowledge. Well, we do not live long enough to acquire much knowledge on our own; if he wants knowledge this person needs teachers, advisers and eventually intellectual peers to learn from. He will need justice to govern his dealings with them, and also honesty and generosity at least in respect of the sharing of discoveries. Someone for whom the Aristotelian answer failed completely would be someone very odd indeed.

Nevertheless, he exists as a possibility, and this is another area that some people find unsatisfactory about neo–Aristotelianism. It is deeply embedded in our thinking about ethics that in *some* sense it 'applies' to everyone. *If* people take that sense to involve ethics providing reasons for action for everyone then they may want to reject neo-Aristotelianism on the grounds that it does not yield such a result. This too is a debate that I cannot begin to settle here; however, in relation to it I should mention the very important senses in which neo-Aristotelianism does have general application to nearly all, albeit not quite all, human beings. For they are, I suspect, essential to the very possibility of ethics or morality as a subject-matter. If they were not true, morality would not exist, or would be unimaginably different.

According to neo-Aristotelianism, in brief, human beings are 'for the most part' (a) the sorts of creatures that can flourish, and (b) do so in the same way as each other, and (c) flourish side by side, all together, not at each other's expense. The significance of these three points emerges most clearly when we see under what conditions each would be false.

For instance, (a) would be false if we were characteristically neurotic, bent on misery and self-destruction and in some sense genuinely not interested in flourishing. It would also be false if we characteristically had bad emotional tendencies which were uncontrollable. (It is certainly part of Aristotelian theory that we are subject to bad emotional tendencies, but also part of it that they can all be trained to accord harmoniously with each other and with reason.) It would also be false if certain racist or sexist claims were true. Some of these have indeed amounted to claiming that to be a black or a female human being is to be subject to uncontrollable emotional tendencies which make it impossible that one should flourish – at least in this life. But according to neo-Aristotelianism, (nearly) all of us can flourish. We can make our lives successful in the fullest sense.

(b) would be false if another sort of sexist claim were true; if, for instance, men and women really were so different that different virtues and vices were appropriate to them. It is implicit in what some people have said that courage is a male virtue and compassion a female one, as if women did not need courage, and cowardice was no vice in them, and men did not need compassion, and callousness was no vice in them. But according to neo-Aristotelianism, the same answer to 'How should I live?' works for each of us in (nearly) every case.

(c) would be false if, facetiously, we were vampires. More seriously, it would be false if something like Mother Teresa's life, a life devoted to the relief of human suffering, really were the best life for a human being. For, without in any way decrying her, it must be said that her life is predicated on, not only the suffering, but also the evil actions, of others. If her life were paradigm, ideal, human flourishing then we couldn't all flourish. A less surprising way for (c) to be false would be the answer we were considering earlier, 'Acquire power'. If exercising power were the best life for a human being then, once again, not every human being can lead the best life. If there are to be flourishing human beings who get their own way by pushing other people around, there must be some non-flourishing ones who get pushed.

Closely related to this answer would be (something like) the Homeric one, that the best life is the one of military endeavour and glory. Centuries of literature have represented this life as noble and honourable and perhaps indeed it can be. But it does require that the condition of human life be war, not peace, and in war many people's lives are the reverse of flourishing. But it is built into the answer given by neo-Aristotelianism that, in theory, it can work not only for (nearly) each one of us but also for (nearly) all of us.

It is a contingent fact that we are one of the sorts of creatures who can only flourish living together, and another contingent fact that in theory, ideally, we can *all* flourish living together. If the latter were not true – if it were part of the concept of a flourishing human life that not everyone could lead it, even ideally and in theory – then, I suspect, the whole history of Western moral philosophy would have been different.

Notoriously, Aristotle himself did not, in fact, believe that we could all flourish. Embarrassingly for his supporters (particularly his female ones) he not only believed that some people were 'naturally' slaves, but also that women were, as such, defective human beings. But his lamentable parochialism in these matters does not infect the theory; his (and Plato's) concept of a flourishing human life as something that, ideally and in theory, we could all lead together, persisted through the moral philosophy of the Romans and became part of Christianity. Subsequent generations of Western moral philosophers have been students of the ancient Greek and Roman moral philosophy, or been Christian; indeed, until very recently, most have been both. Some aspects of Judæo-Christian morality do not mesh well with ancient Greek ethics, but others have meshed so well that it is now extremely difficult to be clear about which aspects of our moral thinking are genuinely secular and which require a theological backing to make sense. The rather general idea that morality 'applies' to everyone, or that everyone 'ought' to be moral, or has reason to be moral, no matter how 'unnatural' or atypical a human being they are, is doubtless connected (whether one realizes it or not) with the Judæo-Christian idea that no human being can escape God's commands, and with the Christian idea that any human being, no matter how psychologically odd, has an immortal soul which can be saved or lost by acting as virtue requires. But it also, I suspect, is connected (once again, whether one realizes it or not) with the Aristotelian idea that the best life for (nearly) all human beings is the life we live together, practising the virtues to our mutual benefit and enjoyment.

3   THE THEORY APPLIED TO ANIMALS

At the beginning of this chapter, I said I would be reflecting neo-Aristotelianism back on the theories considered in the earlier chapters and trying to show that it could accommodate what was right about them. This will also serve the further purpose of continuing with the exposition of the theory, clearing up some points that will have been left unclear in the previous section. The theoretical backing to the person view was the general idea that morality is not essentially about human beings – members of a certain species – but about *persons*; and although, as I argued, there is much that is wrong with this idea, there is certainly something right about it too. So I shall now turn to the quite general question of whether there is something wrong with saying that morality is species-specific – a question that one can reasonably wonder about quite independently of the views one holds about the neutrality or wrongness of abortion and infanticide. If saying this is 'speciesism' what, if anything, is wrong with speciesism? Why is it so tempting to say that morality cannot be (just) about human beings as such?

There are, I think, two quite different intuitions behind this. One is (very roughly) the idea that morality cannot just be about human beings because it would obviously be very wicked of us to treat a species of aliens the way we treat, say, sheep, if they were a species of *persons*. I shall discuss this view in the next section.

The second intuition is the view enshrined in the quotation

from Bentham (p. 148 above) that with respect to the infliction of gratuitous suffering, *the* question is not 'Are they human?' but 'Can they suffer?' If one says that morality is essentially concerned with human beings as such, that they are the ones who matter morally, it seems that at worst this entails that no treatment of animals, however frightful, counts as wrong, or at best that torturing them might count as incidentally or derivatively wrong, through making the torturer more likely to beat his children for example. And many people want to say that much of our treatment of animals *is* wrong and not merely incidentally so but intrinsically so. Morality cannot deal only with how human beings should treat other human beings, leaving animals out of account. So it cannot be (just) about human beings as such. (Though note that this intuition does not give one any reason for introducing 'person', since *the* Benthamite question is not 'Are they persons?' either.) Well, is neo–Aristotelianism 'just about human beings as such'?

The question neo–Aristotelianism answers is, 'How should *I* live in order to flourish?' This began by sounding like an egoistic or self-centred question, calling for an answer particularly tailored to *my* requirements. But the plausibility of the answer that can be given to (almost) any one of us, 'You should be virtuous', an answer that depended on facts about what (nearly) all of us are naturally like, shows that in a way the question was not necessarily about *me* at all. I might have asked instead 'What's the best way for me, as a human being, to live?' or indeed, given that I am not a human being in any idiosyncratic way, I might have asked quite generally 'What's the best way for a human being to live? What constitutes a flourishing/successful/human life?' And the answer, 'Acting virtuously, i.e. being honest, generous, just, courageous, benevolent, compassionate ...', though not tailor-made to my individual characteristics, is tailor-made to the specific characteristics of human beings. It is species-specific.

It is clear that, in being species-specific, the view of morality just outlined is guaranteed to be 'about' human beings as such in the same sort of way that medicine, concerned with the question(s) 'How should we human beings live in order to be healthy?' (or 'What's the healthiest way for a human being to live?'), is about human beings as such, not about other terrestrial animals (or imaginable aliens). Does it then run counter to the intuition about animals?

Clearly not, for what we have now discovered is an innocuous way for morality to be 'about' human beings. That morality is 'about' human beings as such, in the way that has now been outlined, in no way entails or even suggests that moral rules or principles are concerned *only* with how human beings should treat other human beings, leaving animals (and aliens) out of account. So this version of the claim that morality is essentially about human beings need not be thought of as being in opposition to the intuition about animals.

Indeed, if one thinks that the wickedness and folly of our present treatment of animals goes far beyond our infliction of gratuitous suffering on them, neo-Aristotelianism may well be the only available theory which gives one the background to argue for this.

As we have seen (p. 154), utilitarianism cannot protect animals from being exploited to satisfy our trivial or self-indulgent or even cruel desires unless it starts appealing to some ideals about what sort of 'happiness' or 'pleasure' we are supposed to be maximizing. If by 'happiness' is meant something more akin to *eudaimonia*, then it will indeed be possible to draw distinctions between pleasures that should not be indulged and pleasures that should, between desires that should not be satisfied and desires that should. But making any such move towards *eudaimonia* involves moving away from consequentialism; acts become intrinsically right or wrong, rather than simply right or wrong according to their consequences. Moreover, as we saw (p. 152), the quite general problem utilitarianism has in giving any account of why killing is wrong guarantees that only the *ad hoc* introduction of a number of non-utilitarian principles or considerations can impose what many will want to say are the correct moral restrictions on our treatment of animals.

A theory which corrects the most notorious flaws in utilitarianism by appealing to rights runs into grave difficulties if it tries to ascribe appropriate rights to all animals but becomes implausibly *ad hoc* when just some are ascribed to some. It also becomes simply incoherent when rights are ascribed to species *per se* (e.g. the right of The Whale, though not of any individual whale, to exist.)

Moreover, neither of these sorts of theories apparently has any direct connection with what non-philosophers deeply concerned about our treatment of animals talk about. Many of them emphasize the wonder and beauty of the animal kingdom, showing how touching and lovable, or strange and fascinating, instructive, inspiring, amusing, life-enhancing and so on animals are or can be, and the emphasis goes along with a more generalized stress on the environment and our relation to it. Factory farming not only involves animal suffering but is also deplored as expressive of the general attitude to nature which has led to the destruction of hedges, the creation of dust-bowls, the introduction of cheap or visually attractive food which is poisoning us and so on.

It might be said that much of this is typical, non-philosophical, emotional waffle which the philosopher has to systematize, sorting out the wheat from the chaff. But even supposing that is so (a large supposition), there is no reason to assume initially that the only grains of wheat or truth are either (a) that animals can suffer (the truth isolated by utilitarianism) or (b) that animals have rights (the (probable) falsehood isolated by rights-theorists).

I would not claim for a moment that these few paragraphs show that utilitarianism and rights-based theories cannot provide a suitable background for arguing against our current treatment of animals; I wanted only to suggest the most obvious difficulties to highlight what neo-Aristotelianism has to offer.

The virtue of 'animal-concern'

On a neo-Aristotelian view one would immediately think of casting one's theoretical net well beyond just suffering or rights. Just as generosity is having the right attitude to personal possessions, and courage the right attitude to danger and death, so we could maintain that there is a virtue which consists in having the right attitude to animals. There are a number of ways in which we can go wrong in relation to animals and this virtue (let us christen it, for the moment, 'animal-concern') would be the corrective to all of them. So, at its simplest, granted that it is cruel and callous to inflict unnecessary suffering on animals, the virtue of animal-concern rules that out.

But 'having the right attitude' involves much more than that. One cannot have the right (i.e. correct) attitude to something if the attitude involves a lot of false beliefs about it, and 'the ways in which we can go wrong in relation to animals' covers the variety of false beliefs about them we are prone to. These include, for instance, both 'animals are so much better – wiser, more innocent, more understanding ... than we are' which can give rise to the failings of sentimentality or misanthropy, and also 'animals are so inferior to us – so irrational, savage, asocial ...'. This last belief, particularly when it involves smugness about oneself *just* because one is rational, can give rise to such a wide variety of failings that it is unsurprising that animal lovers and 'liberationists' find themselves fighting on so many fronts at once, in the way I have sketched (very briefly) above.

'Having the right attitude' to something, when this is a virtue, not only involves having true beliefs about it and acting properly in relation to it, but also doing the latter willingly or gladly, because one's feelings as well as one's reason prompt one to act in that way. If it is true that we should not be inflicting gratuitous suffering on animals, or killing them off, then it should be possible for us to find these actions painful or distressing. Moreover, if it is true that we should be increasing their happiness and preserving them then it should be possible for us to find these actions pleasant and enjoyable.

That such feelings are possible, at least with respect to particular animals, is something that animal lovers and liberationists emphasize and encourage. They are sometimes accused by their opponents of 'being emotive' or 'appealing to people's emotions' as though this were guaranteed to be somehow wrong and non-rational. But this accusation embodies a confusion about what the proper business of moral argument is. Part of the point of publicizing the suffering of animals in factory-farming and laboratories is to get us to make our emotions engage with the facts rather than allowing ourselves the irrational comfort of false belief. To think 'Oh, what's going on isn't so very terrible' is, for many of us, a comfortable but entirely ill-grounded belief; there is nothing inconsistent with the canons of reasoned debate in the animal liberationists' saying, at length, in detail and with photographs, '*This* is what is going on'.

The writings of some also illustrate how, in many cases, increased knowledge of particular species may simply change our emotional reactions to them and it is in this connection that the appeal to the wonder and beauty of the details of the animal kingdom appears as more than mere rhetoric. We are, psychologically, the sort of creature that comes to care about things which we find interesting. Someone who has been enthralled by the details of the ways in which bees live, probably (though, I agree, not necessarily) ceases to swat them as uncaringly as she used to.

Finally, in order to make out that a certain character-trait – a pattern of acts and feelings (and hence reactions) – such as 'animal-concern' is a virtue, one has to make out that it benefits its possessor, that a typical human being is better off with this character-trait than without it. For it is virtues that answer the question 'What's the best way for a human being to be?' How this relates in detail to the tautology that it is 'best' not to 'go wrong' is a major question in neo-Aristotelianism and cannot be considered here. But it is not hard, I think, to see how one would begin to argue that 'animal-concern' would indeed benefit us. Our lives are enriched by our relations to animals we love, and seeing ourselves and them clearly as all part of the same environment would save us from many mistakes. Even if it were maintained (as I think is plausible) that as things are in the world at the moment, a highly developed 'animal-concern' would be inappropriate, assuming that many people in the Third World could not maintain it and survive, that would not show that 'animal-concern' was not a virtue. For we are talking about the *best* way for a human being to live, and that is quite consistent with maintaining that we have made such a mess of things so far that it is not possible for human beings to live the best way.

Having recalled the 'egoistic' aspect of neo-Aristotelianism, I must say something to block what may seem an obvious objection to 'animal-concern'. It may seem that, contrary to part of the intuition about animals, neo-Aristotelianism will grant animals only derivative, not intrinsic value. If I go in for 'animal-concern' because I believe it will benefit me, this human being, and if, in general, we should go in for 'animal-concern' because it will benefit us, the human beings, as neo-Aristotelianism holds, is this not just as wrongly anthropocentric as a view that says it is wrong to torture animals (simply) because doing so will make us more likely to hurt or torture each other?

To say this is to make a standard mistake about Aristotelianism, to confuse two separate issues. In maintaining that honesty, for example, is a virtue, that a human being has reason to acquire and practise it because it is part of flourishing, i.e. will benefit its possessor, I do not say anything about the reason the virtuous person has for telling the truth on any particular occasion. I probably do not acquire the virtue of honesty because I have figured out that it will benefit me, but because I have been brought up and influenced by the people around me in a certain way, but even if I had set about acquiring it because I thought it would benefit me, that still would not make it the case that I told the truth when I did because, and only because, I thought doing so would benefit me.

Acquiring the virtue of honesty is getting into the habit of telling the truth for the right reasons; I tell the truth because I think one must, or because I think one cannot lie, not even to save one's own skin, or because I love truth, or for its own sake or indeed because it does not occur to me to do otherwise, on some occasions. Similarly, the virtue of 'animal-concern', once acquired, brings its own reasons for acting, and acquiring the virtue involves learning to act for those reasons, not for what one thinks humans, or this human, will get out of it. So one refrains from beating or torturing animals for the Benthamite reason – that *they* suffer – not simply because their suffering makes one uncomfortable, or might make one callous, though this may be importantly true. One refrains from killing them because it is wrong to kill *them*, not because, say, one will upset the local ecology, though this may be importantly true. I play with my cat mostly because *we*, he and I, both enjoy it, and sometimes when I am tired just because he wants me to, but never because I think this is a good way of ensuring that I shall have comforting company when I am sick or lonely, though it is an important fact that domestic animals can give such comfort. There is no reason, according to neo-Aristotelianism, why animals should not be treated as 'ends in themselves', or as having intrinsic value, just as other human beings, and truth, and knowledge, and virtue itself, are.

Conclusions

So I conclude that the intuition about animals is not only consistent with the neo-Aristotelian claim that morality is about human beings as such, but further, that the latter theory looks as though it may provide it with hospitable accommodation. I should add that I do not base this confidence merely on the small sketch given here, but more generally on the rich variety of arguments and considerations given in Stephen R. L. Clark's *The Moral Status of Animals*. Clark disarmingly describes himself as 'an Aristotelian on Mondays and Wednesdays, a Pyrrhonian Sceptic on Tuesdays and Fridays, a neo-Platonist on Thursdays and Saturdays and [someone who] worships in the local Episcopalian church on Sundays';[4] if this is so, a lot of the book must have been written on Mondays and Wednesdays. Clark is particularly powerful when arguing that our failure to have the right attitude to animals (and act accordingly) is intimately bound up with a whole range of vices or failings we are prone to and which inhibit us from flourishing – arrogance, pride, self-deception (particularly as exemplified in the fantasy that we are the masters or rulers of the rest of creation), dulled sensibility or insensitivity, materialism, a terrifying willingness to excuse wrongdoing as 'necessary', and many others.

There is, inevitably, much in Clark's book with which one might fairly disagree. Even if there were not, the wide range of considerations he brings in illustrates how very complex any attempt to bring neo-Aristotelianism to bear on specific moral issues must be. Since the theory puts the fully virtuous and wise agent at the centre, it is debarred from giving simple answers to questions about the rightness and wrongness of most sorts of actions. For these turn into questions about 'What would (or would not) the fully virtuous agent do?' and any such question makes room for the counter-question 'In what circumstances?' Hence, in particular, the theory is not going to yield a simple answer to 'Is it wrong to kill animals? Is it wrong to experiment on animals?'

An action that was absolutely wrong, according to neo-Aristotelian theory, would have to be an action which the fully virtuous agent would *never* do (deliberately), *whatever* the circumstances, and it is questionable that any such actions can be specified in a way that makes clear exactly what should and should not be done. Can we say that, for instance, the fully virtuous agent would never (deliberately) 'inflict suffering on an animal' or 'kill an animal', whatever the circumstances? Obviously not, for the circumstances might make either the right thing to do. The kindest vet will sometimes make an animal suffer, or kill it, for its own sake. Can we say that the fully virtuous agent would never 'inflict gratuitous suffering on an animal', never 'treat an animal with wanton cruelty', whatever the circumstances? Obviously so – but what counts as 'gratuitous' suffering or 'wanton' cruelty is precisely part of what we want to know when we are wondering what our treatment of animals should be.

Let us suppose we do agree that much of our animal experimentation is gratuitous or wanton. That still leaves us with the question – but to what extent, if at all, may we inflict suffering on animals in order to acquire knowledge, particularly knowledge which will spare human beings suffering? Actions that are absolutely wrong can never be justified, whatever the circumstances. Actions that are wrong, *simpliciter*, may be defined as actions which call for a special justification. They are the sort of thing a fully virtuous agent would never do ordinarily, but might do in special circumstances. So for example, one might say that the action of 'inflicting suffering on animals solely in order to acquire knowledge when the knowledge could be acquired without causing suffering' was wrong, calling for special justification, but could perhaps be justified. Suppose the knowledge was very important and needed urgently, and the only way of acquiring it without causing suffering would cost more than the research grant covered and take many years longer. Perhaps, under those circumstances, a fully virtuous agent would do the experiments, or give a scientist the go ahead to do them.

But by this stage, and in the present context, it is really not for me to say. I am offering neo–Aristotelianism as the right framework within which to think about moral issues; I am certainly not claiming that I myself am virtuous and wise enough to know what should be said about them. The theory tells us quite generally that how it is right (or wrong) to treat animals is determined by how the fully virtuous agent would treat them. If I am right about there being some virtue such as 'animal-concern', then the theory tells us (a) that this is a character trait we each have reason to acquire (since it is a virtue) and (b) that in order to acquire it one thing we should do is listen to someone who we think has the character trait and who we think is, in general, (at least fairly) virtuous and wise, and be guided by them over how we should (and should not) treat and think about animals.

The requirement that such a person should be at least fairly well endowed with the other virtues, and the wisdom that is inseparable from them, is very important. It reminds us of the standard of correctness which is built into every virtue. Someone who really does have the *right* attitude to animals is someone who thereby knows how important their lives and sufferings are in relation to other important things such as the relief of future suffering, human or otherwise, and the attainment of knowledge. So someone with the virtue of 'animal-concern' is not someone who goes around blowing up laboratories in protest against animal experimentation. But just what they do do I am not sure, since I am not one myself, nor do I know well anyone who is. The fully virtuous person, with full wisdom, would be the person who *knew* what to do or think in exactly those circumstances that many of us find so deeply puzzling (such as what should one do about wantonly cruel animal experimentation, given that one thinks that there must be some experimentation). If the fully virtuous is described that way, it becomes clear that she is an ideal. We go for guidance to, or try to model ourselves on, the people who approximate to that ideal. Insofar as each of them fails to attain it, some will be better exemplars of certain virtues than of others. As things are at the moment, Western society does not seem to contain many exemplars of 'animal concern'; however, as I said above, that need not lead one to suppose that it is not a virtue and part of the best, ideally best, human life.

4 THE THEORY APPLIED TO ALIENS

The other intuition that I claimed (p. 237 above) lay behind the conviction that there must be something wrong with 'speciesism' was derived from the thought-experiment about aliens, which is taken to show that we do not think that any treatment of any aliens, no matter what they were like, would be morally permissible or neutral. The thought-experiment takes us well beyond the first intuition because we may imagine aliens who can not only suffer, but who are 'like us' in being responsible for their actions. We want to say that morality not only deals with how we should treat them, but also with how they should treat us.

In what ways do we think the aliens must be 'like us' for this to be so? In 'morally relevant respects' of course, and it seems obvious to many that the aliens' *having two legs* or *being warm-blooded* and so on would not matter and could not be called 'morally relevant'. At this point it seems that we not only have a reason for saying that morality is not about human beings as such, but also for saying that it is about persons. Insofar as typical members of the alien species have the personal characteristics – are a species of person – morality is about them as well as us. To see this, it might be said, is a real advance on saying that morality just is about human beings and that is all there is to it. For (a) it provides the explanation of *why* that is so (we are a species of person), and thereby (b) it fixes in advance what we ought (to be consistent) to say about creatures of another species. The first is important because it satisfies a general rational requirement; the second may seem particularly important morally. To insist that the concept of morality is fixed by its present parochial application, that 'right', 'wrong', 'just', 'cruel', 'dishonest', etc. are all used in relation to human beings and that to use them in relation to aliens would be a new and 'extended' use about which nothing can be said in advance – this sounds dangerously anthropocentric. It sounds as though we could be justified in enslaving a species of alien persons just because we did not extend our talk about rights, justice, autonomy, etc. to cover them. And this is clearly outrageous. So morality is not, and could not be, about the species *homo sapiens*; it must be about species of *persons*.

The neo-Aristotelianism that has been outlined claims to be a plausible answer to the question 'What is the best way for *a human being* to live?' It is not made out to be, nor could it be made out to be, a plausible answer to the question 'What is the best way for a member of *any* species to live?' And, as 'person' is standardly defined, it is not, and could not be made out to be, a plausible answer to the question 'What is the best way for *a person* to live?' or 'How should *a person* live in order to flourish?' Indeed, it is impossible to imagine there being any answer to this question at all, since 'person' has not been defined in a way that determines a sense for 'personal flourishing' or 'flourishing as a person'. So it seems that we do have here a view of morality according to which it is essentially about human beings as a species and not only is not, but could not be construed as being, about persons.

Put this way, it seems that neo-Aristotelianism and the intuition about aliens must be totally opposed. But this is not so. Let us return to the medical analogy. Our medical science, concerned as it is with the question 'How should we human beings live in order to be healthy?', could not apply to *any* species, and could not apply to *persons* as such. But just as our medical science would apply to an alien species which was sufficiently like us in physical/biological respects, so our moral 'science' would apply to an alien species which was sufficiently like us for their flourishing to be like our flourishing.

When I was discussing Tooley's argument for his claim that moral principles must contain no references to particular species I showed that one could keep such a reference while avoiding speciesism by the simple expedient of adding an extra clause about 'relevantly similar species' (p. 110). So, for instance, one could maintain that it is human beings, not persons, that have a right to life without being speciesist if one said 'Human beings and members of relevantly similar species have a right to life'. Now although it is unquestionable, I think, that this is formally correct, it might well strike one as a merely formal and basically quite empty move. For what on earth could be meant by 'relevantly similar species'? But the neo-Aristotelian view yields a richly particularized answer to this question. A species is 'relevantly similar' to ours if its members are naturally prone to the same sorts of emotions and tendencies; if they want, enjoy and find satisfying the same sorts of things, if they are subject to the same sorts of temptations, fears and failings, if they respond to the world and each other in the same sorts of ways as we do, then our morality applies to them. And if not, not.

Now this, I would claim, captures everything that is correct about the intuition about the aliens. Could one complain that the neo-Aristotelian view amounts to the insistence that morality just *is* about human beings and that is all there is to it? Perhaps in a way, but it does provide a sort of explanation of this, *viz.* that morality is concerned with how human beings can flourish – it does not just leave the reference to human beings as a brute fact – and that explanation is enough to fix in advance what we ought to say about creatures of some other species.

It might be thought that the view was still improperly anthropocentric. It does require that the aliens be *very* similar to us in an enormous variety of ways, whereas, it might be said, the point of the intuition about the aliens is that concepts such as 'rights', 'autonomy', 'right', 'wrong', 'just', 'cruel', 'dishonest', etc. could be used in relation to beings whose only similarity to us was that they were persons. But if anyone really does claim this, they have, I think, gone wrong.

Compare the neo–Aristotelian emphasis on the complex ways we feel, act and react (in relation to ourselves and to each other and to the rest of the world) as of central importance to morality with the thin specifications that are standardly given of what is required for something to be a person and thereby the sort of thing about which morality is particularly concerned. Tooley, for instance, puts in nothing but the capacity to have desires about one's own future states. Others have suggested that the capacity to communicate, while not necessary, might well be sufficient for personhood. But this yields very little when we remember to consider the theoretical possibility that something that had the capacity to communicate might yet have no desire ever to do so. Others have suggested that consciousness, particularly the capacity to feel pain, and self–motivated activity would be sufficient for personhood. But here again, this yields little when we consider that though, perhaps, pain is necessarily undesirable, a creature might, in some incomprehensible way, pursue painful experiences a lot of the time. (To grasp this as a possibility, imagine how incomprehensible the Martians would find our subjecting outselves to certain sorts of physical stress until they understood, if they ever could, that we regard climbing mountains as a challenge and winning races at the Olympic Games an honour.) It is noteworthy that the capacity to have any emotions at all, let alone the same sorts as ours, is rarely mentioned and never insisted upon. And *nothing* is said about persons' attitudes to other persons.

Now it need not be supposed that these are the only possible specifications of 'person'. But these do stand squarely in the tradition of trying to specify the sorts of creatures with which morality is concerned solely in terms of non-emotional capacities. And any such attempt is, I would claim (though I cannot argue it here), doomed to failure.

Describing the aliens

It is worth reminding ourselves at this point that most science fiction which purports to describe our interaction with some species of alien, our treating them well or badly and being treated well or badly by them, standardly does describe the aliens as being remarkably similar to us in just the ways that neo-Aristotelianism requires. In fact, much science fiction is basically description of human beings in fancy dress – wearing masks with extra eyes, or green costumes with extra legs or fins. Only the most imaginative writers manage to get beyond even such basic similarities as that our species is two-gendered and our reproduction is heterosexual. There is an unusually interesting Isaac Asimov novel in which he attempts plausibly to describe a species in which there are three 'genders' whose simultaneous co-operation is required for reproduction. What is particularly instructive about this is that making the description even initially plausible involves him in finding models or correlates for the great variety of feelings, actions, and reactions that we have relating to the facts that govern our reproduction – about mothers and fathers, lovers, offspring, the sexual act, masculinity, femininity, homosexuality, friendship, being an adult, growing up, and so on. Unsurprisingly, he is quite unable to do it, but notably the mere sketch that he gives goes miles beyond what is usually offered.

From the perspective of a certain philosophy of mind (or of language) this is not only unsurprising but inevitable.[5] It is only of creatures very similar to us in a vast variety of ways that it would even make sense to describe them as having a language, acting intentionally, having thoughts or desires . . . and so on. From this perspective, indeed, one would say that the 'thin' or non-anthropocentric specification of a 'person' was simply a verbal trick. Any 'person', i.e. any creature of which it makes sense to say that it has a concept of its continued existence, or of its self or whatever, must already be a creature similar to us in the ways neo–Aristotelianism requires; the ascription of a so-called 'personal' characteristic brings all the rest of the 'human characteristics' package with it.

Although I think this view is right, the case against 'persons' does not have to rest on it. Let us, contrary to what this view in the philosophy of mind takes to be possible, try to imagine and describe entirely 'inhuman' beings which fit some of the standard thin specifications of 'person' and see what our intuitions are about them. One sort of creature or being to try to imagine would be a sort that had the fewest conceivable emotions or emotional reactions. They do not feel anything about any other member of their species; they lead totally solitary lives; they are not frightened of death or pain or damage; nothing, not even the frustration of their own desires, upsets them; they are sublimely indifferent to everything. Can they then count as having desires about their own future states or going in for self-motivated activity or valuing their own continued existence in some sense? Well yes, if we imagine that they do pursue something, say getting into a rather complicated position holding certain objects every day. In order to achieve this objective they will go to great efforts. They will also kill or inflict pain on each other, or indeed anything else. Let us suppose for example that one of the objects to be held is the *recently detached limb* of a member of their own species and that they show themselves willing to consider our limbs as acceptable substitutes. But if something else makes it physically impossible for them to achieve this objective, they do not mind.

Someone might object that this thought-experiment is too far-fetched, since such a species, entirely indifferent to killing and maiming its own members, indeed, bent on doing so, could not survive. But this need not be so; we can suppose that these aliens are the dominant life form on their planet through the happy accident of greatly superior size and the fact that they reproduce, asexually, as abundantly as fish.

The other sort of creature to try to imagine would be a sort that was, as far as is conceivable, the emotional opposite of us. What inspires 'love' in us inspires hatred in them, and vice versa. So, for example, they particularly hate their own offspring and parents. (We must imagine that they reproduce in very different ways from us, in order to allow, once again, for the possibility of such a species surviving at all, but let us indeed imagine that – they really do produce 'people-seeds' and it requires luck or great effort to identify one's own offspring or parents in order to make them suffer as much as one can.) They are immensely attracted by other members of their species who treat them badly. What are we to imagine about how they want to treat the people they 'are attracted by'? ('Love' really would have been difficult here.) Well, let us say that they passionately desire to make them suffer, not by way of revenge, but for them to be attracted to another person is simply characterized by an intense desire to see the other suffer. They frequently kill each other, and often kill themselves, or allow themselves to be killed, with a sort of fierce enjoyment. They go to great trouble to build elaborate and beautiful objects which they then go to great trouble to destroy. They hate colour and variety, and often make a point of damaging their own sense-organs.

Anyone who claims that neo-Aristotelianism is too anthropocentric, and that 'being a person' is all that matters, must be prepared to say either (a) that there is not the slightest difficulty in regarding these two sorts of alien as 'part of our moral community' or (b) to provide a new specification of 'person' which, while avoiding anthropocentricity, rules them out. The second alternative generates an open-ended debate, the question being whether, for any such specification, I can produce another example of peculiar aliens which count as 'persons' but which my opponent will agree are not what she wants to include.

With respect to the first alternative, I have no further argument. All I can do is state the opposite conviction that, far from thinking it obvious that because all these beings are 'persons' they must form part of our moral community, I think the more and more unlike us human beings we imagine them as being, the less sense it makes to apply moral categories to them. I do not understand what would count as being kind or cruel to such creatures, nor what would count in general as respecting their rights, treating them justly or unjustly.

None of this entails that, if the aliens are sufficiently alien, it is morally open to us to do anything we like to them. To suppose this would be to fall back into the particular crudity of the person view, the error of supposing that if they are not part of our moral community we can treat them in any way we choose no matter how gross, or destructive, or wanton our acts, or with Tooley that *rights* are the only feature which imposes moral restrictions on what we may decently do. Many animals are very unlike us, but, as I argued in the preceding section, neo-Aristotelianism does not allow our treating them in any way we like. If it were clear, for instance, that, like terrestrial animals, the aliens felt pain *and* felt about it in much the same way we do (unlike the examples I have envisaged), though wildly unlike us in many other ways, then we could, minimally, make sense of being cruel to them, and that would be wrong. The mere fact that they are, *ex hypothesi*, a wholly different life-form might be enough to guarantee that it would be arrogant and presumptuous to interfere with them in any way at all.

'But what', someone might ask, 'if they came and interfered with us?' This is part of the standard fare of science fiction, and it is worth reminding ourselves again of what we may be assuming without noticing it. If the aliens come here, in space-ships in the standard way, then we are assuming (unless some special story is told to the contrary) that, like us, the aliens engage in certain co-operative ventures. They have a science which yielded the knowledge to build the ships, and that requires not only a system of communication but social practices which involve some method(s) of education and the exchange, the pooling, and the mutual development of knowledge. The ships were built, and that too requires certain social practices to do with the division of labour and the following of instructions. If all this mutual enterprise is to take place a fair number of the aliens must spend a fair amount of their lives together. So they are, like us, social animals, who go in for communi-cating, pursuing knowledge, teaching each other, learning from each other, working together, giving and receiving orders and requests, and so on. Once we have imagined them to be as similar to us as all this entails, it is not clear that the problem, 'What should we do if there were an alien invasion?', is very different from the familiar, albeit very difficult, questions about our dealings with each other at the national or international level. If two very large social groups of co-operative creatures cannot, for some reason, get on with each other as things are at the moment, and also, for some reason, are in competition for the same bit of the globe, what is the just solution?

Conclusions

Perhaps the most useful aspect of the person view is that, in rejecting it, one is forced to look with a freshly enquiring eye at the idea of the 'morally relevant' features of human beings. The realization that we would find it impossible to ascribe moral responsibility to aliens who were sufficiently different should help us to understand the problems we have in knowing what to say about human beings who are very deviant in certain ways. We may call them mad, and lock up or execute those whose madness takes particularly horrible forms, but, especially within the terms of a secular morality, the more certain we are that they are mad, the less certain we are about whether they are morally responsible, and what counts in general as our treating them as virtue requires.

In trying to imagine apparently quite minor ways in which aliens might differ physically from us (for example, in their mode of reproduction, in their life-cycle, in their life-expectancy), we are led to reflect on the role that these biological facts about us play in our physical *and* psychological life, the extent to which they determine what flourishing is for us.

One upshot of that reflection is the following. As a species, we go through a major stage in our natural life-cycle; it is the stage that one hopes all human beings will develop into and stay at until they die. When human beings do not develop into that stage fully, or, having done so, decline from it because of brain-damage or ageing, we think of this as a tragedy, even if the humans in question are happy and enjoying life in their own way. Now *if* 'person' is defined in such a way as to embrace children, it is not correct to describe this stage as the stage of 'being a person'. For we think of human beings who do not develop mentally beyond childhood as being amongst those who, tragically, do not go through the major stage. But it is only while we are considering the concept of a person within the straitjacket of expecting it to solve the abortion issue that we are anxious to make sure that children at least qualify as persons. If we think abstractly, we need not suppose that the specific point of the concept of a person is to single out those creatures it is wrong to kill, and we can consider more carefully who is embraced by the 'we' in '*We* are paradigm persons'. The original arguments for the person view, the aspects that continued to look plausible even when other weaknesses in the view had been exposed, suggest, not a limited application to killing, but this much.

(1) That we have the non-biological concept of a person as well as the biological concept of a human being (a member of the species *homo sapiens*).

(2) The concept of a person singles out what is especially important about human beings. This involves both (a) that it singles out what distinguishes us, as a species, from most if not all terrestrial animals, and (b) that it distinguishes us in terms of what we think of as being very important or significant. (We can, for instance, be distinguished from all the other animals as being the only *featherless biped* which would satisfy (a). But we do not think that our being featherless bipeds is an important or significant fact about us; so this would not satisfy (b).)

It is beyond doubt that (1) is true – that we have the concept of a person. I would also take it to be true that in a manner of speaking we need it, insofar as it does the job described in (2). But insofar as we have a concept which genuinely does the job described in (2), it is, I would claim, the concept of what I have called our 'major stage'. This is, obviously, not the same as the concept of a human being, since it is, parasitically, the concept of *a stage in the life of a human being*. That we go through, or enter into and persist in, this stage, distinguishes us as a species from most if not all terrestrial animals. We think our entering it and persisting in it is of the greatest importance and significance, to the point where, when human beings do not go through it, or decline from it before they die, we think this is a tragedy, even if they do not suffer at all. We think that deliberately preventing a human being from persisting in it – by, say, destroying parts of the brain so that they become mentally deficient – would be (almost) as bad as murdering them. Some people would say it was worse. Similarly, we think it would be wicked beyond compare to do something to a five or ten-year-old's brain with the intention of preventing them from developing mentally into an adult.

Moreover, we think of it as being important and significant in that it is what would particularly interest us in the aliens; do they have this stage in their lives or not? To see this as striking we could try to imagine a species of alien who were remarkably like human beings except for the fact that they were remarkably like us at five years old or younger. It can be agreed that five-year-olds can be rational, self-conscious, autonomous to a certain extent, can have a moral sense to a certain extent and so on, but the most generous scope of the 'to a certain extent' will still not make a whole society of alien five-year-olds into a community that we can readily imagine dealing with as moral equals.

Finally, when exponents of the person view say 'We are paradigm persons; it is *being a person* which matters about us, not our being human', this is particularly plausible as an appeal to what I have called 'the major stage' precisely because it is only human beings in the major stage who read the books, or attend to the lectures, in which such things are said.

I have not given a definition of 'the major stage' or of 'being a person' in this final sense. The task of doing so, if indeed it could be done, would form a very significant part of moral philosophy, for it would involve specifying what was needed for *maturity*. We can all see that, in some obvious sad cases, human beings who have lived for well over ten years are 'like children' and we all know that in order to be an adult one must put away childish things. But when we think about ourselves and other ordinary adults, we tend to find that we too are 'like children' in certain detailed respects, some of which seem more lamentable than others. In arguing with each other about whether doing or wanting such and such is childish or not, we may find that it is very hard to be clear about what 'the childish things' that have to be put away are. Maturity is emotional or psychological as well as intellectual, and it is part of our concept of it that with maturity comes wisdom. The sort of wisdom it brings is not the sort that can be learnt entirely from books or lectures, but the sort that comes from experience of life, and it is wisdom *about* life. And this is precisely the wisdom which, according to neo-Aristotelianism, is fully possessed only by the fully virtuous human being.

This is not to say that 'the major stage', or 'being a person' in this sense, should be defined in such a way that only the fully virtuous turned out to be persons. It is to say that a definition of 'the major stage' could not be independent of neo-Aristotelian considerations about what constitutes the flourishing human life, i.e. of considerations that, as we have seen, turn out to be what we call moral considerations. The flourishing human life certainly has to contain, and indeed largely to consist of, the major stage. If Aristotle is correct in thinking that the way to flourish is to acquire and exercise the virtues, then doing so will be the activity particularly appropriate to the major stage. So the correct specification of the major stage would have to reflect that fact.

NOTES

1 Etymologically it means 'well (*eu*)-demoned/geniused', i.e. blessed with a good genius or attendant spirit (*daimon*).
2 Though perhaps not incomprehensible, if we can understand a certain sort of neuroticism in which the person seems bent on misery and self-destruction. Aristotle appears not to recognize the existence of such people.

3 This is not strictly Aristotle's answer, since his list of the virtues is not the same as ours, though having much in common with it. Moreover, the Greek term that we translate as 'virtue' (*arete*) has no specifically moral overtones and, if we were concentrating on what Aristotle said, would be better translated as 'excellence'. This is the neo-Aristotelian answer.

4 Clark, S. (1977) *The Moral Status of Animals*, Oxford University Press, p. 5.

5 *Cf.* Wittgenstein, Ludwig (1953) *Philosophical Investigations*, tr. G. E. M. Anscombe, Basil Blackwell, 2nd edn, 1958.

CHAPTER SEVEN

What is wrong with utilitarianism

1 WHAT MORALITY REQUIRES

Having introduced neo-Aristotelianism, and reflected it back on the person view, I now want to return to the topic of utilitarianism.

The point I have stressed most often in objecting to utilitarianism is the fact that it yields morally unacceptable conclusions. The 'sometimes right, sometimes wrong, according to the consequences' aspect of utilitarianism covers not only the sorts of actions described as, for example, 'abortion', 'infanticide', 'lying' and so on. It also applies to actions described in such a way as to make clear the character of the agent. So 'being callous', 'being cruel', 'being unjust', 'being selfish', 'being self-indulgent' are sometimes right, sometimes wrong, according to their consequences.

The simplest example of this point (that utilitarianism yields 'morally unacceptable conclusions') is standardly one in which utilitarianism has it that an action is certainly *right* which anyone, prior to embracing the theory, would say was certainly *wrong*; for example, killing one person in order to use their organs to save five others. In connection with this sort of example, one may think of utilitarianism as encouraging, or leading us towards, acting wrongly.

But although this sort of example tends to dominate the discussion, it is important to remember that this is not the only way in which utilitarian conclusions conflict with those of more conventional morality. Utilitarianism also judges actions to be certainly *wrong* which conventional morality would usually judge to be, if not certainly right, at least perfectly acceptable.

As we have noted on several occasions, it excludes, as irrelevant to moral right or wrong, considerations of special relationships between people. In deciding what I ought to do, I do not consider 'That's my child, mother, brother, husband, friend, etc.', but only consequences concerning maximizing anyone's or everyone's happiness. So if I save the life of one of them instead of saving the life, or worse, lives, of strangers who would have contributed more, or will be mourned more, what I do is straightforwardly wrong by the utilitarian criterion. But we ordinarily allow that special relationships do make an important difference in some circumstances. It is not always wrong to be partial; if my choice lies between saving my child (or my parent or someone close to me) or sparing them pain, and saving a stranger or even two or three strangers, or sparing them pain, it will certainly not always be wrong of me to save or spare the pain of the one I am specially related to. Sometimes it may be wrong of me to do otherwise – irresponsible or neglectful of what I owe to the person in question. And here too, one might think of utilitarianism as encouraging us to act wrongly, though not perhaps in as startling a way as we considered before.

But in other cases, amongst them the sort that are described as moral dilemmas, it may not be clearly *wrong* to exclude the claims of a special relationship as utilitarianism would have me do, nor indeed clearly right. There can be cases in which either acting in accordance with the special relationship or acting with impartial, impersonal benevolence is permissible or justifiable. So, for example, I might make my will in favour of my friends and family, or in favour of some charity, and in many circumstances either course of action would count as all right. Or, in conditions of war, I might devote my effort to looking after my aged parents or leave them and join the Red Cross, and once again either course of action may be all right. In the cases that present one with particularly agonizing dilemmas, describing the alternative courses of action as 'all right' would be inappropriate. Rather, either course can be justified by appeal to the circumstance that one had to do one of the two. Some cases of choosing which lives to save would be of this sort. And here utilitarianism runs counter to more conventional morality, not in encouraging us to act wrongly, but in condemning us for doing what morality allows. There are surely cases in which I am not *required* to take account of a special relationship, against the claims of impartial benevolence, but in which I am *allowed* to, and my doing so does not count as wrong; but it will be so on the utilitarian criterion.

Now this serves to remind us of an aspect of utilitarianism I have hardly touched on, namely the way in which one might regard it as encouraging us to act with heroic self-sacrifice. The one example I have mentioned so far was the apparent consequence of the utilitarian view for a healthy woman of child-bearing age, namely that, unless pregnancy and child-bearing will affect her life very much for the worse, making it not worth living, she should produce babies for any couples who want them and who are likely to give them a worthwhile life. In not doing so, she is failing to maximize happiness and thereby doing what is *wrong*.

This example came up within the confines of considering what utilitarianism had to say about abortion. But, looking beyond those confines, we should consider quite generally what utilitarianism expects me to do. It apparently allows me or even requires me to do many things which are wrong; does it also condemn me for doing, or not doing, many things which are all right, expecting me to rise to heroic heights by doing otherwise?

Saints and villains

I mentioned at the beginning of the chapter on utilitarianism something that seems an obvious platitude, *viz*. that a large number of my 'actions' have no moral significance. Think of what one might do on an average day; suppose I skip breakfast as part of a diet, take the children shopping, put off writing a letter I have promised to write, ring my mother, clean the house, do some work at the typewriter, have some friends in for dinner. It would be odd to describe such a day as one fraught with moral significance. I am not living as a saint or a villain, but as an ordinary person. Nevertheless, we might see much of it as in accordance with morality. The requirement to honour one's father and mother does not require that I dance attendance on my mother constantly, but it does require that I do not neglect her and ring her sometimes. Looking after my children does not require that I take them shopping but it rules out my locking them in the tool shed while I go. I do not break a promise by putting off writing the letter, but I must write it some time soon, and so on.

Now it is sometimes thought that this platitude is *only* made possible by a particular feature conventional morality is claimed to have. According to Singer, for instance, conventional morality embodies the view that

> so long as we do not violate specified moral rules which place determinate moral obligations upon us, we do all that morality demands of us. These rules are of the kind made familiar by the Ten Commandments and similar moral codes: Do not kill, Do not lie, Do not steal, and so on. Characteristically they are formulated in the negative, so that to obey them it is necessary only to abstain from the actions they prohibit . . .
>
> An ethic consisting of specific duties, prescribed by moral rules which everyone can be expected to obey, must make a sharp moral distinction between acts and omissions. Take, for example, the rule 'Do not kill'. If this rule is interpreted, as it has been in the Judæo-Christian tradition, as prohibiting only the taking of innocent human life, it is not too difficult to avoid overt acts in violation of it. Few of us are murderers. It is not so easy to avoid letting innocent humans die. Many people die because of insufficient food, or poor medical facilities. Taking the rule against killing to apply to omissions would make living in accordance with it a mark of saintliness or moral heroism, rather than a minimum required of every morally decent person.[1]

Now, putting to one side his claim about acts and omissions (which I shall return to below), Singer has clearly misdescribed ordinary morality, and hence misidentified how we draw the distinction between the saintly, the ordinary, and the villainous.

The relevant feature of ordinary morality is not that moral rules are 'characteristically formulated in the negative' and hence(?) 'not too difficult' to obey. The relevant feature is that morality does not give me specific instructions about how to decide what to do at each minute of the day; rather it leaves me to get on with my own life subject to certain constraints and directives. Ordinarily, people who do that count as ordinarily decent people, and people who do not range from the ordinarily bad to the villainous.

Against this background we can introduce the notion of the saintly or heroic as contrasted with the ordinarily decent and bad.

Saintliness or heroism comes about in at least two different ways. There are statistically unusual (though by no means extraordinary) circumstances in which living subject to the constraints and directives of morality calls for an unusual amount of sacrifice or effort. One of my parents or my children may develop an illness; it may be that only I can give them the care they need. Then the directive to look after my children or honour my parents – usually a directive that ordinarily decent people find 'not too difficult' as Singer puts it, to live in accordance with – may become extremely demanding, and I may count as a saint or a heroine if I do it. The prohibition against lying tends to be so lightly regarded nowadays that in many cases someone would be counted as a fool rather than a heroine if they refused to lie when the temptation was very great. But even that is not always so; we admire people in politically repressive countries who refuse to recant their views and are sent to gaol or lunatic asylums as a result.

Similar cases came up in the discussion of the Thomson article. Someone who neglects their children in the ordinary way of things is being callous, selfish, irresponsible. But someone who, under extreme pressure, reneges on their responsibilities towards their disabled child does not manifest those vices, nor necessarily any others. It may be that they fail to rise to the occasion, that they show themselves as lacking in the particularly admirable virtue of someone who manages to cope, but they can still count as ordinarily decent people.

'Don't kill', as ordinarily understood, is indeed usually easy for ordinarily decent people to obey. But statistically unusual circumstances can make it difficult – as when we praise the heroism of people in lifeboat situations who choose to die all together rather than draw straws over who shall be killed. And it is certainly a difficult and demanding rule for women to obey if one takes it as prohibiting abortion as stringently as it prohibits infanticide.

The second way, I think, in which saintliness or heroism arises is when someone in statistically normal circumstances takes one of the constraints or directives much more seriously than most people do and ceases to lead an ordinary life thereby. Within the tradition of the Christian Church one of the directives is to love God; many of the Christian saints are to be found amongst the people who turned their whole lives over to following this directive. Contrary to what Singer says, 'Don't let innocent people die' is a prohibition that is recognized in ordinary morality; it prohibits, for example, my passing by on the other side when I see someone bleeding to death, and my shutting the door saying 'Not my responsibility' when I find a baby abandoned on my doorstep. Someone who does these sorts of things is not ordinarily decent, but villainous, or at least bad. But the ordinary interpretation of the prohibition is as a constraint on the ordinary living of my own life; only someone saintly like Mother Teresa turns their whole life over to it.

Ceasing to lead an ordinary life by taking 'Don't' kill' particularly seriously would be doing something of a different sort. One example would be, harking back to Schweitzer's description of what was involved in 'really' believing in the sanctity of life (p. 133), someone who entirely reorganized their lives to avoid killing insects. A less extreme example would be people who are not just vegetarians but Vegans.

These cases might well be disputed on the grounds that taking 'Don't kill' to apply to insects or animals as well as to humans is not taking it 'more seriously' than the rest of us, but mistaking, or misinterpreting it. Rather than go through arguments about that again, let us consider another example. I read of someone who was the innocent cause of someone else's death in a car accident. (He was, according to his witnesses, driving carefully and conscientiously, but a bicyclist turned straight under his wheels without any warning and was killed.) Although everyone agreed he was not guilty, the event made him so conscious of the fact that cars are death-dealing machines that he resolved never to run this risk of killing anyone again, and stopped driving.

This does not count as saintly or heroic, but does count as particularly high-principled. Everyone but the unjust and callous takes the prohibitions against killing and maiming seriously and everyone who is ordinarily decent naturally assumes that, since killing and maiming people are wrong, we are all supposed not only to avoid doing them, but also to avoid running the risk of doing them accidentally 'where possible'. Hence our concepts of criminal negligence, of being criminally or wickedly irresponsible, of acting with a wanton disregard for others, even when no one is killed or harmed. But the 'where possible' is ordinarily understood as being considerably limited by the ordinary running of our lives. Until comparatively recently, many people did not think of drunken driving as particularly irresponsible; in that climate of opinion it was only strong-minded and high-principled people who made a point of keeping sober at parties if they were going to drive. In the present climate of opinion, driving a car is regarded by many people as necessary. 'I couldn't do without it', they say, meaning by that that doing without it would require a complete upheaval of their lives. Someone who then does completely reorganize their life in order to avoid driving, because they believe they (morally) cannot run the risk of killing or maiming people which driving a car involves, is someone who stands out as particularly admirable.

I am not for a moment claiming that it is easy to make out when someone is 'ordinarily decent' and when they are saintly or heroic, or, come to that, when someone is ordinarily bad, and when they are villainous. The distinctions are tricky in themselves for several reasons.

One is that people's character and dispositions are often

not all of a piece. Someone may be utterly irresponsible and cowardly about one thing, pretending to himself that he has not even heard the screams of someone being beaten up in his street, but rise remarkably to some other occasion. Another reason is that it is often difficult to distinguish someone's being saintly from their being a crank, since this involves the judgement about what ought, ideally, to be done. Are people who are not merely vegetarian but Vegan, because they take the constraints and directives about not making animals suffer and respecting life particularly seriously, saintly? Or if not saintly, particularly good? Or are they cranks, albeit well-meaning ones? Is someone who devotes her whole life to fighting social injustices a heroine or a crank? Or does it depend at least in part on how she sets about it and which causes she fights for?

The distinctions are not only tricky in themselves. It is, moreover, difficult to get them right without falling into one of the vices of smugness or hypocritical remorse. If I say that only the saintly give a fair proportion of their income to the people who are starving in other countries, and that I can count myself as being ordinarily decent without doing so, I sound intolerably smug. If, on the other hand, I say that morality requires us to give away everything we do not actually need to help the starving, that our not doing so is just like murdering them and that we are all as wicked as people who murder for financial gain – then this is just posturing. I do not, as I sit in my warm house, typing these words into my expensive word-processor, really mean them. Nor do I expect my reader to believe them and instantly abandon the pursuit of academic philosophy. For either of us to rend our hair, saying 'Oh, I'm as bad as the Kray twins', is hypocritical.

Difficult as the distinctions may be, we can, and do, make them. We distinguish between the saintly or the heroic, the ordinarily decent and the villainous, by distinguishing the reactions people have to the constraints, directives and ideals contained in morality. We are supposed to be unselfish rather than selfish, high-minded rather than exclusively pleasure-seeking, generous rather than mean about our personal possessions, industrious and public-spirited rather than lazy and parasitic. Some people fail completely in this and are selfish, hedonistic, totally materialistic, and live entirely off other people's backs. Most of us are not so bad, but reflection on the plight of people in the under-developed countries should lead many of us to acknowledge how very far from perfect we are, wedded as we are to our comforts and luxuries, the enjoyment of wearing fashionable clothes and eating different sorts of food, being entertained by television, going on holidays ... Given that we grow up in a rich and materialistic society, it is very hard for us not to be attached to these things and regard them as essential to living well, and precisely because it is hard, the few people who manage to break away from the attachment, and, for example, live very simply in order to give half their income to Oxfam, count as particularly admirable. But it is not so hard to give something, and not hard at all for entrepreneurs to find ways of making money which do not involve exporting poisoned food or dealing in heroin with a complete callous disregard for the deaths and suffering that they cause, so the few people who do that sort of thing count as particularly despicable.

As my constant use of virtue and vice terms indicates, this is all part and parcel of neo-Aristotelianism. We are taught the concepts of the virtues and vices against the background of ordinary life. Against that background we compare the ordinary with the ordinary in minor ways, recognizing that, say, *A* is a bit mean about drinks and that *B* is endlessly patient with her difficult child. We are also struck by the cases in which people do 'rise to the occasion', when we see how much more than the ordinary is called for, and use their example to highlight the failure of people who do not even behave well when it is easy to do so. And finally, the news media, and, before its day, literature and folk-tales, present us with the examples of the out-of-the-ordinary people who exemplify at least one or two of the virtues or vices in a particularly full-blooded form.

Can utilitarianism draw these distinctions? For if it cannot we may have here a much more general expression of the objection that its conclusions are widely at odds with ordinary morality.

Some statements of utilitarianism do seem committed to denying the distinction. For example, Smart states the utilitarian view as the one which holds 'that the *only* reason for performing an action *A* rather than an alternative action *B* is that doing *A* will make mankind (or, perhaps, all sentient beings) happier than will doing *B*'.[2] He elaborates this later to '*the* rational way to decide *what to do* is to decide to perform that one of those alternative actions open to us (including ... the doing of nothing) which is likely to *maximize* the probable happiness ... of humanity as a whole'.[3] So it is not open to me to get on with my own life within the constraints and directives of morality; to decide *what to do* at any minute of the day I should consider every alternative open to me and choose the one that maximizes happiness for humanity as a whole. I cannot buy tomatoes for some reason such as having had potatoes yesterday – my *only* reason for doing one thing rather than another is supposed to be that the one will make mankind happier.

Smart considers a form of the objection that, according to utilitarianism, I must act heroically or do wrong, in the following way.

> Baier holds that ... utilitarianism must be rejected because it entails that we should never relax, that we should use up every available minute in good works, and we do not ordinarily think that this is so. The utilitarian has two effective replies. The first is that perhaps what we ordinarily think is false. Perhaps a rational investigation would lead us to the conclusion that we should relax much less than we do. The second reply is that ... utilitarian premisses do not entail that we should never relax. Maybe relaxing and doing few good works today increases threefold our capacity to do good works tomorrow.[4]

It is not clear what the point of having these two replies is. Should the (presumed) effectiveness of one not make the (presumed) truth of the other irrelevant? In fact, these two replies can be regarded as relevant only on the assumption that they supplement each other to form a single joint reply. Suppose we summarize the objection as 'Utilitarianism entails that we all have to be like Mother Teresa, and that it is wrong to act otherwise. But we do not ordinarily think this is so; it is not wicked of us not to act as she does.' Then Smart's single reply goes (taking the second bit first), 'No, utilitarianism entails only that we have to be much more like Mother Teresa than we are (obviously very few of us are capable of giving as unstintingly of ourselves as she is). And that is perfectly reasonable, because a rational investigation would lead us to the same conclusion.'

This reply, though relevant, is hardly effective, for the 'rational investigation' surely does not lead us to anything like the 'same conclusion'. As I said above, reflection on the plight of people in under-developed countries should certainly lead most of us to the conclusion that it is wrong of us not to give more than we do. But it does not lead to the conclusion that we are wicked in not drastically curtailing our lives. People who do that, though still not as saintly as Mother Teresa, are particularly admirable. The gap between what utilitarianism requires and what we think is required in the way of avoiding wickedness is still vast.

Might it be possible for utilitarianism to be stated more modestly? Could it, for instance, be expressed in terms of *moral* reasons, or *moral* decisions? On the face of it, this seems unlikely, for according to utilitarianism there are no sorts of actions, such as *killing*, or *allowing to die*, or *neglecting* and so on, which are the particular concern of morality. All that is ever relevant to morality is consequences, and every action (including doing nothing) has consequences.

Another possibility is that something has gone wrong with this very notion of *consequences*. Can it really be said that people are dying in other countries, or indeed in this one, *as a consequence* or *a result* of my doing the things I do on an average day, such as reading a book or going shopping? It is true that in some sense people are dying 'because' I am not doing anything to prevent it. But, by the same token, people are living because I am not doing anything to prevent that either. As Don Locke has neatly pointed out, if we read things one way we are all monsters and murderers; 'as a consequence' of what I am doing (shopping, reading, not saving) people are dying whom I could have saved. But read exactly the same facts a different way and I am a heroine; 'as a consequence' of what I am doing (shopping, reading, not killing) people are living whom I could have killed![5]

Now this does indeed suggest that something has gone wrong with the notion of consequences when it is used to maintain that, quite generally, people are dying 'as a consequence' of my going shopping. People die as a consequence of my going shopping in only very restricted circumstances – say, when I accidentally kill someone when I am driving to the shops, or when my ailing parent who lives with me has a heart attack while I am at the shops which they would have survived had I been on hand to give them their pills.

Might it be then that utilitarianism could avoid the implausibility of insisting that there was no difference between the ordinary, the villainous and the saintly *if* its proponents cleared up the notion of consequences? On its own that is a very big 'if', but even if we were optimistic about it, the answer would still be 'No'. For even given a suitably restricted notion of consequences, the consequences must be, within the constraints of utilitarianism, assessed as good or bad in terms of their maximization of happiness, interests, preferences or whatever, *impersonally described*.

In passing I mentioned earlier (p. 141) an oddity of utilitarianism which often goes unacknowledged – the fact that it imposes on me no special requirement to consider other people's happiness (or interests or preferences or suffering, etc.) *rather than* my own. What I am supposed to do is maximize, and if on some occasion my choice lies between increasing your happiness or my own, or between reducing your suffering or my own, the only relevant consideration is, which would yield the biggest return? If acting on my own behalf would, that is what I am *required* to do. If there is nothing to choose between them as far as maximum yield is concerned then there is nothing to choose between them morally speaking, I can act on my own behalf, or on yours, it makes no moral difference. So, for example, if my choice lies between your life and mine and there is nothing to choose between them as far as future expectations of amounts of happiness, unhappiness of friends and family and so on is concerned, then I might just as well kill you. When we emphasize this aspect of utilitarianism, it appears that in some areas it does not demand as much as ordinary morality. For unselfishness, generosity, tolerance, respecting other people's rights often involve the agent in considering other people's happiness or interests or preferences *rather than* her own.

What is more usually acknowledged is the other side of the same coin; namely that utilitarianism allows me no special justification for considering my own happiness or suffering rather than anyone else's. So if my choice lies between your life and mine and your expectations of happiness are greater than mine, or more hangs on your death than mine, then I am required to kill myself. If one of my kidneys will spare you the misery of being on dialysis then I am required to donate it to you, albeit at the risk of needing dialysis myself at some later stage of my life. If someone is very much in love with me and will be heartbroken if I reject him, and if I think that, being fairly cheerful and resilient, I could endure a year of his company, repulsive as I find him, without actually suffering, I am required to put myself in his hands. When we emphasize this aspect of utilitarianism it appears that in some areas it demands a great deal more than ordinary morality. For unselfishness, lack of callousness, respecting other people's rights while exercising one's own, are often consistent with the agent's considering her own happiness, interests or preferences *rather than* other people's.

But utilitarianism cannot allow that any such 'agent-relative' priority could be given to people's happiness or suffering either way. And since what counts as, for instance, being utterly selfish or callous on the one hand, or heroically self-sacrificing on the other, or ordinarily decent in the middle, depends on the way the agent gives priority or not to her own concerns or those of others, utilitarianism is committed to denying that these distinctions can be drawn.

'The' acts and omissions doctrine

If utilitarianism cannot draw these distinctions – if, that is, it does yield the conclusion that it is wicked of us not to be (at least very) like Mother Teresa – it must fall back on strengthening Smart's appeal to a 'rational investigation'. It must maintain that some such investigation leads not merely to the conclusion I drew, namely that most of us should give more than we do, but indeed to the 'same conclusion' as is drawn by utilitarianism. And several recent utilitarians do make this move. They maintain (a) that the distinction between what only the saintly do, which is not required of us, and what morality does require of us, which ordinarily it is wicked to flout, relies on 'the' acts and omissions doctrine, and (b) that 'the' acts and omissions doctrine is false. So, they conclude, rational investigation yields, independently, the same conclusion as utilitarianism – that the usual distinctions between the saintly, the ordinary, and the wicked cannot be drawn.

The two questions here are (i) does the distinction between what only the saintly do and what morality requires of us depends on 'the' acts and omissions doctrine, and (ii) is 'the' acts and omissions doctrine false? (And we should note here that it is essential that these two points should be established *independently* of utilitarianism.)

Now a major difficulty in discussing either of these questions lies in understanding what 'the' doctrine is, which is why I have put scare quotes around the 'the'. Glover characterizes it as 'The belief that there is an important moral difference between acts and omissions, say between killing and "not striving to keep alive"'[6] or, as he says elsewhere, between killing and letting die (or killing and allowing to die, or killing and not saving). But one immediate problem here is that the example itself is tendentious. For some philosophers maintain that the difference between killing and allowing to die is *not* a distinction between act and omission. Discussing the distinction between active and passive euthanasia, Philippa Foot says:

> In some ways the words ['active' and 'passive'] are themselves misleading, because they suggest the difference between act and omission which is not quite what we want ... the act of turning off a respirator should surely be thought of as no different from the decision not to start it; if doctors had decided that a patient should be allowed to die, either course of action

might follow, and both should be counted as passive rather than active euthanasia if euthanasia were in question.[7]

In a later article she maintains that the difference between 'doing' and 'allowing' cannot be the difference between act and omission because 'then it would be possible to change the moral character of certain trains of events by such simple expedients as building respirators which needed to be turned on each day'.[8]

The distinction she is here referring to as 'the difference between act and omission' could also be described as the difference between (deliberate) moving as against (deliberate) not moving, or between action and inaction. This distinction has, in the past, been confused in the literature with the distinction between killing and letting die, but I think we can now safely assume that this confusion has been cleared up,[9] and follow Foot in putting it aside. Belief in the distinction between killing and allowing to die is *not* the same as belief in a distinction between moving and not moving, nor between action (in one sense) and inaction. As Don Locke has pointed out, 'it is possible to kill someone by not doing something, e.g. by failing to feed them, or neglecting to turn on the oxygen during an operation.'[10] It is also possible to allow someone to die by doing something, as when they insist that I detach them from the equipment that is keeping them alive and I do so.

Given this, what should we say about the belief in 'the' acts and omissions doctrine? Does Foot, believing in a distinction between killing and allowing to die, believe in it or not? Well, once we are clear about what has been put aside, there is no point in quarrelling about vocabulary. It would certainly be perverse to describe her as *agreeing* with Glover and other utilitarians that 'the' doctrine is false. So let us amend Glover's characterization of belief in the doctrine as follows: it is the belief that there is an important difference between acts and omissions, say between killing and letting die, where this is *not* taken to be simply the difference between doing and not doing (say, turning a machine off/on or not turning it on/off).

Now the problem is, what *is* it to believe that? Is it to believe that, for instance, there is *always* a moral difference

between killing and (deliberately) letting die, namely, that
the first is always worse than the second? Perhaps some
philosopher has held that, but such a position is indeed open
to some fairly standard counter-examples. Suppose I am on
my way to kill a child who stands between me and an
inheritance. As I arrive at the bathroom door, intending to
drown it, I see it slip, bang its head, and go under. I do not
need to push its head under and drown it; all I need to do
is stand by and let it drown. How could it be plausibly
denied that in this case my letting it die is just as wicked as
my killing it? I take it that this would not be plausible; i.e.
killing is not always worse than letting die, there is sometimes
no moral difference between them.

Suppose one believes that there is not always, but sometimes, a morally relevant difference between killing and
(deliberately) allowing to die. Suppose that my sister has
asked me for a commitment to allow her to die 'with dignity'
if and when the time comes, and not have her subjected to
prolonged life-saving treatment. But she has not asked me
to promise to kill her rather than let her linger on, since she
thinks that would be a wrong thing to do. Then, according
to how her illness progresses, it may turn out that it would
be right for me to allow her to die – indeed, wrong of me
not to – but still wrong for me to kill her.

Now if I agree with these judgements about what it would
be right and wrong to do in this sort of case, do I believe
there is sometimes a morally relevant difference between
killing and letting die? Surely I must – yet this has been
denied. James Rachels, in his most recent publication on the
topic of active and passive euthanasia, has come to agree
with Philippa Foot about this sort of example, while
continuing to maintain what he calls 'the Equivalence Thesis'
which 'says that there is no morally important difference
between killing and letting die'.[11]

His position (if I understand him correctly) is that *the*
morally important difference in the above case is the
difference between what I have been given permission to
do, and what I have not been given permission to do.
('Permission', he says, 'may, indeed, be a crucial matter, as
Foot says.') And the difference between killing and letting

die is merely 'correlated' with this.[12] 'I . . . can easily concede', he says, 'that, in some cases it may be permissible to let die but not to kill. Likewise, in other cases it may be permissible to kill but not to let die. This is perfectly compatible with the Equivalence Thesis. All the Equivalence Thesis requires is that, in such a case, it is some *other* feature of the case that makes the difference.'[13]

But the difficulty here is to distinguish between cases in which there 'really' is another feature, which makes the difference, and cases in which there is not. Suppose we attempt to compare, as Glover attempts to compare, the case of the Chancellor of the Exchequer who fails to increase the old-age pension adequately, with the predictable consequence that a number of old people die of the cold, with the case of the man who 'takes a machine-gun to an old people's home' and massacres a number (the same number) of people in it.[14] Is the distinction between killing and letting die crucial here, or is it merely 'correlated' with some other difference? Even Glover, speaking as a utilitarian, admits that there is a difference between what is manifested in the way of character in the one case and the other. 'The Chancellor who fails to put up the pension merely exhibits lack of imagination or concern', he says, whereas 'the man who massacres the old people exhibits some hostile motive or an unrestrained violence.'[15]

Or suppose we were to compare ourselves, leading our ordinary lives (in which we give something, perhaps even quite a lot, to charity, but do not reduce ourselves to starvation level), to a Mafia gangster, who profits from heroin traffic and kills not only people who get in his way but the innocent relations of people who inform on him, and say that there is an important difference between what he does and what we do. Is the distinction between killing and letting die crucial here, or is it merely 'correlated' with some other difference, or differences?

By this stage, at least within the context of the present argument, it seems pointless to pursue the dispute any further. For we can present the utilitarian with a dilemma. Either (a) the distinction between killing and letting die (or 'the' acts and omissions doctrine) is not crucial here, in which case the usual distinctions morality draws, between the saintly, the ordinary and the villainous, do not depend on it (contrary to the first point I mentioned above); or (b) 'the' acts and omissions doctrine is crucial in these examples, in which case we have not been given any reason to regard it as false, and it is (prior to accepting utilitarianism) overwhelmingly plausible (contrary to the second point).

Of course, utilitarianism unmodified by any autonomy principle will not agree with Rachels and Foot that 'permission may be crucial'. Nor does utilitarianism allow that 'the' difference manifested in character makes a difference to the rightness or wrongness of the act. But prior to accepting utilitarianism with its rejection of rights we can say that permission is often crucial. Prior to accepting its single criterion for the rightness and wrongness of acts, we can say that what the Chancellor does is (perhaps) inhumane, or indeed, disgracefully 'utilitarian', but nothing like as wicked or insane as what the mass murderer does; and that what we do is not vicious, utterly callous or cold-blooded the way the actions of the Mafioso are. So the utilitarian does not have an independent way to establish his two required points.

So complicated has the discussion of 'the' acts and omissions doctrine become in recent philosophical literature, even with respect to the single, limited example of killing and letting die, that I have myself lost a clear grasp of whether I believe in it or not. One thing that emerges from all the recent discussion is that 'the' doctrine is, at least, 'correlated with' (whether or not it is 'crucial to') a number of distinctions or considerations that I certainly do 'believe in'. These include not only the two just mentioned (concerning rights and what morality requires) but a number of others.[16] With regard to a great range of examples, an act and an omission may have the same outcome as far as the number of deaths is concerned and yet be significantly different in other ways. (Though not invariably in a way that makes the act worse than the omission. Sometimes the opposite is true; and sometimes both may be equally bad but still different.) Now, the utilitarian cannot say that I believe there are all these differences between examples *because* I believe in 'the' acts and omissions doctrine and then go on to cut the ground from under my feet by maintaining (let alone proving) that the doctrine is false. The differences do not depend on 'the' acts and omissions doctrine; if anything the order of dependence is the other way around. It is because I believe there are all these differences that, in a sense, I believe in 'the' acts and omissions doctrine, the relevant (and only) sense being that it would be disingenuous of me to say that I agreed with the utilitarians that 'the' doctrine was false. So it comes to this: I say there are all these differences, and the utilitarians say 'But, according to utilitarianism there aren't'. At this stage, I think I might claim to have plausibility on my side and thereby a general sort of objection to utilitarianism. If it entails that there is none of these differences, *and* there is, then utilitarianism is false. But plausibility is not the same as victory. Only one side can win, but both sides can claim plausibility. Few modern utilitarians deny that, with respect to the sorts of examples that have been the subject of this section, I have plausibility (or commonsense, or ordinary morality) on my side. But, they say, on their side is the overwhelming plausibility of the utilitarian theory itself, the theory which, *par excellence*, embodies or reflects all that is right in commonsense or ordinary morality. True, it has these few rather odd and disconcerting upshots, but they are as nothing in comparison with how *convincing* the theory is.

It would be unwise for an anti-utilitarian to deny that utilitarianism is plausible and convincing. I think it must be immediately conceded that it is. The next move is to try to uncover *why* and, in doing so, display the plausibility as merely specious. This I attempt to do in the next section.

2   BENEVOLENCE AND THE OTHER VIRTUES

Suppose one simply began with the following line of thought: 'Wouldn't it be nice if everyone could have what they wanted, be perfectly happy, satisfied and contented. Of course this isn't actually possible, because people get sick, and the people they love die. But it's also true that there's a lot of needless suffering around. It's not only all the people suffering because they are starving and have preventable diseases but we *create* a lot of unnecessary suffering for ourselves and each other by hanging on to an irrational conviction that some sorts of actions are intrinsically right or wrong. Look how miserable the Victorians made themselves and each other because they were hung up about sex, for example, and to this day some people are still unhappy because they think they "ought" to stay married, when it would obviously be best for everyone concerned if they got divorced. Look at what miserable lives homosexuals used to lead, and what miserable lives some of them still do lead, because they think that homosexual sex is "wrong". Any suffering is bad, but unnecessary and preventable suffering is a tragedy. A lot of it has been, and is being, caused in the name of "morality". But what any decent morality should surely be doing is trying to prevent it, and trying to make everyone as happy as possible.'

Very often, though doubtless not invariably, it is some such line of thought which prompts people towards utilitarianism. It contains the two aspects which yield a utilitarian theory. On the one hand is the idea that a lot of things that people used to say are intrinsically wrong, and make a lot of fuss about, are *not* wrong; we may recall Singer's proud claim that 'a utilitarian can never properly be accused of a lack of realism, or of a rigid adherence to ideals in defiance of practical experience' (see p. 135). No one, it is claimed, who is realistic or practical or rational could think that lying or breaking promises was always wrong or that masturbation ever was. This idea is captured in utilitarianism's consequentialism: that acts are right or wrong only insofar as they have good or bad consequences.

On the other hand there is a conviction about what really is wrong – making people unhappy or causing suffering. There is nothing wrong with masturbation precisely because it does not hurt anyone. It is obvious, it is claimed, that, far from always being wrong, lying and breaking promises are sometimes right, precisely because it is obvious that sometimes the lie or the broken promise, far from hurting anyone, actually spare people suffering, or make for much more happiness all round than there would have been if one had rigidly adhered to some idealistic principle. This idea is captured in the second aspect of utilitarianism – the way in which it specifies what count as good or bad consequences; they are good insofar as they increase happiness or well-being or give people what they want or reduce suffering, bad insofar as they reduce happiness or well-being or deprive people of what they want and increase suffering.

The distinctly startling upshots of relying on consequentialism have been thoroughly explored in the earlier chapter on utilitarianism. It is the second aspect of utilitarianism which I shall concentrate on here.

The definition of 'happiness'

I mentioned at the beginning of the chapter on utilitarianism a very general objection to it, namely the claim that there is no specification of the good consequences we are supposed to maximize under which utilitarianism can be preserved as a plausible and coherent moral theory (p. 136). In order to let the discussion of the utilitarian attitude to killing get off the ground, I shelved this objection, allowing utilitarians who apply the theory their working assumption that we all understand *roughly* what is intended by 'happiness' or 'well-being' or 'giving people what they want' and can rely on the theoreticians to work out the details in time. But it is now time for us to turn a sceptical eye on that assumption.

Many people are immediately struck by the plausibility of the view that the promotion of the greatest happiness for the greatest number is of central importance to morality, perhaps indeed, the only thing that matters. But even those who are so struck may naturally worry about the definition of 'happiness'. 'What *is* happiness?', it is natural to wonder. 'How can it be measured and how can the happiness of two very different people be compared? If someone says she is happy but is a slave can that be true happiness? If someone says he can only have a happy sex-life if he has sex with children am I supposed to hope some willing children can be found, or does that sort of happiness not count?'

Perhaps the only upholder of utilitarianism who has ever thought that there was *no* difficulty in defining, measuring or comparing happiness is its founder, Jeremy Bentham. Bentham briskly equated happiness with pleasure, and famously said that 'quantity of pleasure being equal, push-pin is as good as poetry'. But his immediate successor, John Stuart Mill, not only drew a distinction between higher and lower pleasures but also, in neo-Aristotelian style, insisted that virtue gave pleasure (of the highest sort) to the lover of virtue.

The very general objection to utilitarianism with which I am here concerned is not 'It is impossible to decide which is the right definition of "happiness" – Bentham's or Mill's or someone else's – and hence impossible to work out what utilitarianism would have us promote or maximize'. The objection is: 'Whatever definition we take, maintaining that acts are right or wrong only insofar as they promote or reduce "happiness" is implausible.'

Broadly speaking, the problem could be expressed as follows. On a view similar to Bentham's it seems that the morally ideal state of the world is the one in which we are all hooked up to pleasure-machines which are not only life-support systems but which also, by stimulating some appropriate bits of our brains, maintain us on the equivalent of a life-long, harmless, heroin high. This would guarantee that *everyone*, if asked 'Are you perfectly happy?', would say 'Yes' (supposing they could answer).

Not many people think that this is the sort of state of the world we ought to be trying to bring about, and their objection is not merely that this 'ideal state' belongs only in the realms of fantasy or science fiction. The deeper objection which is often made is that achieving guaranteed pleasure and freedom from pain or misery *at the price* of giving up rational autonomy and personal relationships is not desirable. Agreed, loving people is giving hostages to fortune; agreed, maintaining one's autonomy is courting suffering – nevertheless, many people want to say that these things are worth the price. Some pleasures or enjoyments are more valuable or important than others.

To say this is to move towards introducing a more

distinctively human interpretation of 'happiness', an interpretation that is somehow more appropriately tailored to our distinctive capacities to take non-sensual pleasure or enjoyment in such things as acquiring knowledge and exercising the virtues. And making this move, as Mill did, has always been the obvious block to the Benthamite idea that all pleasures are equally valuable or desirable or worth having. But to interpret 'happiness' in terms of some such rich notion resembling Aristotelian flourishing, is to introduce the idea of there being good pleasures and bad pleasures and then, far from aiming at giving everyone what they want, a utilitarian starts aiming to give them what they *ought* to want, or *would* want if they were not such fools and pigs. And utilitarianism thereby loses that very aspect which first made it intuitively appealing and becomes oppressively paternalistic.

Concluding his discussion of the higher and lower pleasures, Mill says:

> It is better to be a human being dissatisfied than a pig satisfied; better to be Socrates dissatisfied than a fool satisfied. And if the fool, or the pig, are of a different opinion, it is because they only know their own side of the question. The other party to the comparison knows both sides.[17]

Now it is one thing to believe, with Mill and Aristotle, that 'true happiness' involves acting virtuously and exercising one's intellectual capacities. It is quite another to believe it is right to impose this view on others, particularly other adults, against their wishes. Most of us do believe it is better for an intelligent human being to be educated rather than not (that people are more likely to be happy, have a greater chance of success, of leading flourishing lives, if they are literate and can enjoy poetry as well as 'push-pin') and in the light of this belief we send our children to school, frequently against their wishes. But not many of us would think it right to seek out the few illiterate adults in our population and force them to learn to read, nor to rout out the literate push-pin players and force them to go back to poetry.

Benevolence

Viewed from the perspective of a theory of virtue, utilitarianism may be seen as a theory of general benevolence (or charity in the old sense), the concern for the happiness or well-being of others. It is basically from the point of view of benevolence, loving one's neighbour as oneself, that the consequences of actions are assessed as good or bad. The qualification 'basically' serves to remind us that this is not entirely accurate, since as I have pointed out before, utilitarianism strictly involves counting one's own happiness as being just as important as anyone else's – we are duty bound to love ourselves as much as our neighbour. Notwithstanding this point, utilitarianism is usually thought of as the ethic of perfect benevolence, and the idea that benevolence or charity is, if not the only, at least the most important of the virtues, has a perennial appeal. 'For now abideth faith, hope and charity, these three; but the greatest of these is charity' says Paul (Corinthians 13:11) and he claims if I 'have not charity, I am nothing' (ibid. 13:2). The faith and hope to which he refers are theological virtues; hence it would seem that in a secular morality, charity is indeed the only virtue. Mill himself says:

> In the golden rule of Jesus of Nazareth, we read the complete spirit of the ethics of utility. To do as you would be done by, and to love your neighbour as yourself, constitute the ideal perfection of utilitarian morality.[18]

But when utilitarianism is viewed from this perspective (a neo-Aristotelian theory of virtue) not only its appeal, but also some of its flaws show up particularly clearly.

The idea that benevolence or 'charity' is at least the most important of the virtues has, as I just said, a perennial appeal, and it seems particularly appealing when we regard benevolence as including the twin virtue of compassion – the concern with the suffering of others. Many people live in conditions so frightful that they cannot flourish. Insofar as we can do something to ameliorate these conditions, benevolence urges us to do it, and this is something that utilitarians concerned with practice (rather than pure theory) standardly stress. It is no accident that the great nineteenth-century utilitarians were social reformers and indeed laid the foundations of the present welfare state, and no accident that modern utilitarians are so frequently to be found arguing against our relative indifference to the plight of people suffering in the Third World. However much room for disagreement there is about good and bad pleasures, about what pain or suffering it is worth risking or enduring, it is plausible to maintain that there are some sorts of suffering, notably sorts produced by extreme poverty, which everyone would agree we would be better off without. It is also beyond question that there is much that could be done to eliminate such suffering which has not yet been done and that this must be a matter of concern to anyone interested in morality. In emphasizing this, utilitarianism undoubtedly has right, and plausibility, on its side. But mention of the welfare state and aid to the Third World should remind us of a familiar set of problems concerning people's autonomy. One can provide, for instance, free dental care; but forcing people to have regular check-ups is something else despite the fact that many people, if not forced, will not go regularly and will suffer accordingly. We encounter the same sorts of problems in bringing up our children. We may bring them up as best we can, protecting them from suffering as much as possible, but there comes a point at which we have to let them lead their own lives and suffer the consequences of their own mistakes.

The 'nice' thought behind utilitarianism is that one should *make* other people happy, producing their happiness *as a consequence* of one's own acts. But this cannot always be done. Sometimes all one can do is cross one's fingers and wish people well. 'Benevolence' indeed literally means no more than 'well wishing', but in practice, a fair amount of beneficence or 'well doing' is needed to manifest a genuine rather than an idle wish. So benevolence urges us to eliminate those conditions which make it impossible for people to be happy as far as we can, to avoid cruelty and unkindness, to create conditions which make it easier for people to be happy as far as we can – but in some circumstances and at some stages benevolence requires that we only *wish* others well, not that we go out and interfere. My wish that, for example, my best friend should be happy does not count as idle just because I stand by helplessly as she embarks on a disastrous marriage.

The sad fact that one cannot *make* other people happy, that people's happiness is, to a certain extent, in their own hands is particularly obvious if one thinks of 'happiness' in terms of the rich notion of Aristotelian flourishing or living well. I cannot act so as to make you flourish, or live your life for you, well or badly. You have to do your own flourishing, developing your own virtuous character traits and acting in accordance with them, just as I have to do mine. Thinking of 'happiness' as flourishing or 'true happiness', I cannot make you happy by telling you comforting lies either; people whose lives are based on falsehood are living in a 'fool's paradise' and only think they are happy. But the point need not depend on the correctness of the Aristotelian view of 'happiness', since any view of happiness which allows for individual autonomy is bound to acknowledge that letting people do as they choose will sometimes lead to their (avoidable) suffering, but that people are unhappy and frustrated when they are prevented from doing as they choose. But the Aristotelian emphasis on individual lives and activity, in contrast to passive states of pleasure or enjoyment, makes the point especially vivid.

So the first flaw that I claim to find in utilitarianism's appealing benevolence is that, as a guide to what it is morally right to do rather than morally right to wish, it cannot be extended far beyond trying to make it easier for people to be happy. Though the urgent importance of doing a great deal more about this than is done at present can hardly be over-emphasized, it should not be described as *making* people happy, nor should we pretend that it is possible to produce other people's happiness as a consequence of our own acts.

We 'cannot' make other people happy or prevent their suffering in another sense too. Sometimes there is, straightforwardly, nothing to be done, as when I have set my foolish heart on someone who you know will make me wretched. At other times, there will be something which it is physically possible to do, but it will be something that 'cannot' be done morally speaking, as when there is 'nothing that can be done' for the patients who need transplants until a suitable donor or corpse turns up. Obviously it is physically possible to kill another patient – the others 'can be saved' as far as physical possibility is concerned – but we cannot kill one patient in order to provide organs for others. And the second flaw that I claim to find in utilitarianism's appealing benevolence is that it makes benevolence (supposing this includes compassion) the *only* virtue, whereas it is, though very important, but one virtue amongst many.

In concentrating exclusively on benevolence utilitarianism ignores the claims of the other virtues, most notably those of justice. 'Let justice be done though the heavens fall' (or 'the world perish') goes the saying and what that saying captures is the fact that acting justly may well have consequences which, from the point of view of pure benevolence, are deeply regrettable. All my benevolence and compassion might cry out against someone's determination to waste her life by devoting it to someone worthless, or to live out its last agonizing months. But I owe it to her not to interfere; though benevolence makes me long to, justice demands that I do not. The virtues of fidelity (in the sense of 'being true to one's word' or keeping promises) and honesty may also set restraints on what can be done in the name of benevolence. One can view with compassionate regret the fact that someone is going to suffer through being told the truth, or lament the fact that someone would be happier if a promise were broken, and still believe that, in each case, the truth must be told, the promise must be kept.

Benevolence, moreover, is in one sense an impersonal virtue, directed towards everyone's well-being. But there are other virtues, such as those of friendship, or being a good parent, or a dutiful daughter or son, which are particularly concerned with the happiness and well-being of just a few people one is in some relationship to. Literature has familiar examples of people whose moral failing is that they neglect their family for the sake of the more general and impersonal claims of benevolence; someone who is totally committed to the well-being of humanity at large has no time to spare for the special attentions that are due to friends, due even when the friends do not actually need them.

Now it is noteworthy that if we tried to obey the instruction 'Act benevolently' we would not necessarily find ourselves acting against the claims of justice, honesty, friendship and so on. Whatever the opposite of benevolence is (strictly it should be malevolence, but let us say, roughly, cruelty and, sometimes, selfishness) we do not always count someone as acting cruelly or selfishly when they let other people bring misery on themselves, or tell someone a painful truth, or keep their promise to one person when others would have been better off if the promise had been broken and so on. And it would never occur to us that one way to obey the instruction was to kill one person in order to provide essential parts for five others. This is, I take it, because our concept of benevolence is the concept of one virtue among others. To think of perfect benevolence is to think of the perfection of that virtue in combination with others, not as existing on its own. (This is not to deny that we may think that perfect benevolence is incompatible with perfection in *some* of the other virtues. Perhaps being a perfect friend and family person really does involve a little insensitivity to the well-being and suffering of strangers, and is hence incompatible with perfect benevolence. But to say we (might) think of perfect benevolence as existing without the virtues of friendship and being a good parent is a far cry from saying we (might) think of it as existing without any of the other virtues.) One can be perfectly benevolent without always acting benevolently, because (since benevolence is one virtue amongst others) sometimes what is called for is not benevolence but some other virtue such as justice.

Since our concept of benevolence is like this, there are limits to what a moral theory that concentrates exclusively on it can say. Suppose utilitarianism said 'Act benevolently', or rather, 'Acts are right insofar as they are benevolent, wrong insofar as they are malevolent'. Then this theory would not require us to do a lot of things that were contrary to the other virtues; it does not tell us that it would be right to kill the person who would be better off dead even though they do not want to die, or that it would be wrong to tell the truth to someone if the truth were a painful one. For, as we just saw, sometimes what is called for is not benevolence but justice or honesty, and being just or honest does not count as being malevolent. What would be mistaken about this theory is not that it would label as right many actions that are wrong (and vice versa) but that it would be so incomplete. Benevolent acts are right, malevolent ones are wrong – but what about the ones that are neither, i.e. some of the just ones and the honest ones, or some of the family-neglecting and promise-breaking ones? The theory has not said anything about them, right or wrong, at all, and hence is, as a moral theory, glaringly incomplete.

Suppose instead that the theory said 'acts are right insofar as they are benevolent and wrong *otherwise*'. This theory would be complete in the sense that it says something about every act; for every act is either benevolent or not. But the trouble is now that the theory does not provide me with clear guidance about what to do. Should I kill this one person to provide essential parts for five others? No, because we agreed above that this does not count as a benevolent act. Well, should I refrain from killing him? No, that is not benevolent either; it is required by justice, not benevolence. So it is wrong to kill him, and wrong not to kill him, because neither is an act of benevolence. So the theory gives me no guidance as to what to do in such a case.

Utilitarianism is complete and does guarantee guidance as to what to do. How does it achieve this despite concentrating exclusively on benevolence? In effect what it does is take the concern of benevolence – people being happy, and the more the better – and say 'Make this your only moral concern'. That is, acts are right insofar as they increase happiness, wrong otherwise. (Or we could add: it takes the concerns of benevolence and compassion – the latter concern being for people suffering, the fewer the better – and says 'Make these your only concerns'.)

It is true that being told to make the concern of benevolence one's only concern is not the same as being told to act only benevolently and no other way. As we saw above, if I am told to act only benevolently I have not been given clear instructions – it is wrong to kill the one for the five and wrong not to. But if utilitarianism were explicitly expressed as 'Make the concern of benevolence your only concern' we would, I suspect, find a similar difficulty in working out what we were supposed to do; it would also strike one more forcibly that what one was being told to do was give up the concerns of justice, friendship, family loyalties, honesty, etc. But when the theory is expressed in the standard utilitarian way, these difficulties are not at all obvious. We do not realize that we are supposed to do a number of frightful things, nor that we have been told to give up so much.

These two factors are just two sides of the same coin, and in a way amount to what is by now familiar ground – that utilitarianism describes as right a lot of actions that common-sense morality holds to be wrong (and vice versa). But now, instead of the piecemeal production of examples of such actions, we have a general characterization of how they arise. Wherever common-sense morality has it that in these circumstances what is called for is not benevolence but justice, or honesty, or fidelity to promises, or friendship and so on, it is on the cards that utilitarianism and common-sense morality will conflict. (They may not, because sometimes 'everything works out for the best' as we say, and justice or honesty or some other virtue require just what benevolence would have wanted.)

If utilitarianism were expressed as 'make the concern of benevolence your *only* concern' it would also be clear how the difficulty I noted in the previous section arises. If the general good is to be my *only* concern then I must also give up the concerns of everyday life (except insofar as a concern for the general good is held to involve my own). That is, what morality requires of me is that I be a saint or heroine – there is no way to be an ordinarily decent person.

Conclusions

As I said at the end of the previous section, few modern utilitarians deny that, with respect to some examples, their theory runs counter to common-sense morality and to that extent is radical and revisionary rather than the embodiment of what we all believe. But Singer, for instance, maintains that utilitarianism is radical only insofar as it repudiates what he regards as the irrational convictions of a bankrupt Christianity. If we could but rid ourselves of these we would realize that the so-called counter-examples are quite innocuous and that, when we can manage to be consistently rational and high-minded, we really do believe in utilitarianism, or at least ought to. But the general characterization we have now discovered of how the counter-examples arise should make us suspicious, whatever our religious allegiance, of claims that we ought to be utilitarians because utilitarianism is the rational result of discovering the intellectual inadequacy of conventional moral thinking, or that this thinking becomes manifestly outmoded as soon as we distinguish it from its Christian backing. In a piecemeal discussion of particular examples one might be momentarily convinced of this, but no such discussion should convince one that benevolence is the only intellectually respectable virtue nor that justice, honesty, friendship, etc. require a Christian backing whereas benevolence uniquely does not. Notwithstanding the 'neo-', neo-Aristotelianism is as secular a morality as original Aristotelianism was. It can quite readily be made consistent with Christianity, and indeed Christianity can give it a particularly powerful backing, but it does not need that backing. It can stand on its own without it.

Finally, let us recall the doctrine of the sanctity of life, which utilitarians say we should abandon. I suggested, when discussing it, that, within the terms of a secular morality, the belief in it consisted of no more than (but no less than) a larger or smaller set of other beliefs, such as – killing adult humans is wrong, infanticide is wrong, killing persons is wrong, killing animals is wrong, etc. Such a belief, expressed as it may be in a variety of ways connected with a number of the virtues, is not, and need not be, peculiar to people who give it a theological backing. Justice, friendship, fidelity to promises, and benevolence, any one of them may rule out killing on some occasion. On others what may be called for is risk or sacrifice of life for the sake of saving others; though this may sometimes involve mere maximization of lives to be preserved in a utilitarian way, it will not always do so and the decisions will, rather, be expressive of the idea that each individual life is of incommensurable value.

This idea 'that each individual life is of incommensurable (or, as people sometimes say, 'of infinite') value' is, I suspect, just another version of the doctrine of the sanctity of life. Perhaps what this way of expressing it particularly brings out is that it is only utilitarians (who really have abandoned the doctrine) who would ever think that, quite generally, questions about who to save, or kill, or let die, should always be determined by a head count (other things being equal). When just one or two people are trapped down a mine, or on a mountain, or in some other extremely dangerous circumstances, it is quite common for *lots* of people on the spot to rally around and risk their lives in the attempt to save them. I am not saying that considerations of whether so many can be risked for so few are never relevant. I am merely pointing out that there are *some* circumstances in which if someone said, 'Oh but there is only one of them, and the lifeboat or rescue party will need three people – it's obviously not worth it', we would think they were quite mad to try to weigh human lives against each other in this way. It may be indeed that this idea is part of the concept of benevolence itself. It is not only, as we noted above, that we do not expect the benevolent (or compassionate) person to kill one to provide organs for five; we do not expect the benevolent person even to hope that the one will die. To someone who wishes her fellow human beings well, the unlooked for death of one who had many good years before them, regardless of the excellent consequences for others, is an evil in itself, not merely a figure in a calculation.[19]

NOTES

1   Singer, Peter (1979) *Practical Ethics*, Cambridge University Press, pp. 149–50.
2   Smart, J. J. C. and Williams, Bernard (1973) in *Utilitarianism, For and Against*, Cambridge University Press, p. 30; my italics.

3   *Ibid.*, p. 42; my italics.
4   *Ibid.*, p. 55.
5   Locke, Don (1982) 'The Choice Between Lives', *Philosophy*, vol. 57.
6   Glover, *op. cit.*, p. 21.
7   Foot, Philippa (1977) 'Euthanasia', *Philosophy and Public Affairs*, vol. 6, no. 2.
8   *Idem*, 'Morality, Action and Outcome', in Honderich, Ted (ed.) (1985) *Morality and Objectivity*, Routledge & Kegan Paul.
9   See in particular, Don Locke, *op. cit.*
10 *Ibid.*
11 Rachels, James (1986) *The End of Life*, Oxford University Press, p. 111.
12 *Ibid.*, p. 127.
13 *Ibid.*
14 Glover, *op. cit.*, p. 93.
15 *Ibid.*, p. 111.
16 See again Don Locke, *op. cit.*, and Philippa Foot, 'Morality, Action and Outcome'.
17 Mill, J. S. (1871, 4th edn) *Utilitarianism*, London, Chapter 2.
18 *Ibid.*
19 In this Chapter I am indebted to a number of articles by Philippa Foot, cited *en passant*, and quite generally to Don Locke *op. cit.* In neither case do the references adequately reflect the debt.

CHAPTER EIGHT

The special position of women

One important upshot of neo-Aristotelianism, as we have seen, is that most actions are indeed 'right in some circumstances, wrong in others', but not at all in the way that utilitarianism holds. The reason why particular sorts of actions such as killing, or infanticide, or abortion, can be right or wrong, is not because their morality varies according to their consequences, but because the fully virtuous agent acts differently according to the circumstances.

This means that a certain sort of cultural relativity is built into neo-Aristotelianism, for the same virtues and vices can be manifested differently in different cultures. There is much variety, for instance, in what counts as 'honouring one's dead'; we bury or burn ours, but in other cultures proper respect was shown, for example, by eating them. We are brought up to regard cannibalism as out of the question, beyond the pale, disgusting, horrific – so anyone who, despite this upbringing and in defiance of it, tries to cook and eat human flesh, counts as perverted. But if one had been brought up to regard it as an integral part of a fairly serious family ceremony, something one did every now and then from toddlerhood up, a restricted form of cannibalism would be perfectly proper.

This does not mean that whatever people in another culture do is right as long as they believe it is. There is no theoretical reason why we should not criticize another culture for having the wrong idea of human flourishing. Moreover, as I have stressed several times, built into the concept of the virtues is getting things *right*, where this includes 'correct'. A culture whose members share a collection of false beliefs about the inborn vices or failings of some subset of them – say, the black ones, or the female ones – is off to a bad start as far as the manifestation of the virtues is concerned.

There is more truth in the converse: that whatever people in another culture (or ours) do is wrong if they think it is. But this is not because 'values are culturally determined'. It is because, quite generally, it is wrong to do what you think is wrong, to act against your conscience. We do not always insist on this, for sometimes we want to describe someone as 'realizing deep down' or 'in their heart of hearts' that such and such is not wrong, despite the fact that in some sense they think it is, and praise the triumph of good instincts over bad moral teaching. But in order to do so, one needs to be fairly sure about the good instincts; not just any case of rebelling against bad teaching would count.

Closely related to the built-in cultural relativity, is a form of built-in circumstantial relativity. As I noted when considering how saintliness or heroism arose, a course of action such as 'honouring one's parents' might become exceptionally demanding, and in those circumstances, failing to do it may exhibit no more than ordinary human weakness. But in ordinary circumstances, failing to do it would usually be to exhibit selfishness, or irresponsibility, or callousness and cruelty, and so on. The ideal of the fully virtuous person provides one with a standard according to which one can judge that an action was wrong in some sense and yet not, given how demanding the circumstances were, wrong in being selfish or callous or whatever. Ordinarily, it should not be particularly hard for the ordinarily decent person to avoid wrongdoing, but circumstances can make it particularly hard.

However, if we bring this quite general point to bear on the issue of abortion, a rather startling consequence emerges. Nothing could be more ordinary and familiar than the fact that women get pregnant unless they remain chaste or (in developed countries, and only relatively recently) take the most painstaking care with contraception. Are we to say then that it is not particularly hard for the ordinarily decent woman to avoid the wrongdoing of having an abortion? But the alternative, in many cases, will be the arduous business of carrying a child to term. Is that to be described simply as doing what any ordinarily decent person would do in ordinary circumstances? Was there not *some* truth in Thomson's claim that women who went through with their pregnancies frequently acted, not just as Minimally Decent, but as particularly Good Samaritans? Thomson based her claim (a) on the working assumption that the fœtus was a person from the moment of conception and (b) on the unargued for assertion that I am not morally required to stay hooked up to the violinist. I have rejected both these assumptions, but might we not be able to find some other grounds from which to argue that women who bear children act not merely ordinarily, but particularly well?

In this chapter I try to provide such grounds, by bringing into neo-Aristotelianism some of the special facts about our biology, and the effect they have on our physical and psychological life. This will provide us, at long last, with the material to say something, albeit something tentative, not only about abortion, but also about surrogacy.

1   THE AVERAGE WOMAN

It is often held to be an important part of our moral thinking that in *some* sense all human beings are born morally equal, neither superior nor inferior to each other. Insofar as some desirable characteristics – such as beauty or intelligence – are characteristics that some are (unfairly) born with while others are not; insofar as one is born into a particular position, rich or poor, or born black, white or mixed, or born female or male, we say that these characteristics do not make one a morally better or worse person; they are 'morally irrelevant'. That whether one is male or female is 'morally irrelevant' is a claim that is often made in the context of arguments against sexual discrimination and in favour of equal treatment. In such a context, the parallel with the claim that one's race or skin colour is 'morally irrelevant', which is put forward to combat racial discrimination, is obvious. The characteristics and actions that make for being a morally good person are those that anyone might acquire or do; short of being born mentally defective in a certain way (e.g. incapable of becoming mentally more than a child), we are born in *some* sense with an equal chance of becoming good (and insofar as we are not, because, say, some are born into particularly deprived and damaging environments, this is one of the greatest social injustices).

This apparently supports the following: suppose we have two people, *A* and *B*, who, morally speaking, behave exactly in the same ways for years and years. Most of the time they act with at least minimal decency, in accordance with virtue. Very occasionally they act particularly well and do something quite admirable, acting as a really good Samaritan would. More frequently, they make the ordinary mistakes and fall prey to the ordinary temptations – they are occasionally unjust, sometimes a bit dishonest or callous or selfish or self-indulgent and so on. It seems that they are two ordinary decent average people, and surely morally on a par, since we have mentioned the only things that count.

Now if *A* and *B* are both men, the chances are high that they will have achieved this rather ordinary standard without a great deal of difficulty. But if one of them is a woman, the chances are that she, in achieving this rather ordinary standard, will have done something distinctly demanding, *viz.* carry and bring forth a child, at no inconsiderable risk to her health and life. The average woman has done this at least once, if not twice, by middle-age; although some men may have done as much, no *average*, ordinary man will have – and yet Mr and Mrs Average will count as morally on a par, that is, as two ordinarily decent people.

Given the brute fact that it is women who get pregnant, can we really continue to maintain that there is a sense in which all human beings are born equal and that whether one is male or female is 'morally irrelevant'? For, if abortion is usually wrong, then it seems that nature has unfairly arranged things in such a way that it is harder for women to avoid wrongdoing than men. Human beings are equally prone to thoughtlessness, to the seizing of the present pleasure regardless of future consequences, but in relation to the particular temptations of sexual pleasure, the consequences for women are far more serious. A moment of ordinary thoughtlessness or imprudence does not, in the natural way of things, standardly land men in situations in which they may be tempted to infanticide or some other particular wrongdoing. But in the natural way of things, it standardly lands women in the situation in which they may be tempted to abortion, since the alternative is the arduous and often frightening business of child-bearing. In order to avoid being faced with this predictable temptation, a woman must opt for chastity, or long periods of sexual abstinence or (more recently) the most painstaking care with contraception. Moreover, she needs to do this from an early age – an age well below the bottom line at which we usually think it reasonable to expect much foresight, prudence, resolution, self-control, or independence; all of which may be called for. And even if she opts for chastity (or abstinence, or the wrong sort of contraceptive) this will still leave open the possibility that, due to rape, she will find herself pregnant anyhow.

It seems that to many people nowadays, the idea that nature could have stacked the cards against women in this way is so intolerable that they feel compelled to get out of it by maintaining that there is absolutely nothing wrong with abortion. Men and women *are* equal, so no more than men are women morally obliged to make the extraordinary, beyond the average, efforts of chastity, abstinence, painstaking contraception or pregnancy to avoid acting wrongly by having an abortion. No more than men are women morally debarred from exercising their right over their own bodies in ordinary circumstances by aborting a fœtus that is in it and part of it. For having an abortion is not acting wrongly. This satisfies the common intuition that, particularly in respect of the fairly young, two people who try to be responsible about their sexual activity but are occasionally thoughtless or careless or carried away by passion, are morally on a par, and also the intuition that if a pregnancy is due to rape, it is the rape that constitutes all the wrongdoing; there can be *nothing* wrong with a subsequent abortion. The idea that women, and particularly girls, are set up by nature to have to take on the heavy burden of pregnancy or act wrongly in having an abortion is too unfair to be tolerable.

So Mr Average who has occasionally been thoughtless about contraception, and Ms Average who has too, and has had an abortion, count as morally on a par.

But, quite aside from the dissatisfaction many people feel with saying there is nothing wrong with abortion, this line still does not seem to do justice to Mrs Average. Although the average woman, unlike the average man, has borne two children, there is nothing in the view that abortion is perfectly permissible which will give us grounds for saying that she has thereby done something of moral significance, something that counts. Indeed, *if* what we are trying to maintain is that (somehow) nature could not be so unfair as to stack the cards against one sex, that 'all humans are born equal', in some sense important to morality, then we shall have to deny that Mrs Average has done something of moral significance. For otherwise nature would have unfairly stacked the cards against men.

But suppose we give up trying to maintain that. I suggest that we should; that we should abandon the attempt to maintain that there is some important moral sense of 'all humans are born equal', according to which any biological differences between being male and being female are 'morally irrelevant'. Instead we should acknowledge the relevance to morality of the brute fact that women get pregnant and men do not. Part of the point of doing so would be to bite on the bullet of saying that women, even young girls, just *are* faced with a greater liability to act wrongly than men are, given that abortion is usually wrong. But, having accepted that, we would find compensation or understanding in the fact that women are, in one respect, born superior to men – superior in the straightforward sense that they are born with a capacity to do something worthwhile, *viz.* bear children (and no corresponding incapacity, such as being unable to think logically) which men lack.

The point of the clause about 'no corresponding incapacity' is to emphasize that this suggestion is far more radical than the traditional exaltation of motherhood. For the traditional moral systems which have professed to honour women's peculiar capacity to bear children have always assumed that men characteristically and peculiarly do something else (or indeed more), something women cannot do, which equals or matches it. But this is just to make again (at best) the very assumption in question – that in some moral sense we are all born equal, that Mr and Mrs Average are morally on a par. But I am suggesting that we give up the idea that in some sense men and women are born 'morally equal' and acknowledge that in bearing children, Mrs Average does something morally significant and worthwhile which Mr Average does not match, whereby they are not morally on a par.

So usual is it for women to care for and bring up the children they bear that it is important to emphasize at the outset that I shall be concerned only with the business of bearing children. It would be comparatively easier to maintain that, in their selfless devotion to their children, at least in the earlier years, many women achieve a level of acting well which few men match. But this difference between women's and men's achievements is not fundamental in the way the difference between child-bearing and not child-bearing is. It is not uncommon for women to be bad mothers, and perhaps equally common for men to be selfless fathers. Moreover, though it is clear that nature has laid it down that women bear children and men do not, it is far from clear that nature has laid it down – at least to anything like the same extent – that women and not men do care passionately about their young children. We know that some men do care passionately, and perhaps more would if they were given the opportunities that women have. Pending the proof that males really are born naturally self-seeking, destructive and indifferent to their offspring, whereas females are born altruistic and compassionate, we have as yet no reason to abandon the idea that males and females are born with an equally good chance of acquiring the virtue of being a good parent. To claim that in her rearing of children the average woman acts well in a way unmatched in the life of an average man would be to claim that, as a matter of (underrated) fact, cases in which women are no more than ordinarily decent (or, conversely, in which men achieve even that standard) are much rarer than is usually acknowledged. But to claim this would not be to call into question the fundamental principle that all humans are born equal. It would only be to say that judging them (as the principle requires) by the same standards, we find that many if not most men tend to behave rather badly and selfishly, whereas most women behave rather well and altruistically. Whether or not this is true I do not know; but its truth, as I say, is not part of my concern here. It is certainly true that most women bear children and that no men do, and it is the significance of this unquestionable fact in which I am interested.

Describing the putative significance in question as 'moral' seems to me obvious and natural, but if, agreeing with everything *else* that I am about to say, someone wanted to deny me this use of the word 'moral' I should not be particularly concerned. Indeed, what follows may be regarded as being in part a tentative attempt to say something about the extraordinarily difficult question of how our concepts of 'the moral', 'the morally relevant', 'the significant', 'the worthwhile' and so on, fit together.

Child-bearing and choice

'I would rather stand three times in the battle line', says Euripides' Medea, 'than give birth once.' When men or women go into battle they are praised for their courage; when they suffer pain and sickness uncomplainingly they are praised for their fortitude; when they struggle on from day to day fighting a constant battle against exhaustion we admire them for their endurance. And if you can make light of these things – joking in the trenches, saying that the sickness will pass, or is not bad all the time, enjoying much of your day despite the exhaustion, this counts as particularly admirable. Most pregnancies and labours call for courage, fortitude and endurance, though most women make light of them – so why are women not praised and admired for going through them?

It might be said: well the *average* ordinary woman goes through this, it is an everyday occurrence, and we do not praise and admire people for doing what is done every day. But in fact, taking the human race as a whole, *people* do not go through this sort of thing every day; bearing children is not something the average ordinary human being does. Indeed, in relation to sex-determined characteristics, functions, or activities, it is obviously nonsense to talk about 'the average human being'.

'Still', one might say, 'isn't it the case that nature compels women to go through bearing children? It's not really a matter of deliberate choice, like going into the battle line and standing firm. And without deliberate choice we do not have an action or a "doing" of the sort that is relevant to morality. It cannot be said that a woman who has borne children has *done* something except in a few exceptional cases. If it were entirely a matter of deliberate choice then, given that one can see the point of Medea's remark, perhaps many fewer women would go in for it. And then things would be very different, perhaps unimaginably so.' This apparently simple line of thought contains in fact many strands which need to be teased out at some length.

Let us begin by asking why it might be said that bearing children is 'not a matter of deliberate choice'. One reason that may be given is that, as a matter of fact, women do not, by and large, decide *to bear a child*. Usually women just get married (and in many countries, and throughout much of our past, that is not and was not a matter of choice) and get pregnant (also not a matter of choice for many women past and present) and are then more or less stuck with carrying the thing through.

In response to this we may note that the lack of deliberate choice or foresight about getting pregnant or bearing a child should not, on the face of it, impugn a woman's courage, fortitude and endurance. For we praise other examples of the exercise of these virtues even if the agents have or had 'no choice'. Even if the alternative to fighting in the battle is being shot by your own commander, even if people will only tell you to shut up and treat you unkindly if you try complaining about your pains, even if you must struggle on

despite your exhaustion or die – what you do still counts as
admirable. And that you did not choose to get yourself into
the situation that calls for the exercise of these virtues is not
relevant either; these are precisely the virtues that the virtuous
person may, consistently with virtue, hope she never has to
exercise. We are not expected to hunt out opportunities for
being courageous, only to be ready to cope with them when
they befall us.

However, an important point may have been glossed over
here, concealed in the ambiguity of 'what you do counts as
admirable'. It is true that we tend to praise and admire people
for doing what virtue requires even when circumstances are
such that they have little or no 'real' choice. But perhaps
we do so only because we give them the benefit of the
doubt, assuming, for example, that the soldiers would have
fought even if their commander had not threatened to shoot
anyone who tried to run away. There will, after all, often
be no way of telling whether someone would have done the
admirable thing anyhow, and it would seem unduly cavilling
to withhold praise when it has been done. It may seem too
that the very fact that the agent didn't break down under
the strain calls for some praise. Nevertheless, though we
may often find it difficult or impossible to apply the
distinction between 'doing what virtue requires' and 'acting
virtuously' (or between 'doing what virtue requires but not
for the right reason' and 'doing what virtue requires for the
right reason') it is a distinction that we think very important.
And perhaps what should be said about women's bearing
children and manifesting courage, fortitude and endurance
is that though such women do what virtue requires they do
not act *virtuously*: they do not do it for the right reason but
because they have no choice.

But in what sense do they have no choice? After all, not
every woman who gets pregnant makes a good job of
bearing the child. Not only do some break down, but others
moan constantly, take to their beds, insist on continuing
with, or being given, dangerous drugs to make themselves
feel better, refuse to do what is required during labour.
Others opt for abortion. It is true that 'whether or not to
break down' may not be a matter of choice, but whether or

not to act in any of the other ways surely is. But, notwithstanding the recent enormous increase in abortions, it is still true of the average woman that she does not act in any of these other ways; she bears the child and makes a good job of it. So it seems that to say she has no choice but to do so (and moreover does it because she has no choice) will not work.

But is there nevertheless not something correct about saying that she does not choose in the way that acting virtuously requires? This needs further exploration. It might be said 'It is true that the average woman "has a choice" in that the options of bearing or aborting, and bearing well or badly are there. But the fact is that women do not usually see things that way. At least until the last twenty years or so (and in a small number of countries at that) women who found themselves pregnant did not usually deliberate about whether or not to have an abortion and make a principled decision not to; nor did they consider and consciously reject the idea that they might take to their beds, demand constant attention and sympathy, be excused from ordinary duties, be entitled to more drugs or drink. They just went ahead and bore the child well unthinkingly, and it is because women bear children unthinkingly in this way that it is correct to say that they do not act virtuously in doing so. They do not see the situation as presenting them with a choice, so they do not choose to act well in the way that acting virtuously requires.'

I suppose some people would object to the claim that most or even many women bear children unthinkingly in this way. If we continue to hold firmly in mind that we are trying to generalize properly about all women, not limiting our discussion to modern, Western, educated, liberated ones, I do not see why we should object, but either way, it does not matter. We can surely object to the argument itself, in the following way. Not seeing the situation as presenting you with a choice is very often just what acting virtuously involves. Someone needs help or attention or their lives saving, and it is a frightful nuisance but, one says, 'There's nothing else to be done. There's no choice, we'll just have to make the best of it.' If it were pointed out that there *is* something else to be done, one does have a choice, this would, in many circumstances, simply be rejected by the virtuous person as a bad joke. We *cannot* or we *do not* take up those sorts of options; they do not get into the running as courses of action to be deliberated about.

The occasions on which the *average* ordinary human being unthinkingly acts virtuously in this way are presumably either not very common or tend to be *so* ordinary that they hardly count as positively acting well at all. On this latter point, there is a nice example[1] about responding honestly to a request for information in the street ('Is this the right way to the station?' 'Can you tell me the time please?'). Doing this unthinkingly is so ordinary that one tends to think that anyone who made a point of deliberately taking up the option of misleading a stranger over such an issue would be really odd, rather than thinking that this is the sort of occasion on which most of us are *exercising honesty*. Bearing children is in one sense common and ordinary enough but, as I have already noted, only for half the human race. Exercising unthinkingly the virtues required is common amongst women, to the point where we may think it really odd if, without some special reason, a woman takes up the option of doing it badly, but though common and average amongst women, it is not amongst men. A man who goes through something like what women go through in child-bearing (such as a painful illness or operation) with the same unthinking courage, fortitude and endurance is counted as particularly admirable, as are women who go through anything other than child-bearing which calls for the same exercise and do it well.

So it seems that to say that the average woman, in bearing a child and doing it well, is not making a deliberate choice to do so, and hence not acting virtuously, will not work; that is, the inference does not go through. But I think the content of the idea that she is not acting virtuously because she is not acting 'for the right reason' has not been exhausted yet.

When 'the' idea is expressed, not in terms of lack of choice, but as I just expressed it, in terms of 'not acting for the right reason', people come up with two very different considerations. One is that the average woman *wants* to have children. The other is that some (not the average) want to have children for the wrong reasons — as toys, or to show they are adults, or to keep their husbands, or to secure the inheritance. As considerations that people simply volunteer spontaneously in the course of the argument, these are difficult and suggestive. The second consideration suggests the existence of a contrast between wanting to have children for the right reason(s) and for the wrong reasons. If we recognize the examples just given as examples of wanting children for the wrong reasons, what is (or are) the right reason(s)? Presumably, it is the very reason given in the first consideration; the right reason for having a child is that you *want* to have a child 'as an end in itself', not as a toy, or as heir to the estate, or because people expect it of you, or for ulterior reasons. But if this is the right reason, how does the first consideration manage to suggest that the average woman is not acting virtuously in bearing a child and making a good job of it because she is (only) doing it because she wants to have a child?

This might simply be the effect of the muddled belief that no one counts as acting well unless they are doing so unwillingly, against their own inclinations. This would mean that the only women who acted virtuously in bearing children were those who did not want them at all, but went through it all simply out of duty. I do not have the space to argue against this view of moral virtue here; so I shall simply assume that it is revealed as implausible as soon as it is made explicit. (It entails, for example, that if I give you something of mine gladly, not begrudging it, and pleased to have been able to be of help to you, I act with *less* virtue than someone who is too mean to take any pleasure in helping others, hates parting with his possessions and, bitterly begrudging it, helps you only because he thinks he ought to.)

Closely related to this view of moral virtue, though distinguishable from it, is the idea that acting well, even if it need not be punitive, must nevertheless not be selfish or self-seeking. Saying that most women *want* to have children may make it sound as though they have them for selfish reasons. So does the first consideration amount to saying that women do not act virtuously in bearing children because they go through it for selfish reasons? But this way of interpreting the first consideration is undercut by the second. The examples of wanting children for the wrong reasons were precisely examples of wanting them for selfish reasons, and these *contrasted* with wanting to have a child 'as an end in itself'.

Nevertheless, the grandiose phrase 'wanted as an end in itself' or 'for its own sake' does not, one might say, guarantee the right kind of purity of motive which is needed for acting well or virtuously. People want all sorts of daft and trivial things as 'ends in themselves' such as leaping a motor-bike over thirty cars. Wanting to do this is not what would ordinarily count as selfish or self-seeking; and in pursuit of such an end or aim some people exhibit daring and grit which are closely allied to courage and fortitude. But the thing in question so clearly fails to be worthwhile that we see something merely self-indulgent and unadmirable in the pursuit of it. 'Yes', we say, 'people who go in for this sort of thing risk their lives. They face, and often endure, a lot of pain but, well, in some sense, it's their choice, they don't have to. They're only pleasing themselves.'

With this thought, I think, we have (at last) exhausted the topic of choice and moved decisively in the direction of considering whether bearing children is 'morally significant' or 'intrinsically worthwhile' (whatever these exceptionally difficult phrases mean). If you go in for something insignificant or worthless then you count as 'only pleasing yourself' however much pain and effort and grit it calls for. But, it seems, if you go in for, or do, something significant or worthwhile you do not count as *only* pleasing yourself. We would not say that Mother Teresa was 'only pleasing herself' despite the fact that what she does is her choice, she doesn't have to do it. Nor does this seem to be limited to the *morally* significant or worthwhile. We do not describe Beethoven as 'only pleasing himself' when he went on composing and conducting after having gone deaf. So let us now turn to the topic of the worthwhile.

2 BEARING CHILDREN AS INTRINSICALLY WORTHWHILE

It seems that some people feel compelled to say there is nothing intrinsically worthwhile in bearing children in order to express their contentment with not having done so, or with being unable to do so. Women who are childless by choice and are convinced that their choice was not a mistake, men who think how frightful it would be to be a woman rather than a man, such people may want to dismiss the bearing of children as of no account.

Suppose that such people are rightly content with, or even rightly proud of, their lives. This gives them no reason to deny that bearing children is worthwhile. For one can lead a worthwhile life without its containing everything that is worthwhile – such lives can take many different forms. Women who are childless by choice are usually women who have not only chosen not to bear children, but not to bring them up, thereby choosing to lead a different sort of life. But that some action or activity would not be a worthwhile part of the sort of life I wanted myself should not lead me to say that it is not a worthwhile part of anyone's. I might think of some of the houses my brother has built as being worthwhile achievements – they are beautiful and built to last and their owners love them – and acknowledge that I have never done anything like that. But I chose to become an academic; I developed an intellectual skill instead of a technical one, choosing to lead a philosopher's life in which there is not enough time to devote to his sort of activity. I am convinced my choice was not a mistake and that the pursuit of philosophical truth is worthwhile, but it would be a poor thing if I were led from saying that I rightly chose a different sort of life, in which building houses well cannot figure, to decrying his achievements.

I am not sure whether there is any sort of intrinsically male life with which one can be rightly content. But let us suppose there is – perhaps what they say about the emotionally disturbing effects of carrying around so much biological equipment whose function is parturition is true; then a man who wanted to lead an ascetic life might thank his lucky stars that he was not a woman and could not bear children. But, unless he maintains that this is the only worthwhile sort of life, once again, he has no reason so far for decrying the bearing of children as not worthwhile.

What about people who are *wrongly* contented with, or mistakenly proud of, their lives? The opinions of some of them (people who are very corrupt) can be safely dismissed on the grounds that they have such a faulty conception of the worthwhile anyhow, but what about the ordinary, non-corrupt but somewhat smug? Many of us, after all, though willing to acknowledge outstanding virtue and/or achievement in others, like to think of ourselves as 'as good as the next person'. Hence the naturalness of the move I just made above, where, acknowledging something worthwhile in someone else's (fairly ordinary) life, one hastens to think of something that matches it in one's own. And hence the difficulty of acknowledging that someone else fairly ordinary has done something worthwhile that one cannot match.

The fact that it is difficult, and that one is tempted to dismiss what one cannot match as something that 'doesn't count' does not, of course, justify doing so. And, it might be said, we can understand only too well why men have for so long not acknowledged that bearing children is intrinsically worthwhile since they cannot equal this, and any other achievement they do bring off is one that some woman who has also borne a child may match (assuming, as I did above, that women have 'no corresponding incapacity'). That the refusal to recognize bearing children as worthwhile, on the part of men and women childless by choice, is suspect does not, of course, show that it is unjustified. But perhaps one could say that to a certain extent it shifts the burden of proof. Many women have thought and do think it worthwhile; if it is to be said that they are mistaken in doing so, some argument should be given.

But here we encounter a difficulty common to both sides: how *does* one argue about the worthwhile? What are the starting points and what does one bring up as relevant facts? The 'argument' that I am about to produce is perhaps too loosely structured to merit that label; in effect what I try to do is say 'If we are going to talk seriously about things being worthwhile, then child-bearing fits in like this ...' I take as my starting points a number of bald assertions. I do not assume that these are beyond question but I am assuming, perhaps wrongly, that anyone who wants to talk seriously about the worthwhile will, as a matter of fact, agree with them.

The worthwhile

Children figure as 'goods' in our conceptual scheme. I do not mean by that that they figure as merchandise, but as 'good things' like health, knowledge, pleasure and virtue. Just as a special context is needed to make sense of 'What do you want to have health (or knowledge, or pleasure or virtue) for?' so is one needed for 'What do you want to have children for?' Unions are 'blessed' not cursed with issue; those who have children are 'favoured by fortune'; the childless are 'unfortunate'; to be unable to have children is a lack, a privation, a misfortune. And once again, special backgrounds are needed to reverse these platitudes.

To say that 'children' figure as goods is not the same as to say that *human life* (or *lives*, or *another human life*) figure as goods to us. People do not just want there to be *another human being* or even *another child/member of the next generation* as such. They want *progeny* or *offspring* – their *own* children. This is not to deny that couples go in for adoption happily, nor that some high-mindedly adopt, believing that it is better to change an existing unwanted child into a wanted one than to procreate a wanted one. And of course adoptive parents can make a child their own, just as genetic parents can abandon a child or alienate it. But it is, and would be, odd, to want *to have a child* (i.e. be a parent) as an end in itself (i.e. not to secure the inheritance nor as a publicity stunt) without at all wanting *to have one's own child* (in the biological sense).

Agreed, any child necessarily is another, or a new, *human being* or *human life*, and our thoughts about having children are hence inextricably bound up with our thoughts about human lives – including such thoughts as that death is (usually) an evil, that correspondingly life is, except in rare cases, a benefit to its possessor, that murder is wrong, that lives should (usually) be preserved, that somehow each human life (except perhaps in rare cases) is uniquely valuable and cannot be weighed against other lives and found to be dispensable, that it is tragic when people die in the flower of their youth, that there is something particularly horrifying about the possibility of our wiping out the human race in a nuclear holocaust . . .

It is tempting to say that all such thoughts are grounded or underpinned by a belief in the sanctity of life, and to try to see our attitude to procreation as worthwhile as simply expressive of the belief that *a human life is worth creating* just as a human life, being 'sacred' in some way, is worth protecting, worth preserving, worth living to its end.

But, as I suggested at the beginning of Chapter Four, this would be a mistake. Without the special sense that can be provided for 'the sanctity of life' by a theologically backed morality, there is nothing more (though nothing less) to the belief in the sanctity of (human) life than some such set of moral beliefs and attitudes as I just sketched above.

In that chapter on utilitarianism I began by giving a very small set of beliefs and attitudes, all concerned explicitly with killing, but in the course of it, pointed out that beliefs about the right to life could form part of such a set too. At the end of the last chapter I pointed out further that the belief that each human life was of incommensurable or infinite or unique value was another way of expressing belief in the sanctity of life. To believe in it, within a secular morality, is not only to believe various things about the wrongness of killing but also to believe the sorts of things I mentioned above, amongst them that a human life is worth protecting, worth preserving – and worth creating. So the belief that *a new human life is a good in itself* (because a human life is a good in itself) does not *underpin* our attitude to procreation; if anything, the order of explanation is the other way around. We think that a human life is 'a good in itself' insofar as we have the attitude towards having children that we have – *and* a whole lot of other beliefs about murder and saving lives and people being irreplaceable and so on.

But this is not the only reason why it is a mistake to think that our attitude to procreation as worthwhile is *based* on a belief in the sanctity of life. For utilitarians (of course) do not make that mistake. But they too consider procreation only in relation to its producing a *new happy human life*. A *happy human life* is worth protecting and preserving (other things being equal), and similarly worth creating. And procreating is discussed within utilitarianism solely in these terms. However, our beliefs about having children are not connected solely with beliefs about the value of a human life, happy, sacred, or whatever.

The deep reason why it is a mistake to regard our attitude to having children as merely expressive of a belief that a new human life is good in itself is that our beliefs about having children are inextricably bound up with a second set of thoughts, thoughts about the value of love, of family life, of our proper emotional development through a natural life-cycle and what count as enrichments of this emotional development. In connection with these thoughts, children do not figure as goods insofar as they are *new human beings, extra human lives*, but as *progeny* or *offspring*, as *my* or *our* children. Though I said at the outset that I would be concerned with bearing children, not with bringing them up, that does not debar me, in the present context, from appealing to the obvious fact that most people who get married expect and hope to 'have children' in a sense that covers the whole process of the couple's generating them, the woman's bearing them, and their all living together as a family. It is in the context of these thoughts, not the ones about the sanctity or value of human life, that couples who are childless by choice are sometimes described as 'selfish' or 'irresponsible' or 'refusing to grow up' or 'not knowing what life is about'. One may well not agree with this, but one can see what point is being made and the point is not that *refusing to create a new life* is selfish and irresponsible the way *refusing to save someone's life* is. The claim is (something like) *refusing to be a parent, to have your own child*, is not being prepared to submit to the insensate demands of children, trying to maintain all through your life the life that courting couples lead, avoiding giving hostages to fortune – and this is being selfish, irresponsible, childish and so on.

These thoughts about (roughly) family life and the first set of thoughts about (roughly) the sanctity of life do not exhaust the (just) distinguishable sets of thoughts in which the thought of procreation plays an important part. Procreation is *creation* and hence connects with a vast array of thoughts we have about that, particularly the creation of the new and the beautiful. In connection with such thoughts children may figure simply as goods insofar as we think of them as beautiful things which exist independently of us (like sunsets, or trees, or spring, or cats) but more commonly they figure as new and beautiful creations of ours, like works of art. People describe their children as their works, each one a miracle they have wrought, their living monuments, their finest creation, and conversely, we may describe our works and artistic achievements metaphorically as our children and stress what labour was needed to bring them forth.

No doubt further and different things could be said in support of the view that children (offspring) are goods, desirable as such (*as* offspring), but surely no more needs to be said. I shall take it, anyhow, as being established that they are (insofar as one can establish such a thing). And if *our* or *my* own child is a good in itself, then having *our* or *my* own child is intrinsically worthwhile. And although, for a man 'having our or my child' can only be playing his part in its generation and later on having it in his family, for a woman it is not only that but also bearing it. So since for a woman bearing a child is in part constitutive of having a child, and since having one's own child is intrinsically worthwhile, bearing a child is intrinsically worthwhile.

This conclusion seems to have emerged rather suddenly, so we should pause to consider some objections to it. Someone might say, 'There is nothing intrinsically worthwhile in *bearing a child* – that whole ghastly business of pregnancy and labour. It just happens to be the only way of getting what is, I agree, good in itself, namely a child of one's own. So it's only instrumentally good, only good as a means, not good or worthwhile in itself.'

It must, indeed, be agreed that if going through 'pregnancy' and 'labour' was not a process that characteristically terminated in the birth of a living baby, it would not be worth going through – it would not have any point. And thereby, one might say, 'bearing a child' contrasts with 'generating a child'. Just as bearing a child is going through pregnancy and labour, so is generating a child going through the sexual act, but the latter would still be worth doing even if it never generated a child, if only for the pleasure.

(Whether 'the sexual act' would be expressive of love and union in the universal absence of any connection with generation, and indeed whether 'it' would be 'the sexual act' in such circumstances, are both obviously problematic. When I say 'universal absence of any connection' I do mean just that, not the existing circumstances in which there is a connection, notwithstanding the fact that some people are sterile, and some sexual unions are between people of the same sex, and sexual union continues past child-bearing age. I am imagining the possibility of some alien species who reproduce by, say, splitting, quite independently of an activity they go in for which in its manifest physical details is just like our sexual act. Whatever one thinks about this, one can still see the point of saying that we can imagine there being such an act as 'coupling' which was worth doing in itself because it was so pleasurable.) And the thought might be: sex is pleasant, and bringing up a child is rewarding, interesting, enriching and all sorts of other things, but pregnancy and labour are just travail. So bearing a child is just travail which, as it happens, is the only way of getting what is good in itself.

But the fact that it is 'the only way' makes, I think, all the difference. (I will say something about *in vitro* development and surrogacy shortly.) Suppose someone said: 'Philosophical knowledge is good in itself, and having it is bliss, but acquiring it is just travail. All those months and years of struggle and boredom and despair; as it happens, it's only by going through this that one can acquire the knowledge, but how much better things would be if we could acquire it in our sleep, or something like that.' (Similarly, a composer might say 'A beautiful symphony is good in itself, and conducting one's own composition is bliss, but composing itself is just travail; how much better things would be if one could just wake up in the morning with the whole thing complete in one's head.')

One thing that is wrong with this way of talking is that our concept of *having knowledge* (or of *producing* or *creating a work of art*) is in part determined by how 'as it happens' we acquire it (or produce it). If somehow we all became cleverer and cleverer without any effort, the concept of knowledge – as something worth pursuing, as something I can have which will be an achievement of *mine* – would be quite different. But as things are, though the struggle does indeed involve boredom and despair, it is also intensely satisfying. One does not just want to know, to be told, one wants to find out for oneself; one wants the knowledge to be one's own doing. Similarly, if one is an artist, one wants one's works of art to be one's own doing.

And the fact that bearing a child *is* the way, for a woman, of having a child in part determines our concept of having one's own child – progeny. As has recently been made vivid by the discussion of surrogacy, the business of going through pregnancy and labour makes the resulting child the bearer's in a way that is not overridden by the facts of its generation, nor by facts about contracts and promises about the baby's being handed over, nor by its subsequent upbringing. A child that is the genetic result of A and B, and borne by a surrogate mother C is, of course, truly describable as 'mine' or 'ours' by all three people, as 'my' or 'our' doing by all three. But it is the genetic mother A's sense of 'mine' and 'ours' which suffers the diminution. (It is worth noting that women who want to be able to employ surrogate mothers generally acknowledge this: surrogacy is regarded as a poor second best to bearing one's own child. No doubt there are some women who would choose surrogacy while perfectly capable of bearing their own children in order to avoid the travail, but this is simply a mistake, just as it is a mistake to think you can acquire the good of knowledge by plagiarizing or by cooking your results, and a mistake to think you can acquire the good of artistic creation by stealing someone else's ideas.)

In all the three ways I sketched above in which offspring

figure as goods in our conceptual scheme, the business of bearing them in the ordinary way has a central role to play. Both the man and the woman are responsible for generating a new human life, but it is the woman who, in bearing it, preserves that life, makes sacrifices and risks her own to keep it going and bring it forth. It is in this connection that one can see why it is tempting to regard bearing a child as analogous to sacrificing a fair amount of time and effort to saving someone's life (*cf.* the Thomson cases).

In bearing the child, the woman makes it particularly and peculiarly *hers*, *part of her* life-cycle, *her* family. In so doing, she enriches her own life and that of those who form part of it. In bearing it (in standard circumstances) she gives her husband the outcome of their union, she makes them not just a couple but a family, she gives her other children a sibling, she gives her and her husband's parents a grandchild, her friends or extended family a new member of their group. And she gives herself the outcome of her union with her husband, she goes through what her mother has been through, what the majority of women have gone through, thereby sharing something with almost half the rest of the human race.

And all of this can properly be described as her doing. She can look upon her children as *her* achievements, her works of art, the result of her efforts and suffering. She has not only played her part in generating them but has, on her own, borne them.

So, I conclude, bearing children is intrinsically worthwhile. To do it, and do it well, is to have done something morally significant. Doing it well involves exercising courage, fortitude and endurance, and moreover, exercising them in the achievement of something worthwhile, not, like being a wall-of-death rider, something worthless. What is done is, I claim, not just worthwhile and significant but *morally* worthwhile and significant, because of its connection with, on the one hand, the value or sanctity of life and, on the other, with what I have roughly categorized as 'family life' – the field of our closest relationships with other people. For these two areas are the concern of morality if anything is. (Its connection with the third area, that of artistic creation, is not irrelevant, for aesthetics and morality shade into one another in many ways, but I would not want to stress this to support the view that bearing children is morally significant. And I do not think there is any necessity for relying on it.)

Tentative conclusions

Suppose that all this is right. What, if anything, follows from it? To block a number of objections that might be brought, I should begin by saying what does *not* follow from it. It does *not* follow that women who have been, and are, forced to endure numerous pregnancies should, if sufficiently high-minded, be able to find doing so satisfying and worthwhile. To claim that bearing children is intrinsically worthwhile is not to deny that bearing them, especially lots, in some circumstances, can be hell; indeed it provides the grounds for saying that a quite particular wrong is done when it is made hell. It is not only that things are running amiss because lots of people are suffering (women who are pregnant when they do not want to be, children who are suffering because they are unwanted and their mothers are too exhausted to give them care), though this is important. Things are running amiss also because a great good is being missed out on or wasted.

Nor does it follow that women ought to bear children and that they necessarily miss out on doing something worthwhile if they do not – not, at least, on any ordinary understanding of 'miss out'. For, as I made a point of emphasizing at the outset, we are in the happy position of there being more worthwhile things to do than can be fitted into one life. To recognize that bearing children is intrinsically worthwhile is not to deny that women should be free to choose whether or not they go in for this worthwhile activity or some of the many others; a woman who has never borne a child, whether by choice or happenstance or perforce, may be rightly content with her life.

Nor does it follow that women who have borne children well are in any obvious sense morally superior to people who have not, that Mrs Average is necessarily more sensitive or unselfish, wiser or more courageous than Mr or Ms Average.

But what does follow, difficult as this may be for many to accept, is, I think, the following. All ordinary childless women and all ordinary men, who are content with their lives, and think of themselves as being 'as good as the next person' (albeit not as good as the outstandingly virtuous) are open to the question: 'As good as Mrs Average? Why? She has borne two children and done it well. What have you done to match that?' And they may not have an adequate answer. I should emphasize again that mentioning some worthwhile things in one's own life does not make for an adequate answer unless it is clear that Mrs Average has not done them too; there is, after all, no reason to suppose that bearing children is the only worthwhile thing she has done.

However, I am not particularly concerned to force this question on childless women and men. There may be, after all, something wrong with this crude comparison between the 'average' childless, and Mrs 'Average'; perhaps when we try to think seriously about comparing lives we are forced to consider particulars (rather than statistics) which cannot be described as 'average', though they may well be 'ordinary' rather than extraordinary. Moreover, when we do consider particulars, it may well be, I acknowledge, that the notion of *matching* which the question relies on, fails to get a grip. Suppose a particular Mrs X has borne two children well and I have not done that, but have supported a number of friends through adversity (which she has not done). There seems something amiss with the idea that these two things can be weighed on some scale and it be found that they 'match' or that 'this outweighs that'.

Perhaps the general conclusion to be drawn from *any* serious discussion of 'the worthwhile' is that *all* of us who lead ordinary lives should consider whether:

> The world is too much with us; late and soon,
> Getting and spending, we lay waste our powers;
> Little we see in Nature that is ours;
> We have given our hearts away, a sordid boon!
> (William Wordsworth,
> 'The World is Too Much With Us')

Then the particular conclusion to be drawn from the particular discussion of the worthwhile we have been going through in this section is that no woman who has borne children well in the ordinary way should say humbly to herself, 'Well, I haven't done anything with my life really; I've "laid waste my powers"', for she can say, 'I have done *this* much'. But anyone who has not borne children well *might* have to say, 'I haven't done anything with my life really'.

3   SURROGACY

To say that an activity (bearing children, pursuing knowledge) is intrinsically worthwhile is to talk about how things are usually or 'in the ordinary way', not to say that every case of going in for it is. It would be cruel mockery of a woman whose child had been still-born or which was doomed to die shortly after birth to say, 'Oh well, you achieved something worthwhile'. As I emphasized in the preceding section, bearing children is intrinsically worthwhile because it is, for a woman, in part constitutive of having offspring, and it would not be worth going through if it were not a process that characteristically terminated in the birth of a living (and healthy) baby. To go through it in the hope and reasonable expectation of having one's own child only to be denied this good at the last moment is quite a particular tragedy.

But what of women who are denied this good anyhow, because for one reason or another they cannot go through successful pregnancies? This raises the issue of surrogacy, recently an issue that has been discussed both in connection with a woman's right to decide what happens in and to her body and in connection with a woman's right (more rarely a *couple's* right, or simply *the* right, of anyone) to have children. I mentioned some of the obvious flaws in the most common arguments above[2] but we should now look at the debate more carefully.

Ever since artificial insemination has been used by infertile couples, there have been objections to it, and it is important to distinguish objections which are fairly general from those which relate only to surrogacy (or perhaps even commercial surrogacy).

There is a quite general objection to AIH, AID (see Glossary) and surrogacy, which is that they are unnatural, a claim that always generates a quick preliminary skirmish. Supporters of whatever has been objected to as unnatural point out that most, if not all, Western medicine is unnatural, from heart transplants to toothpaste and spectacles and dental work; do the objectors want to maintain that toothache and myopia, measles and gangrene, high infant mortality and leprosy, are natural and thereby good?[3] The objectors counter this list of advantages that being 'unnatural' has brought us with a list of the disadvantages ranging from the horrors of nuclear war and radiation, through pollution and various ecological disasters to lung cancer, white bread and the widespread use of tranquillizers. So far we have a stand off.

But there is a better version of the 'unnatural' claim; one that involves invoking not Nature in general, but, as neo-Aristotelianism does, human nature. Humans, it might be said, are the sorts of creatures who go in for biological pairing (as, for instance, swans do and rabbits, despite their reputation, but cats and dogs do not) and reproduce by sexual intercourse (like all other mammals and unlike, say, most fish) and raise their own young (unlike, say, cuckoos). This is part and parcel, not just of our physical nature, but of our emotional and psychological nature too. And to try to act against our emotional and psychological nature is at worst dangerous and potentially destructive and at best utterly futile, since we will not succeed. And the activities and practices that may count as trying to act against our natures in this sense include: AIH, AID, surrogacy, promiscuity, homosexuality (in either sex), contraception and abortion (a fairly familiar list so far), also chastity, solitude and adoption.

One deep difficulty about using these facts about human nature as a basis for a blanket condemnation of 'unnatural' practices is that, as we noted before, facts about species are only ever facts about what is true of most of their members. As a species we are sighted, but some people are born blind;

as a species we are five-fingered and five-toed, but some people have extra fingers or toes; as a species our females suckle their young, but not all women can breast feed; as a species we are male *or* female, but some people are born neither and some are born (almost) both. Similarly, some of us are born sterile, or, arguably, homosexual and, perhaps, though we have no way of telling, some of us are born naturally promiscuous, or solitary, or chaste. Hence, facts about human nature will not guarantee even a risk that in individual cases 'unnatural' acts and practices are either dangerous or doomed to failure.

Moreover, in relation to the various ways of getting around infertility, the 'unnatural' objection bites both ways. We just said that it was natural for us, as a species, to form pairs and reproduce within them and raise our own young. Hence, most of us have a natural desire to do so, and trying to suppress or thwart this desire is as unnatural, as potentially dangerous and destructive or futile as the attempt to get away with doing anything else unnatural. And the whole point of AIH, AID and surrogacy is to find ways which, to varying degrees, succeed in satisfying that desire. This does not mean that they are themselves 'natural', but they count as acting *with* nature, rather than against it.

It is quite possible to maintain that treatment for infertility is unnatural in some cases; for instance, venereal disease can make one sterile and it might plausibly be thought that this is just as well. Cervical hostility (see Glossary) might have been (though apparently is not) a natural mechanism for preventing the conception of the genetically abnormal; if it had been, tampering with it would have been 'unnatural' in the dangerous way the objection points to.

It is also possible to maintain that some forms of treatment are unnatural and bad in that they involve acting against our nature as well as acting with it. And surrogacy is particularly claimed to fall foul of this objection, because of the natural bond that holds between the child and the mother who carries it and gives birth to it.

How is this objection supposed to work out in detail? It begins from the above claim about the natural bond between (carrying) mother and child. This claim has a role to play in other moral arguments too; for instance, it is used to support a mother's special parental right to the children she has borne, a right that is usually allowed to outweigh the father's and not to be lost by putting the child out to adoption or fostering. There is thought to be something particularly wrong in separating a mother from her child, especially when the child is young; it is thought that this causes both mother and child acute and perhaps unique suffering, and is likely to do each of them, especially the child, grave psychological damage, destroying a relationship which is actively good for both parties, and so on.

But what if the mother herself wants to separate them? Suppose that she simply does not feel the pull of the bond and, on the contrary, wants to get rid of the child as quickly as possible, believing she will be much happier if she does? What follows, if anything, about *her* from the naturalness of the bond is that she is not a typical female member of the species (just as women who are infertile or find men disgusting are not typical female members of the species) *or* that she has made a mistake about her own feelings and is more typical than she thinks she is. If the former, then, as I noted above, the 'nature' premise yields nothing in particular about her; given other premises she might be someone to pity, or envy, or simply find rather odd. If the latter, the 'nature' premise yields the likelihood that, if she does not try to love the child but gives it up, she is making a dreadful mistake, both wasting an opportunity for great satisfaction and happiness, and running the risk of making herself utterly miserable in the future. The child is badly off either way, for either way it is going to miss out on its natural mother's love.

Now why has this not been voiced as a vigorous objection to adoption as well as, more recently, to surrogacy? Part of the answer to this is that, in a manner of speaking, it has. Pregnant women are not encouraged to arrange the future adoption of the child they are carrying, and it is thought to be wrong for people who want to adopt to tempt pregnant women to give up their children through avarice or dire economic necessity. Many people also recognize the arrogant folly of some bureaucratic decisions that some women are not fit to bring up their own children. And all these qualifications and hedgings around of adoption reflect the view that, other things being equal, it is best for both mother and child to stay together even if the woman says she wants the baby adopted.

'Other things' of course are not always equal. A woman cannot be forced to give a child love, and if she insists on refusing to keep it, then adoption is the best alternative for the sake of the child though the mother may suffer later. But on the naturalness premise it remains true that the child has been disadvantaged, and this is consistent with recognizing that many, if not most, adopted children flourish and are happy with their adoptive parents.

Adoption, on the naturalness premise, is making the best of a bad job; it can work wonderfully, but that does not alter the fact that a bad job is what it started out as. The relevant difference between adoption and surrogacy is that, in the latter case but not the former, a woman and a couple deliberately set out to bring about this bad job. And that, in detail, is what is held to be wrong about surrogacy as 'unnatural'.

What difference does it make if the surrogacy is not 'commercial' but undertaken between sisters or friends? People's reactions to this vary a lot, since a number of different points can be made. It is said that a child resulting from a surrogacy for love will be 'born out of love and charity, not out of greed'.[4] What difference does this make? It certainly makes a difference to the motive on the part of the surrogate mother; she is intending, perhaps at considerable physical and emotional cost to herself, to do something for someone she loves. As an aim this is admirable, but what about the cost to the child? For the premise we are working with at the moment is that it is best, not only for the mother, but for the child, if the natural bond is not broken. And so the child will count as disadvantaged whether the mother breaks the bond for good or greedy motives. Mary Warnock, in the article just cited, assumes with no justification that in a surrogacy-for-love case the child will wind up with (in some sense) two mothers instead of one and have gained rather than lost; she seems to be envisaging that the surrogate mother will remain around, loving it and having a 'special relationship' to it. Well, this is possible, as in group families and kibbutzim, but it is hardly a paradigm case of surrogacy. The surrogate mother might actively dislike children, or have six of her own and no time or affection to spare. So the objection stands; even if the surrogate mother is motivated by the most charitable feelings for her sister or friends or brother and sister-in-law she is, nevertheless, on the naturalness assumption, deliberately setting out to bring about a disadvantaged child. And her love for the couple involved does not justify this. Nor, it should be noted, does their desire to have a child justify their being party to it.

It was clear from the newspapers when the Baby Cotton case[5] was being discussed that many people do regard commercial surrogacy as much worse than surrogacy for love. Is this just because they have overlooked the above point, or is there something more to it? A comparison that was often made was that commercial surrogacy was like prostitution, whereas surrogacy for love was, by implication, like sex for love. The thought here, I believe, is that sex is bad unless it is for love and similarly surrogacy, or giving away one's child, is bad unless it is a loving gift. But bad in what way? It cannot, as in the preceding version of the argument, be being counted as bad for the child, for then, as I just argued, the good motives of the surrogate mother would not make any difference. Bad, in some way, for society? Just as prostitution is claimed to undermine marriage and hence society, so commercial surrogacy would undermine ... what? Well, some people seem to think it too would undermine marriage and 'the family', but there are no grounds for this which would distinguish at all between commercial surrogacy and surrogacy for love. (Similarly, any grounds there are for saying prostitution threatens marriage and/or the family apply equally well to sex for love outside marriage, and hence fail to distinguish prostitution as particularly bad.)

The remaining possibility is that both prostitution and commercial surrogacy are thought of as bad for the woman or as intrinsically bad. These thoughts may be expressed by saying that they are both morally degrading and debasing. Arguments about this can rage hotly especially if the terms 'degrading' and 'debasing' are used, as they frequently are, in a superior and censorious manner. But the words need not be used that way. They each have a very straightforward meaning: 'to lower in quality or character', which can, for example, apply to minerals. Then the interesting question in relation to prostitution and commercial surrogacy is this. Is it being claimed that the woman lowers *her* (moral) quality or character by acting as a prostitute or commercial surrogate; or is it being claimed that to go in for prostitution or commercial surrogacy, to make a financial business of what should be a matter of love is to lower the (moral) quality of sex or motherhood? The two claims may be related, in that someone might give the second as ground for the first but for the moment I shall try to keep them separate.

To take the second one first, what is it to claim that sex or motherhood has a (moral) quality which can be lowered? Here the discussion in the preceding section stands us in good stead. To claim, in this context, that sex, or motherhood, has a moral quality is to claim (a) that (loving) sexual relations and (minimally successful) motherhood are amongst the human goods or blessings (like health or knowledge), and, moreover, (b) that loving sexual relations and motherhood (unlike health or knowledge) form part of the field of our closest relationships with other people, which is part of the concern of morality if anything is.

As long as we are clear that these are not being claimed as the *only* goods, nor the *only* close relationships with other people, it is fairly widely agreed that sex and motherhood do indeed have this moral quality. It might be thought that it was parenthood rather than motherhood which was the good in question, but that is (also widely agreed) an extra and different claim. What many men envy, and what infertile women who are interested in adoption or surrogacy may still regret, as I stressed in the preceding section, is not parenthood but motherhood – the actual carrying and bearing of a child that one then loves *as* the child of one's body. It is important too to note that one can recognize sex or motherhood as (moral) goods without their having the slightest attraction for one personally; one might even find either or both of them rather disgusting. But though one might not *sympathize* with someone who said that they thought their life had been wasted because they had never once allowed themselves to experience physical love, or someone who deeply regretted not having been able to bear children, it would be silly to pretend one did not understand.

So, bearing the above in mind, how is the objection to prostitution and commercial surrogacy to go? Presumably like this: that all the moral good that can come from (loving) sex and (ordinary) motherhood is made impossible if either is undertaken for ulterior reasons. Moreover, (perhaps) the circumstances which surround the activities when they are done for ulterior reasons make them positively bad (necessitating, for instance, treating other people with suspicion or contempt). So in this sense prostitution and commercial surrogacy are intrinsically bad, involving as they do the deliberate treating of something that can be a moral good, morally worthwhile, in such a way that it is not that but inferior (and perhaps even bad).

If life is a good to the possessor then killing something is the destruction of a good, and hence intrinsically bad. And if pain is an evil to the one who feels it then hurting them is the production of an evil and hence intrinsically bad. But things that are intrinsically bad are not thereby very bad, for we may regard killing animals as intrinsically bad and requiring justification, but also regard almost any justification as sufficient and condemn only wanton slaughter of animals. Similarly, even small hurts are intrinsically bad, but we do not think that to inflict a small hurt on someone else in a fit of irritation is particularly bad.

So, even if it were granted that prostitution and commercial surrogacy were intrinsically bad, involving as they do, not the destruction of a good, but the debasing of one, there would still be the question *how* bad? Can this be answered in terms of the moral quality of people who would do such things? Is either the sort of bad thing one can do without being depraved and corrupt?

Some people seem convinced that this is not so, that to go in for either is the mark of a depraved nature and that anyone decent would rather starve in the streets than do such a thing. A less extreme view holds that a decent person might find it 'necessary' if the alternative were starvation, or even comparative poverty – a decent person could be driven to such a thing. People who hold this view are often rather unclear as to whether the decency can be preserved. They are clear, however, that no decent person would do such a thing unless driven to it; minimally decent people would not go in for prostitution or commercial surrogacy just as an easy way to make a lot of money; only if they were desperate.

The difficulty in either view is that it purports to be a claim about what prostitutes or commercial surrogate mothers will be found to be like which is confidently made in advance of any acquaintance with them and which is not, as far as I can see, borne out by the facts. Are all prostitutes or commercial surrogate mothers known to be markedly dishonest or unkind, or violent, or callous, or selfish? Are they most especially the people who go in for blackmail, betraying their friends, selling their country's secrets, neglecting or being cruel to children, lying, corrupting the young, exploiting the weak or innocent? Apparently not. As far as most of us know and can reasonably infer from the interviews and articles in the newspapers, commercial surrogate mothers are not markedly different from other people except in that one respect – that they have had a child and given it away for money.

It is true that one can say, 'To do so and so is the mark of a depraved nature. Anyone who does that is wicked, and this can be confidently said in advance of meeting them or learning anything else about them.' Many would want to say that about the people who ran the Nazi concentration camps. But to say this is to avow that doing so and so is intrinsically *very* bad, about as evil as one can get, and what we were trying to do was find out how bad prostitution or commercial surrogacy might be thought to be, not settle the question in advance. And I am suggesting that if we do not prejudge the question, but try to settle it in terms of the moral quality of the people who do such things, it does not emerge as particularly bad. Kim Cotton (Baby Cotton's surrogate mother) seemed a fairly ordinary citizen and wife and mother, albeit hardly high-minded.

This suggests that those who want to hold that commercial surrogacy is quite bad should not allow that the question 'How bad?' is to be settled in terms of the moral quality of people who do such things. Rather, they should insist that motherhood is such an important good that to waste it – to debase it by treating it not as an intrinsic good but as a mere means to an inferior end – is correspondingly bad.

This would not be at all an implausible claim, for it has parallels with the way we also talk about 'prostitution'. If one has been blessed with a great artistic talent or an unusual degree of intelligence, it is thought bad to debase these goods by treating them as mere means to some inferior end. Their appropriate ends are the production of beauty and Truth with a capital 'T', where the capital connotes that the truths in question should be important or enduring in some way. When people use their artistic talent to produce the merely pretty or commercial, and when they apply their intelligence to producing trivia, we describe them as prostituting their talents or their art and this counts as a bad thing. People who go in for 'prostitution' merely because they want a larger television set or a bigger car really have, according to neo-Aristotelianism, made a fundamental mistake about what matters in life, about what human flourishing consists in. (To say this is not, of course, to deny that people may be driven to some form of 'prostitution' by economic necessity. If and when they are, this is, once again, a situation in which things are running amiss not only because people are suffering, but because a great good is being missed out on or wasted.)

Conclusions

I have not considered in this section any arguments concerning the legalization or prohibition of surrogacy, commercial or otherwise, nor arguments in favour of the view that commercial or otherwise, it is permissible or morally innocuous. The first omission is part of a general policy which I mentioned in Chapter One, viz. that I am concerned with moral issues not legal ones. The second omission results from the fact that I have not found anything philosophically interesting to be said on the permissive side. Arguments for the permissibility of surrogacy consist, as far as I can see, in issuing a challenge to people who think there is something wrong with it to come up with a good argument for their position. It is acknowledged that a lot of people *feel* very strongly that there is something wrong with it, but this, it is pointed out, is no substitute for argument. This I do not deny, but the philosophically challenging thing to do is to see to what extent these powerful feelings can be traced to fundamental aspects of our thoughts about morality. I have claimed to find at least three: (a) that in general, though not invariably, trying to act against or undo what is natural to us is potentially damaging or destructive (so, in particular, to try to break the natural bond between child and (carrying) mother is potentially damaging or destructive to either mother and child, or at least to the child); (b) that loving sexual relations and minimally successful motherhood are each human goods or blessings and are the sorts of things that can significantly enrich a human life; and (c) the idea that it is bad or wrong (debasing) to treat something with such intrinsic value as though it were merely a means to an inferior end. I have not tried to maintain that the wrongness of surrogacy follows from such premises, nor that they are exceptionless or unquestionable truths.

The first thought – that trying to act against, or undo what is natural to us as human beings is potentially damaging or destructive – is a particularly difficult one. As I noted, it can bite both ways. Moreover, it applies only 'for the most part', yielding a warning to act cautiously in a certain area, rather than a clear deliverance that acting 'against what is natural for human beings' is wrong. So, in a particular case, it might be hard, if not impossible, to find, in anything that has been said here, a firm objection to altruistic, albeit commercial, surrogacy. If a healthy woman was sure that she could carry and bear a child and then kiss it goodbye with no regrets, and was genuinely moved by the plight of childless couples but (contrary to utilitarianism) thought that it was a bit much to be expected to go through a pregnancy for the sake of strangers out of pure altruism with no payment, then the only objection to her being a commercial surrogate mother, in what has been said, is the claim that this is to set about bringing a disadvantaged child into existence. If it is wrong of her to do this, it is equally wrong of the childless couple to want her to do it; but many people find it hard to accept that there can be anything wrong in passionately wanting a child on whom one is expecting to lavish the greatest love and care, and that it is simply implausible to assume that such a child would be disadvantaged in any way. On this point, there may be more to say, but I do not myself know what it is.

The above discussion suggests that the distinction that people make between 'surrogacy for love' and 'surrogacy for money' is slightly, but significantly, misdescribed. It looks like a distinction between the circumstances of the act – it was an arrangement between people lovingly related, or it was a commercial arrangement between strangers. But, if the bases of the objections are as I have described them, it is not the fact of money changing hands which is particularly important so much as the question of pure motivation. The third thought – that it is bad or wrong to treat something with intrinsic value as though it were *merely* a means to an inferior end – does not locate anything wrong in accepting payment for being a surrogate mother, any more than it locates anything wrong in accepting payment for being a nurse, or a musician, or a philosopher. It says there is something wrong in finding no worth in these things except as a means to money. If one thinks of succouring people, or playing beautiful music, or doing philosophy, *only* as ways in which one happens to be handily suited for earning a living, then one has made a mistake about what things in life are really important; and similarly, if one regards bearing a child *only* as a handy way of making money. But one might, having had children of one's own, be most particularly struck by the second thought – of how successful parenthood can significantly enrich a human life – and hence think that being a surrogate mother really would be worth doing, not *for* the money, but for the sake of some childless couple.

But like nurses, musicians and academic philosophers, one might reasonably expect to get paid for doing it.

4   ABORTION

Finally, what conclusions, if any, follow about abortion? I said at the beginning of this chapter that there was a temptation to say something like the following: 'Abortion *can't* be wrong because it *can't* be the case that women, even young girls, face a special liability to act wrongly which men don't face. For men and women are born equal and the differences between them are morally irrelevant.'

If what I have argued for in this chapter is (roughly) right, then this temptation should have been undercut. Men and women are not born 'equal'; though the differences between them are irrelevant in many areas, they are not irrelevant to moral questions about abortion, pregnancy, child-bearing and having children. Women, even young girls, *are* faced with a greater liability to act wrongly than men are, if abortion is wrong; but this is in virtue of the capacity they have to do something intrinsically worthwhile, *viz.* bear children, which men lack. Women, even young girls, are faced with a greater opportunity to act well and to do something with their lives.

But, it might fairly be said, this is still to say nothing about the ways in which abortion is wrong, and in what circumstances it is, and I must now say something about that.

A major aim of this book has been to demonstrate that difficult moral questions really *are* difficult, not to be solved simply, and that abortion, in being so special, is particularly intractable. A second aim has been to introduce neo-Aristotelianism, with all its complexity, as the right way to think about moral questions, but as I said at the beginning of the chapter in which I introduced it, although I claim that the theory gives us the right way of thinking about abortion, I do not claim that, thinking in this way, I have yet managed to come up with the right thoughts. To have all the right thoughts about abortion would be to know

what the fully virtuous and thereby perfectly wise woman
would do in all the different circumstances in which the
question of abortion might arise; and to know that, I would
need to be fully virtuous and wise, which I lay no claim to
being.

However, it would obviously be simply cowardly to
refuse to stick my neck out at all, and so I shall try to sum
up the various strands of thought that have been running
through this book. If bearing children is intrinsically worthwhile, for the complex set of reasons I have given, then we
might expect the ways in which abortion is wrong to relate
to these. Approaching it this way imposes at least some
system on its variety of special aspects.

The fact that abortion is, in some sense, the destruction
of a new human life, and thereby, like the procreation of a
new human life, connects with our thoughts about human
lives and deaths, must make it a serious decision, always
something of *some* moment. To disregard this fact about it,
to think of abortion as nothing but the killing of something
that does not matter, or as nothing but the exercise of some
right or rights one has, or as the incidental means to some
desirable state of affairs, is to do something callous and
light-minded; the sort of thing that no virtuous and wise
person would do. It is to have the wrong attitude to human
life and death, and it is because the three liberal lines I have
discussed encourage us all, girls and women in particular,
to have some such wrong attitude, that I have devoted so
much space to criticizing them. But opting for an abortion
does not necessarily manifest a callous or light-minded
attitude to human life, for a number of reasons. One reason
is that it may manifest the opposite. If one's reason is a
genuinely altruistic desire that new lives should not begin
disabled because, far from being callous, one is sensitive to
suffering, and, far from being light-minded, one is very
conscious of how momentous a thing it is to bring a new
person into the world, then opting for abortion need show
no disregard for the fact that it is the destruction of a new
human life.

It is hard to develop (what I take to be) the genuinely
right attitude to abortion in the case of actual or suspected

disability; for it cannot, I have maintained, be the *right* attitude if it spills into making wrong judgements about people who have been born with various disabilities, or acquired them through accident or illness. Indeed, to have the right attitude to disability quite generally is a very difficult thing for someone who enjoys perfect physical health and capabilities. One needs to be sympathetic without being condescending, and to be conscious of one's own great good fortune without being too reliant on it, and this does call for a great deal of wisdom.

As if that were not difficult enough, one may also find a problem concerning the decisions of some people, women in particular, one finds admirable. Some women decide, together with their partner, or alone, to go through with their pregnancies in cases of actual or suspected disability, saying that they are prepared to welcome and be thankful for whatever child fate has dealt them, or that it is not for them to decide to destroy a new life. Now I can see that some people might reasonably say that this was self-centred ('What *you* will welcome or be thankful for is not the point') or irresponsible ('It *is* for you to decide; face up to the decision'), especially perhaps where the disability in question is one that involves much suffering. And I can certainly imagine its being done in a self-centred or irresponsible way. But I have read and heard the personal accounts of some people who, in making this decision, seem to me neither self-centred nor irresponsible, but admirable. What seems admirable is something like a rich acceptance of experience, an ability to love it in its good and in its bad aspects. One recognizes, I think, the same admirable character trait in people who succeed in accepting their own suffering or disabilities with no diminution of joy, and in people who bring up, or live with, the severely mentally retarded, and take as much joy and interest in their restricted achievements and lives as other people do in the achievements and lives of their ordinary family and friends.

This is one area where I feel the lack of wisdom very acutely. Should one say that, ideally, someone with this admirable character trait should be able to see that, now disabilities are predictable and early abortion available, it is a mistake to embrace *this* bad aspect of life, especially if it involves at least running the risk of forcing someone else, namely the new person that will come to be, to embrace it too? Or is it the case that our psychology just will not work that way; that to have this admirable character trait is always (or 'for the most part') inevitably to be a person who has the sort of 'respect for human life' which rules abortion out? I am still very puzzled about this, and must leave it as a question.

The mention of wisdom may serve to remind us that one of the simplest reasons why opting for abortion may not manifest serious callousness or a light-minded attitude to life is that girls can make this decision when they are far too young for their characters to have formed. The young are, in a way, callous and light-minded, but only in a way that is natural to youth. It would be foolish to deny that many young women who have abortions develop into sensitive, serious-minded people who, moreover, subsequently have children and are marvellous mothers.

This point is connected to the fact of gradual fœtal development. Notwithstanding the fact that there is no place at which clear boundary lines can be drawn, our emotions and attitudes regarding the fœtus do change as it develops, and again when it is born, and indeed further as the baby grows. Abortion for selfish reasons in the later stages is much more shocking than abortion for the same reasons in the early stages in a way that matches the fact that deep grief over miscarriage in the later stages is more appropriate than it is over miscarriage in the earlier stages (where, that is, the grief is solely about the loss of *this* child, not about, as might be the case, the loss of one's only hope of having a child). The mere fact that one has lived with the fœtus for longer, conscious of its existence, makes a difference; so too does the fact that it is very hard to be fully conscious of its existence in the early stages and hence hard to appreciate that an early abortion is the destruction of life. It is particularly hard for the young and inexperienced to appreci-ate this, because appreciation of it usually only comes from experience.

I do not mean 'from the experience of having an abortion'

(though that may form part of it), but quite generally 'from the experience of life'. It is as one learns more about what sorts of things happen in people's lives (one's own included) and how people respond to them, that the appreciation grows. One hears mothers, looking at their grown-up children, saying, 'Would you believe it – I thought of having an abortion! If I had, she would never have been born!'; one hears women, with or without children, saying, 'I had an abortion twenty years ago, and I've never forgotten it; I'm always haunted by the thought of what the child would have been like'; one hears women who have had abortions recently or long ago talking of a feeling of loss – loss of a baby. Short of a particularly intense religious upbringing, it is only through learning about these ways of thinking and feeling that one comes to appreciate fully that even abortion in the earliest stages is the destruction of a new human life; and I am not even sure that a religious upbringing could produce full appreciation of it, rather than a deep-seated but rather uncomprehending belief that it was wrong. Having 'the right attitude to life and death', where this is not only a matter of believing a set of moral principles, but part of one's character, is something that one develops only as one's character forms; and it is formed through experience.

These considerations inevitably bring in the second set of thoughts connected with the thought of procreation as worthwhile; namely, our thoughts about the value of love and family life, and our proper emotional development through a natural life-cycle. Corresponding to these is that aspect of abortion which involves opting for not being a mother (at all, or again, or now), and here again there is room for much variety, particularly in relation to age and experience. A woman who has already had several children and fears that to have another will seriously affect her capacity to be a good mother to the ones she has, does not show a lack of appreciation of the intrinsic value of being a parent. Nor does a woman who has been a good mother and is approaching the age where she may be looking forward to being a good grandmother. Nor, necessarily, does a woman who has decided to go in for a life involving some other worthwhile activity or activities with which motherhood would compete.

Though this much may be clear enough in the abstract, it becomes immensely difficult again when embodied in the actual facts of life, where the decision not to be a mother (at all, again, or now) is often the abortion decision and hence about killing too. If the decision is made with due recognition of that fact, seriously, and for serious reasons involving an understanding of the intrinsic value of being a parent, it would often, I think, be the right decision – the one that the perfectly virtuous and wise woman would make – but not thereby a decision that was not regrettable, in that it would be appropriate to regret that circumstances made it necessary to do this thing.

That circumstances may make it necessary to do what is, in itself, wrong, is not peculiar to abortion. Suppose one compared it to hurting someone very much, against their wishes. I might have to do this for their sake, or for my own, or for the sake of others. Even in the cases when it is quite certain that I really do have to hurt them, there is still much room for regret, some sense that, notwithstanding the fact that the decision was the right one, and that one has done the best thing that could be done, one has still done something wrong, albeit not something one should feel guilty about. One natural expression of the regret is to go on worrying 'irrationally' about whether the decision really was the right one. Another is to reflect on how one got into the circumstances in which it was the right decision in the first place, for guilt will be appropriate if this was one's own fault.

When the decision in question is the decision to have an abortion, reflection on this amounts to reflection on one's sexual activity, and one's choices, or the lack of them, about one's sexual partner and about contraception. Sometimes one will have nothing to blame oneself for here. But very often one will. And then there will be a further sense in which the abortion is wrong; right as the decision may be, it will not be the decision that the perfectly wise and virtuous woman would have made in the circumstances, because she would not ever have got herself into those circumstances.

The mention of the 'virtuous woman', particularly in the context of sexual activity, can be misleading here. Let us recall that it means, not simply 'chaste woman' or anything explicitly related to sexual activity, but 'woman with the virtues, i.e. the character traits necessary to, and partly constitutive of, human flourishing'. Amongst these are such character traits as strength, independence, resoluteness, decisiveness, self-confidence, responsibility, being serious (as opposed to light-minded), being in control of one's own life – and no one, I think, could deny that many women become pregnant, in circumstances in which they do not welcome, or cannot face, the thought of having *this* child, precisely because they lack one or some of these character traits. So even in the cases in which the decision to have an abortion is the right one, it can still be the reflection of a moral failing; not because the decision itself is weak, or cowardly or irresolute or irresponsible or light-minded, but because lack of the requisite opposite of those moral failings landed one in the circumstances in the first place. Hence guilt or remorse can be entirely appropriate feelings about an abortion, even when the decision was the right one.

They are doubly appropriate in the cases in which the decision itself is not, or not certainly, the right one, manifesting not only some lack of due respect for life but also an inappropriate unwillingness to be a mother. It is, presumably, the fact that the decision *not* to have an abortion can be so momentous, that so many childless women, particularly young ones, flinch from making it when they find themselves in an unplanned pregnancy. To decide not to have an abortion, to decide instead to have a child, is, after all, to take at least two futures, one's own and the child's, and quite possibly more, those of one's husband, or the child's father, those of one's parents, into one's hands, and give them a decisive shove in one unalterable direction, for better or for worse. If one has the child 'things will never be the same again' in some really significant way. And it requires courage to make a decision which one knows and clearly appreciates is going to change the future in a substantial way, when the apparently easy alternative of abortion is available.

To flinch from taking one's whole future into one's hands when one is young and irresponsible is not necessarily even cowardice. It might be an appropriate modesty or humility, and the young may say truly 'I'm not ready for motherhood yet'. (Though if they decide to have an abortion, and if this is, rather than pregnancy and adoption, the right decision, it will still often be the case that they should reflect with remorse on how they became pregnant.) But to flinch from it when one is older is to behave *as if* one were young and irresponsible, and that is just refusing to grow up. If one is 'not ready yet' then, according to one's age and circumstances, the pressing question may be 'And why not?'

I said earlier that people who are childless by choice were sometimes described as 'irresponsible', or 'refusing to grow up' or 'not knowing what life is about'. I did not endorse this, for I argued that, on the contrary, we were in the happy position of there being more worthwhile things to do than could be fitted into one lifetime. Though parenthood, and motherhood in particular, are intrinsically worthwhile, they undoubtedly take up a lot of one's adult life, leaving no room for some other worthwhile pursuits. But some women who choose abortion rather than having their first child are not avoiding motherhood for the sake of other worthwhile pursuits but for the worthless ones of 'having a good time'. And some others who say 'I am not ready yet' are making some sort of mistake about the extent to which one can manipulate the circumstances of one's life so as to make it fulfil some dream one has. Perhaps one's dream is of having two perfect children, a girl and a boy, within a perfect marriage, in financially secure circumstances, with an interesting job of one's own. But to care too much about that dream, to demand of life that it will fulfil it, and act accordingly, is to run the risk of missing out on happiness entirely. Not only may fate make it impossible, or destroy it, but one's own attachment to it may make it impossible. Good marriages, and the most promising children, can be destroyed by just one adult's demand for such perfection.

That I say 'adult' rather than 'woman' here may serve to remind us that, with very little amendment, all the above applies to boys and men too. Although 'the' abortion decision is, in one obvious sense, the woman's decision, for her to make, boys and men are often party to it, for well or ill, and, even when they are not, they are bound to have been party to the circumstances which brought it up. No less than girls and women, boys and men can, in their actions, manifest callousness and light-mindedness about life in relation to abortion, can be self-centred or courageous about the possibility of disabilities, need to reflect on their sexual activity and their choices, or lack of them, about their sexual partner and contraception; they have to grow up and take responsibility for their own actions and life in relation to fatherhood. If it is true, as I have maintained, that, insofar as motherhood is intrinsically worthwhile, being a mother is *a* purpose in women's lives, being a father (rather than a mere generator) is *a* purpose in men's lives too, and it is adolescent of men to turn a blind eye to this and pretend that they have many more important things to do.

I have been trying to support the view, all through this book, that abortion is an intensely serious matter, and that the decision to have one, or that one's partner should have one, is, correspondingly, an intensely serious decision not to be undertaken lightly, nor indeed self-righteously. It is a decision, one might say, about 'the meaning of life', in a unique way. It is, for one thing, a decision about the meaning or value of the potential life within one's power which is, in part, of one's own making. And it is also a decision about the meaning, or point, or purpose, of one's own life, and what one is going to do with it and make of it and of oneself.

The event of abortion often does lead people to reflect seriously on these matters. They think 'What sort of person am I?' and realize that they could be a lot better in a variety of ways – stronger, more responsible, resolute and decisive, less aimless, less manipulable, less thoughtless or insensitive, less materialistic, more loving and tender. They reflect on their sexual relationships, sometimes realizing that they have been choosing emotionally shallow ones, or playing a shallow part within them, or not even *choosing* them. They reflect on their past attitudes to other people and realize that they have lacked compassion, or courage, or foresight, or gratitude, or understanding.

To reflect on such matters in the right way is, according to neo-Aristotelianism, part of the process of acquiring that wisdom about life which is virtue, and since it is only by acquiring it that we can live well together, such serious reflection is incumbent upon all of us, from the earliest age at which we are capable of it. In some sense, perhaps, it is never too late to start, though the later we start the more harm we shall probably have done, and the harder it will be to acknowledge our own failings. But the earlier we start, and the earlier we teach our children to start, by example rather than by precept, the greater our chances of mutual success, of flourishing together.

NOTES

1 Harman, G. (1977) *The Nature of Morality*, Oxford University Press.
2 Chapter Two, Section 3.
3 *Cf.* the 'irrationally strong' premise that 'it is wrong to interfere with nature' mentioned in Chapter Two, Section 4.
4 Warnock, Mary (1985) 'Legal Surrogacy – not for love or money?', *The Listener*, vol. 113, no. 2893 (24 January, 1985).
5 The 'Cotton case' was the first, or at least the first publicized, case of commercially arranged surrogate birth in Britain. Mrs Kim Cotton, the healthy mother of three children, was recruited by a commercial agency, the Surrogate Parenting Centre, to act as a surrogate mother on behalf of a childless couple unknown to her, for the fee of £6500.

Human development

At fertilization the female cell (the egg or *ovum*) unites with the male cell (the sperm or *spermatozoon*) to become a new single cell. The nucleus of this cell contains twenty-three pairs of chromosomes, one in each pair from each parent. At this stage the fertilized egg is called a *single-cell zygote*. Usually a woman produces only one ovum a month; if she produces two or more and each of them is fertilized, the result is fraternal twins (or triplets or . . .), who, unlike identical twins (see below), need not be of the same sex, though they may be, and do not necessarily look alike.

In ordinary circumstances fertilization or conception takes place in the upper portion of the fallopian tube, and the *zygote* gradually moves down the fallopian tube into the uterus over a period of four to five days. Within twenty-four hours of conception, while it is still in the fallopian tube, the single-cell zygote divides into first two, then four, then eight, then sixteen smaller cells all loosely clumped together, in an arrangement rather similar to that of a blackberry. The *multicell zygote* or *blastocyst* continues to grow and take form as it moves from the fallopian tube into the uterus and begins to *implant* in the uterine wall. *Implantation* takes six to seven days and is usually complete eleven to thirteen days after fertilization. If implantation does not occur the blastocyst will be lost at or before the next menstrual period.

As the zygote moves out of the fallopian tube into the uterus it triggers the production of a number of hormones and pregnancy proteins. It is now possible to detect these and hence the presence of a zygote even at this early stage; research suggests that at least 40 per cent of all zygotes fail to implant successfully and are lost. It is unclear as yet whether many or most of this 40 per cent are genetically abnormal, or whether most are perfectly normal and lost because of some difficulty with implantation. (Zygotes which do implant successfully, their presence indicated by the familiar signal of a missed period and confirmed by an ordinary pregnancy test, have a further failure rate of about 20 per cent in the form of miscarriages, most of which occur very early in the pregnancy and many of which are the result of extreme genetic abnormality of the fœtus.) This makes for a total failure rate of about 60 per cent.

While the zygote or blastocyst is implanting, its internal development is proceeding too. Around the time of established implantation, the first recognizable feature of the *embryo* appears – the 'primitive streak' in which a number of cells in the inner cell mass of the blastocyst collect together more closely, on about the fifteenth day after fertilization. The Warnock Committee described the formation of the primitive streak as a point that 'marks the beginning of *individual* development of the embryo' ('Warnock Report', p. 66, my italics) and accordingly set the slightly earlier fourteenth day after fertilization as the cut-off point for permissible research. The reason for describing it this way is that this is the latest stage at which identical twins can occur, signalled by the appearance of not one but two primitive streaks. (They can also occur as early as the two-cell zygote stage.) So, prior to the formation of the primitive streak(s) what is referred to as *the* zygote or embryo might be potentially more than one human being.

By the seventeenth day the 'neural groove' appears – the antecedent of the spinal cord and hence the beginnings of neural development – and the cells of the embryo start to differentiate, i.e. begin to assume the characteristics of nerve cells, blood cells, skin cells, etc. Thereafter development is rapid; within the next three weeks rudimentary eyes, ears, liver, kidneys, stomach and nervous system all develop, and the blood system begins to function independently, i.e. the embryo's heart is pumping the embryo's own blood, which may be of a different blood-type from the mother's. At this stage the embryo is about two millimetres long and looks rather like a tadpole, with a clearly recognizable head.

About eight weeks from fertilization the embryo is known as a *foetus*: by this stage, though still tiny (about twenty-five millimetres, or an inch, long) it is recognizably of human form, with arms and legs, fingers and toes, and makes spontaneous movements, squirming and kicking. (This is not to be confused with 'quickening', which is when the mother first feels the foetus move; this happens much later, and can vary from the sixteenth to the twentieth week of pregnancy.) Between nine and ten weeks after conception some foetuses have been observed apparently sucking their thumbs; there is, however, some dispute as to whether they are really sucking.

At this stage, the pregnancy is nearly at the end of the first *trimester*, despite the fact that the foetus has been developing for only nine to ten weeks, not twelve or thirteen. This oddity arises from the preferred terminology of doctors. Well-established medical tradition calculates the date of birth as 280 days or 40 weeks from the first day of the last menstrual bleeding, a date that any woman with reasonably regular periods is likely to be able to recall one, or more likely two, months later when she goes to her doctor first suspecting that she may be pregnant. Applied to women with perfectly regular twenty-eight-day menstrual cycles, this calculation works; what the doctors call a forty-week-old foetus will have been developing and growing for 38 weeks and will be born at the predicted time. Since many women's periods do not conform to this pattern, the predictions are frequently out by a week one way or the other, and quite often by more.

It is important to bear these points about terminology in mind when reading reported claims about the earliest stage at which a foetus has, so far, proved to be viable. Some reports say 'as early as 20 weeks'; others say '24 weeks at the earliest'. There is indeed disagreement here, but if the first reports are expressed in the terminology of 'weeks after conception' and the second reports in the medical terminology of 'weeks after first day of last period', the measure of disagreement is much less than it first appears.

At the moment, the twenty-four-week pregnancy (i.e. the twenty-two or twenty-one-week-old fœtus) is a sort of brick wall for viability because the internal organs are not sufficiently developed to enable the fœtus to survive in an incubator. At about this date, or preferably a week later, it is possible, but only just, to use artificial ventilation to enable the fœtus to breathe. The fœtus's own lung development must be almost complete for this to work; even if it does, it is unlikely that the fœtus will survive the shock of such a procedure. The survival rate at this stage, despite the most sophisticated care, is about 10 per cent. It is very unlikely that medical technology will be able to improve much on this rate, or lower the present age of viability further, without a new breakthrough, such as the invention of something like a surrogate amniotic sac. But in theory there is no reason to doubt that this will be forthcoming.

Viable fœtuses, at about the twenty-fifth to twenty-sixth week of pregnancy, weigh about 700 grams (though premature babies of only 500 grams have been born and survived). The ideal weight for a full-term new-born baby is about three and a half kilos; so, for the third trimester of the pregnancy, the development of the fœtus, all its internal organs and external features complete, basically consists in (more than) tripling its size and weight.

Methods of abortion

The standard forms of abortion practised in the UK at the time of writing are *suction evacuation* and *prostaglandin termination*. The former is the most common and is the sort used when the woman's pregnancy is twelve weeks or less. The mouth of the womb is stretched open and a powerful suction tube is inserted. The fœtus and placenta are torn apart and sucked into a jar. The fact that the contents of the womb go straight into a jar makes this method less harrowing than the earlier *D & C* (dilation and curettage) method which is still sometimes used. This also involves the mouth of the womb being stretched open; the surgeon inserts a scoop-shaped sharp knife with which the sides of the uterus are scraped, cutting the fœtus to pieces; these pieces then have to be removed.

After twelve weeks of pregnancy it is possible to use the other method. A substance called prostaglandin is inserted into the cervix or uterus which causes it to start contracting. If there are no complications, the contractions usually kill the fœtus within a matter of hours and the woman then goes into labour and is delivered of a dead fœtus twelve or so hours later. Sometimes the fœtus is not killed by the contractions, is born alive and dies after a few minutes of oxygen deprivation because the lungs are too undeveloped to operate.

In the United States and Canada the most common method of late abortion is *salt poisoning* (also known as *amnio abortion* or the *saline* procedure). This is done after the sixteenth week of pregnancy when enough fluid has accumulated in the amniotic sac. A needle is inserted through the mother's abdomen into the sac and a concentrated solution of salt is injected into it; this kills the fœtus by poisoning it and burning off its outer layer of skin. This takes about an hour and, if there are no complications, the woman then goes into labour and delivers the dead fœtus later.

Hysterotomy is the abortion procedure often used in the past after the fifth month of pregnancy. It is in fact a Caesarean operation and yields living fœtuses some of which may be viable (see Appendix One). It has generally been superseded in the UK by the prostaglandin method.

Methods of overcoming infertility

'Infertility', when used in relation to people seeking medical treatment to help them to have children, is used to cover difficulty in having children as well as the various cases of complete incapacity. So when a couple are 'treated for infertility' it need not be that either is strictly infertile.

Artificial insemination (AI) is the placing of semen inside a woman's vagina or uterus by means other than sexual intercourse. Semen is collected from the husband or donor through masturbation; it may be used straight away or frozen for later use.

Artificial insemination by husband (AIH) may be resorted to when the couple cannot use sexual intercourse to introduce the man's semen into the woman's vagina, as for instance when the man is severely physically disabled and unable to achieve intercourse. It may also be used when the husband's sperm count is very low, or to overcome 'cervical hostility', a condition in which the woman's cervical mucus reacts to the sperm as hostile foreign bodies and kills them while they are still in the vagina. The sperm is inserted into the uterine cavity in these circumstances but there is apparently no clear evidence that AIH is more effective in these circumstances than natural intercourse.

It may also be used when a man chooses to have his semen frozen and stored for later use in the knowledge or expectation that he may become completely infertile. For example, a man in France deposited some of his semen in a sperm bank having developed cancer of the testicles and been warned that the chemotherapy might leave him sterile.

A child born as a result of AIH to a married couple is, legally, the legitimate child of that couple. There are various complications in different legal systems about the status of a child born as a result of AIH to a widow impregnated after her husband's death by his stored semen.

Artificial insemination by donor (AID) may be resorted to when the husband is sterile and also used deliberately to avoid hereditary diseases which are carried by men and not women. It has been widely used for many years and, in Britain, is provided under the National Health Service in a few places. However, it is not officially part of NHS practice and it is provided on a private, or semi-private basis in many centres. A further oddity is that a child born as a result of AID is, under current law, the offspring of the donor (and the mother). Hence the husband of the mother has no parental rights or duties in relation to 'their' child; the child is, legally, illegitimate. No doubt (in part) because of this much secrecy surrounds how often AID is used. According to the 'Warnock Report': 'In 1982, the latest year for which figures are available, the Royal College of Obstetricians and Gynaecologists knew of over 1000 pregnancies conceived and at least 780 live births following AID in this country' (*op. cit.*, p. 19).

A donor to a sperm bank must do more than masturbate. He must abstain from sexual intercourse or masturbation for three days prior to the donation (to maximize the sperm count) and undergo a rigorous medical enquiry into his own and his family's medical history. Donors for AID are screened in particular to exclude venereal diseases, hepatitis and AIDS. Most countries with sperm banks rely on voluntary contributions, offering small 'fees' by way of compensation for inconvenience. Britain relies heavily on the contributions of medical and other students; the French encourage couples using AID to press their married friends to donate.

Donation, however, need not be to a sperm bank. Women have impregnated themselves by inserting semen into their vaginas with a syringe, semen donated by male friends who, for one reason or another, want to help the woman have the child she wants without having intercourse with her. It can be a simple do-it-yourself matter.

In vitro fertilization (IVF) The artificial insemination described above works only if the woman is producing eggs which can be fertilized by the artificially introduced sperm. Some women produce eggs, i.e. ovulate, but do not have fallopian tubes which allow the egg to pass from the ovary to the uterus. The tubes may be diseased, or damaged, or blocked, or may have been removed by earlier surgery. In such cases it is impossible for the egg to be fertilized *in situ*. Nothing could be done about this (except for tubal surgery which was occasionally appropriate and successful) until a way was found of extracting the egg from the ovary, the main difficulty being to know when it was ripe enough to be fertilizable. This was made possible by the development of 'laparoscopy' during the 1960s. (The laparascope is a kind of very thin flexible telescope with its own light. It can be inserted in the abdomen through a very small cut (half an inch) and used to examine the internal abdominal and pelvic organs, including the ovaries.)

Once ripe eggs could be extracted, fertilization of them outside the womb was possible. (Edwards and Steptoe first reported having done it in the scientific journal *Nature* in 1969, having teamed up only a year before.) The egg is put in a suitable culture in a glass dish and then the semen of the husband or donor is mixed in and usually (the success rate is 50–90 per cent) fertilization occurs. The fertilized egg is transferred to the mother's uterus shortly afterwards – within about two or three days, when it is clear that the cells are dividing (apparently) in the right way.

The difficulty lies in replicating the next natural step – the implantation of the embryo in the uterine wall. Even in ordinary fertilization the rate of implantation is quite low (see Appendix One) and at present still lower for *in vitro* fertilization. It is because of this difficulty that the method of transferring more than one embryo is used. Transferring more than one gives a better probability of one embryo implanting, and there is also evidence that if more than one embryo is transferred they may help each other to implant.

The first 'test-tube' baby was born in 1978 using natural ovulation, but it soon became universal practice to use superovulation methods. Women normally produce only one egg per menstrual cycle, and so must, if there is to be more than one embryo, go on a course of 'fertility' drugs which cause superovulation. This may result in as many as a dozen ripe eggs being extracted on one occasion. If each egg is then mixed with sperm it is likely that several will be fertilized. Some embryos may, in the very first hours or days of their conception, show signs of not developing in the right way and hence of not being suitable for transfer. Thus transferring more than one embryo increases the chances of the couple's success rate in other ways too. There is less chance that the one egg extracted will not be fertilized, and less chance that the only fertilized egg or embryo available will be too abnormal to be transferred.

However, although multiple embryonic transfer improves the chances of successful pregnancy, it also allows for the possibility of multiple pregnancy which can be dangerous for both the woman and the embryos. Hence the availability of 'spare embryos', when the upshot of superovulation and successful fertilization is more (apparently) perfect embryos than the practitioner considers it advisable to transfer (at present three is usually the optimum number). The question may then arise of whether the 'spare' embryos are to be donated to some other woman trying to have a child by IVF.

Some women (or couples) insist that, in their case, no more embryos are to be produced than can be transferred. If the woman then produces more eggs than are needed, she must decide whether or not she is willing to donate the surplus.

Sperm, egg and embryo donation   *In vitro* fertilization is usually discussed in terms that presuppose that any child that results will be the genetic offspring of the carrying mother and her husband or partner. Given the availability of sperm banks, the latter is not necessary and indeed some children have been born as a result of the combination of AID and IVF.

Given present medical technology, egg and embryo donation are more complicated. As yet, eggs which have been frozen and thawed are not unaffected by the process, unlike semen. They fertilize, but they do not develop successfully. So any donated egg must be fertilized immediately; it cannot at present be stored. Evidence suggests that embryos can be frozen and thawed without being affected; experiments involving the freezing, thawing and transfer of embryos of various animals have not produced abnormal results and at least one baby has been successfully born as the result of transferring a thawed embryo. But at the moment using frozen and thawed embryos is simply introducing more risks into what is already a very risky business. So here too the working assumption is that any donated embryo must be transferred when ready.

Some couples are infertile because the woman cannot produce an egg; hence the technological breakthrough of egg extraction does not benefit them directly. Others, who initially appear to be candidates for standard IVF (i.e. with successful ovulation but damaged or non-existent fallopian tubes) turn out to have ovaries which are inaccessible by present techniques. Such women will usually want to have their husband's child; egg donation and IVF make this possible. A donated egg, or eggs, are fertilized *in vitro* with the husband's semen, and the embryo(s) then transferred to the woman as above.

If the couple are such that the woman needs egg donation and the husband is infertile then the only possibility of their having a child is embryo donation. A donated egg or eggs are fertilized *in vitro* with donated semen and the resulting embryo(s) transferred to the woman. The resulting child will not, of course, be genetically related to either of its parents; indeed one of the medical teams who do IVF refer to embryo donation as 'pre-natal adoption'.

Uterine lavage or intra-uterine transfer   This is another form of embryo donation but one which does not involve IVF and does not necessarily mean that the embryo is genetically unrelated to the father. The 'egg donor' is artificially inseminated with semen from the husband (or a donor if the husband is also infertile). A few days later, at the time when the embryo should be in the uterus but not yet starting to implant, the donor's uterus is washed out and the embryo(s) retrieved transferred to the infertile woman's uterus. The resulting child will be genetically related to the husband if his semen was used, and related to neither parent if it was not.

The 'Warnock Report'

The so-called 'Warnock Report' is in fact the *Report of the Committee of Inquiry into Human Fertilisation and Embryology*, a committee that was chaired by Dame Mary Warnock, and set up in 1982. Its brief was 'to consider recent and potential developments in medicine and science related to human fertilisation and embryology; to consider what policies and safeguards should be applied, including consideration of the social, ethical and legal implications of these developments; and to make recommendations.'

Amongst the subjects the Report covered were the two which had created the 'public excitement and concern' which prompted the Inquiry in the first place, namely surrogacy and research on human embryos. Very briefly, the Inquiry came out against surrogacy and in favour of embryonic research (subject to a number of complicated restrictions), but these two brief statements do little to convey the range of considerations, and variety of opinions, that are recorded.

Embryonic research In fact, on the issue of embryonic research, three members of the sixteen-member committee were against it entirely, and a further four against its being permitted on anything but the spare embryos presently produced with a view to helping a woman to have a child. So the majority recommendation of the Report, that research should be permitted on embryos brought into existence specifically for that purpose, had a majority of two.

Many of the recommendations concerning embryonic research are, inevitably, to do with the details of legislation;

so, for instance, the Inquiry recommends that such research should be permitted only under licence from a new, statutory, licensing authority (recommendations 1 and 43), and specifies some of this licensing body's constituents (recommendation 2) and duties (recommendations 16 and 49). Some reflect firm moral judgements which the Inquiry clearly thinks should be enshrined in law rather than left to the deliberations of this licensing body, such as that 'the placing of a human embryo in the uterus of another species for gestation should be a criminal offence' (recommendation 48), and a recommendation to rule out the production of hybrid half-human creatures (paragraph 12.3).

Others reflect a combination (of firm moral judgements and details of legislation) such as 'it shall be a criminal offence to handle or to use as a research subject any live human embryo derived from *in vitro* fertilisation' beyond the limit of fourteen days after fertilization (recommendation 45). This recommendation presupposes a firm, albeit unstated judgement that *some* research on live human embryos is wrong – say, definitely, by the time the 'embryo' is eight months old – but does not, of course, amount to a firm moral judgement that, having been justifiable earlier, it suddenly becomes wrong precisely fifteen days after fertilization. It is the consideration of legislation that requires a firm cut-off point, and the Inquiry does not attempt to argue that fourteen days is inherently a more reasonable limit than thirteen, or fifteen; rather, it 'agreed that this was an area in which some precise decision must be taken, in order to allay public anxiety' and then drew a number of considerations together and threw in an extra day's limit to be on the safe side.

One issue the Inquiry does leave to the deliberations of the licensing body is the question of what sort of research it should grant licences for. It clearly expects that the 'substantial' lay representation on the licensing body will curtail the hopes of any 'mad' scientists to do the sort of research unlikely to be considered 'ethically acceptable' by the public at large (recommendation 49). And it takes it as so obvious that scientists applying to the body for licences to do research would be obliged to show why the research could not be done using other material (such as animals) that it merely mentions this obvious fact in passing (paragraph 13.11) and does not bother to enshrine it in a recommendation. This leaves it all rather unclear whether the Inquiry foresaw the possibility that the proposed research might be not so much 'mad Frankenstein' as purely commercial, and supported for that reason, nor the possibility that people might query the *obvious* propriety of using dolphins and chimpanzees rather than ten-day-old human embryos.

Surrogacy   The Report remains generally uncommitted on the morality of 'surrogacy for love' (though see below), commenting only that it recognizes that 'there will continue to be privately arranged surrogacy agreements' and deciding that the criminal law should not attempt to control this. One reason given for this is that the members of the Inquiry 'are anxious to avoid children being born to mothers subject to the taint of criminality'. However, the Report also recommends that the law should give no support to private surrogacy agreements, and indeed makes this explicit. Recommendation 59 is that: 'It be provided by statute that all surrogacy agreements are illegal contracts and therefore unenforceable in the courts'. The Inquiry also recommends, as a supplement to the existing law, that 'when a child is born to a woman following donation of another's egg the woman giving birth should, for all purposes, be regarded in law as the mother of that child and that the egg donor should have no rights or obligations in respect of the child' (recommendation 55). These two recommendations amount, in effect, to recommending that, if a couple and a woman do enter into a private surrogacy agreement, and subsequently fall out, the child that is born is, by law, the surrogate mother's. So if she decides to keep it, the commissioning couple have no redress against her, whatever promises, for no matter how much money, have been made. And if the couple decide they do not want it, it is her responsibility, even if she had it only on the understanding that they would take it.

With the dissent of two of its members, the Inquiry decided to recommend that the creation or operation of agencies, and even the actions of professionals 'and others', whose purpose is to assist in the establishment of a surrogate pregnancy should all be rendered criminal by law. The two members who dissented pointed out that this not only rules out commercial surrogacy agencies, but also 'would prevent gynaecologists from offering any form of assistance' to couples. They say that a 'particularly unsatisfactory' possible consequence of this is that couples will be driven into 'some sort of "do-it-yourself" arrangement'.

The claim that this is 'particularly unsatisfactory' seems at odds with the previous acceptance of 'private surrogacy agreements' or 'surrogacy for love', but it is not clear what objection the two dissenters have to it. They mention lack of medical counselling services, but lay no stress on this. (Perhaps rightly – an enterprising threesome in the United States managed the whole thing on their own ten years ago by reading up on artificial insemination in the *Reader's Digest Family Health Guide*. (Described in Keane, Noel and Breo, Denis (1981) *The Surrogate Mother*, Everest House.)) Instead, they refer back to a paragraph right at the beginning of the Report (3.2) which recommends anonymity to protect all parties involved in infertility treatment from 'legal and emotional complications'. But this early paragraph is explicitly concerned only with parties to sperm and egg donation, not with surrogacy, and when, five chapters later, arguments for and against surrogacy are given, nothing is said about 'emotional complications' arising (or not) from lack of anonymity. On the contrary, the 'arguments against' include the point that 'Many unforeseen events may occur between the moment of entering into the surrogacy agreements and the time for handing over the child', but the 'arguments for' fail to make the obvious counter-claim, made by supporters of 'surrogacy for love'. As two supporters of surrogacy put it, 'Of course, even in the best of circumstances things can go wrong. Things are markedly less likely to go wrong, however, when people are motivated by love and kindness, and act without demanding a reward' (Singer, Peter and Wells, Deane (1984) *The Reproduction Revolution*, Oxford University Press).

Glossary

abortion According to the dictionary, the term means 'giving untimely birth to offspring', and is synonymous with the term 'miscarriage'. But in common current usage it means 'deliberate termination of pregnancy', one form of which is induced miscarriage. See Appendix Two, 'Methods of abortion'.

AID Artificial Insemination by Donor, i.e. with sperm which has been donated rather than taken from the woman's husband or male partner. See Appendix Three, 'Methods of overcoming infertility'.

AIH Artificial Insemination by Husband. See Appendix Three.

amniocentesis A test for genetic abnormality amongst other things, involving the withdrawal and analysis of the amniotic fluid surrounding the fœtus. The fluid contains cells from the fœtus, and analysis of these reveals some genetic abnormalities including those responsible for Down's syndrome and spina bifida. It also reveals the sex of the fœtus. The test creates some particular moral problems because at present it cannot be carried out until about the fifteenth week of pregnancy and, on top of that, the analysis of the fluid takes at least 3–4 weeks, taking the pregnancy to the eighteenth or nineteenth week at the earliest, well into the second trimester. A further complication arises from the fact that the test has a 1 in 100 chance of causing a miscarriage. When a woman has a higher than usual risk of bearing a genetically abnormal child, as is the case, for instance, if she is over thirty-five, it is standard practice for her to be offered amniocentesis. But doctors are in general unwilling to run the risk of inducing a miscarriage by testing young pregnant women who have no special reason to be worried, even if the women want them to.

anencephaly The congenital absence of all or part of the brain.

cervical hostility A condition in which the woman's cervical mucus reacts to the sperm as hostile foreign bodies and kills them while they are still in the vagina.

Down's syndrome A genetic abnormality, the result of an extra chromosome, which shows itself in subnormal intelligence and the characteristic facial features of what used to be called 'mongol' children. It is often associated with other serious physical abnormalities. Whether or not a fœtus has Down's syndrome can be discovered before it is born by amniocentesis (see above) but not, as yet, by other means.

embryo The young of animals in the womb or the egg. In the case of humans, the unborn is called 'an embryo' until about the sixth week of its development, after which it is called 'a fœtus'.

fertilization The process whereby the ovum and the sperm fuse to become a single cell. See Appendix One, 'Human development'.

fœtus See 'embryo' above and Appendix One, 'Human development'.

haemophilia A genetic abnormality resulting in an impairment of blood clot formation. The defective gene can be present in females or males, but its symptoms are manifested only in males (except in very rare cases). Hence a couple, one of whom has the gene, can predict that if the fœtus the woman is carrying is male the chances are fifty-fifty that if it is carried to term the baby will have haemophilia (and fifty-fifty that it will not have the gene at all); whereas if the fœtus is female the chances are fifty-fifty that if it is carried to term the baby will merely be an unaffected carrier of the gene (and fifty-fifty that it will not have the gene at all).

implantation   The process whereby the embryo becomes implanted in the wall of the uterus. See Appendix One, 'Human development'.

in vitro **fertilization**   Literally, fertilization in glass: ova and sperm are mixed together in a dish (not, in fact, a test-tube, despite the media name, 'test-tube babies', for babies thus conceived).

IUD—Interuterine device.   A 'contraceptive' device, such as the 'coil', which stays in the uterus and prevents, not literally conception, but implantation *q.v.*

spina bifida   A congenital malformation of the spine in which a section of the spinal cord is split – bifurcated – and exposed, instead of being a tube covered with skin. The defect can be very minor and treatable, but when the treatment of spina bifida is discussed it is usually with reference to the severe form. In this, the nerves that run along the spine are damaged and spinal fluid leaks out of the wound on the spine. The damage to the nerves may result in partial or total paralysis of the legs and in double incontinence. It also commonly involves hydrocephalus ('water on the brain') leading to brain damage and hence mental retardation. The further things that can go wrong with spina bifida sufferers include deformation of the spine, hip dislocation, kidney disease, blindness and fits.

trimester   Strictly, a period of three months; hence the (more or less) nine months of pregnancy may be divided into the first, second and third trimesters. See Appendix One, 'Human development'.

viability   The stage at which the fœtus becomes able to survive outside the carrying mother. The laws governing abortion in both Britain and the United States fix viability as the twenty-eighth week of pregnancy; the facts are otherwise. See Appendix One.

Index

of, 357; development of,
341–2; donation of, 350,
350–1; and *in vitro*
fertilization, 44, 79, 349;
mixed-strategy views on,
70; and women's rights,
211

equality, moral, 295–300, 330

Equivalence Thesis, 275–6

*Essay Concerning Human
Understanding* (Locke), 92–3

ethics, Greek view of, 220–6

eudaimonia, 222–5, 231, 239

euthanasia, 9; and the
autonomy principle,
158–61; active and
passive, 273–6; definition
of, xi, 43; involuntary,
144–7, 158–61, 163; law
and morality, 13; and
the moral status of the
fœtus, 29; and the
person view, 123–4, 179;
and the potentiality
view, 75–8; in Tooley,
119–20; and
utilitarianism, 144–7,
155, 158–63; *see also*
fœtal euthanasia

fathers of unborn children:
and abortion, 337–8;
liberal views on, 50–2;
rights of, 206; 213

fertilization, *see* conception

Finnis, John, 195

flourishing: in Aristotle, 232;
and happiness, 285; and
neo-Aristotelianism,
222–3, 232–7; and the
person view, 248; and
the virtues, 226–8, 230–1

fœtal deaths, 341; conservative
views on, 44–6

fœtal development, 342–3; and
abortion, 333

fœtal euthanasia: and the
animal view, 62–3;
conservative views on,
41–3; mixed-strategy
views on, 69–70; and the
potentiality view, 75–8

fœtal research: and the animal
view, 61–3; conservative
views on, 43, 47;
extreme liberal view of,
53–4, 58; mixed-strategy
view on, 70–1; and the
moral status of the
fœtus, 29–31; and the
person view, 89, 90–1,
124–5; potentiality views
on, 78–9, 84; and
utilitarianism, 171; and
viable fœtuses, 53–4

fœtus, moral status of, 10,
27–88; and abortion,
204–5; animal view of,
59–64; conservative
views on, 27, 31–47, 86;
liberal views on, 47–59,
86; and the liberal/radical
view, 17–18; mixed-
strategy views on,
65–72; and the person
view of, 89–130, 156–7;
potentiality view on,
72–86; and the person
view of, 205; in
Thomson, 195–6, 204;
and utilitarianism, 157–8

fœtuses: and the right to life,
112–14, 163–4, 185, 192;
and women's rights,
197–200; *see also* viable
fœtuses

Foot, Philippa, 76, 273–4,
275, 277

generosity, as a vitue, 226,
228

Index by Isobel McLean